Wiener Chic

Wiener Chic
A Locational History of Vienna Fashion

Susan Ingram & Markus Reisenleitner

intellect Bristol, UK / Chicago, USA

First published in the UK in 2013 by
Intellect, The Mill, Parnall Road, Fishponds, Bristol, BS16 3JG, UK

First published in the USA in 2013 by
Intellect, The University of Chicago Press, 1427 E. 60th Street,
Chicago, IL 60637, USA

A catalogue record for this book is available from the
British Library.

Series: Urban Chic
Series ISSN: 2053-7077 (Print), 2053-7085 (Online)
Cover image: Wiener Chic Postkarte (© Horowitz & Weege, Wien).
Cover designer: Stephanie Sarlos
Copy-editing: Janine de Smet
Production manager: Bethan Ball
Typesetting: Contentra Technologies

Print ISBN: 978-1-78320-184-6
ePDF ISBN: 978-1-78320-214-0
ePub ISBN: 978-1-78320-215-7

Printed and bound by Hobbs, UK

To the memory of Lydia Marinelli

Table of Contents

List of Illustrations

We have gone to great lengths to trace and contact the copyright holders of all images in this book. Many, such as the Anzenberger Agency, proved very cooperative, and we would like to acknowledge their generosity. If any copyright holders of images have not been properly credited, please contact the publishers, who will be happy to rectify future editions.

Cover: Wiener Chic Postkarte (© Horowitz & Weege, Wien).

Introduction:
0.1 MQ Summer of Fashion billboard (Photo: S. Ingram).
0.2 MQ Summer of Fashion advertising pillar (Photo: S. Ingram).
0.3 Vienna Fashion Night (Photo: S. Ingram).
0.4 Luxury Mile during Fashion Night 2012 (Photo: M. Reisenleitner).
0.5 *The Third Man* (Images ©1949 London Film Productions/British Lion Film Corporation).
0.6 *The Third Man* (Images ©1949 London Film Productions/British Lion Film Corporation).
0.7 *The Third Man* (Images ©1949 London Film Productions/British Lion Film Corporation).
0.8 Sign on park bench (Photo: S. Ingram).
0.9 Sign on garbage truck (Photo: S. Ingram).
0.10 Showdown in front of the Cafe Griensteidl (Photo: M. Reisenleitner).
0.11 Materials from the Vienna Tourist Board advertising campaign (www.wien.info).
0.12 Eissalon Schwedenplatz (Photo: K. Sark).
0.13 Baroque splendour (Photo: M. Reisenleitner).
0.14 Wiener Chic shop (Photo: W. Fischer).
0.15 *Before Sunrise* (Images ©1995 Detour Filmproduction/F.I.L.M.H.A.U.S. Wien/Sunrise Production/Castle Rock Entertainment).

Part I:
1.1 The Gloriette at Schönbrunn (Photo: M. Reisenleitner).

1.2 "Zu den blauen Flaschen" (The Blue Bottles), Old Vienna coffeehouse scene (anon. courtesy of Creative Commons).

1.3 Haas Haus (Photo: M. Reisenleitner).

1.4 Loos Haus (Photo: M. Reisenleitner).

1.5 Panoramic view from the Belvedere (Photo: M. Reisenleitner).

1.6 *Wiener Chic* (Alphonse Mucha).

1.7 Vienna 1900 exhibition posters in the Wien Museum (Photo: S. Ingram).

1.8 The Schmetterlinge (http://zebrase.wordpress.com).

1.9 *Blutrausch* (Images ©1997 Dor Film Produktionsgesellschaft/Österreichischer Runkfunk (ORF)).

1.10 Willi Resetarits and Ernst Molden in the Kunstzone-Karlsplatz (Photo: Manfred Werner, courtesy of Creative Commons).

1.11 *Blutrausch* (Images ©1997 Dor Film Produktionsgesellschaft/Österreichischer Runkfunk (ORF)).

1.12 *Blutrausch* (Images ©1997 Dor Film Produktionsgesellschaft/Österreichischer Runkfunk (ORF)).

1.13 *Blutrausch* (Images ©1997 Dor Film Produktionsgesellschaft/Österreichischer Runkfunk (ORF)).

1.14 *Blutrausch* (Images ©1997 Dor Film Produktionsgesellschaft/Österreichischer Runkfunk (ORF)).

1.15 *Blutrausch* (Images ©1997 Dor Film Produktionsgesellschaft/Österreichischer Runkfunk (ORF)).

1.16 *Blutrausch* (Images ©1997 Dor Film Produktionsgesellschaft/Österreichischer Runkfunk (ORF)).

1.17 *SOKO Wien* (Images ©2008 ZDF and ORF).

1.18 *SOKO Wien* (Images ©2008 ZDF and ORF).

1.19 Kolaric poster (Initiative Minderheiten).

1.20 *I Love Vienna* (Images ©1991 epo-film).

1.21 *I Love Vienna* (Images ©1991 epo-film).

1.22 *I Love Vienna* (Images ©1991 epo-film).

1.23 *I Love Vienna* (Images ©1991 epo-film).

1.24 *I Love Vienna* (Images ©1991 epo-film).

1.25 *I Love Vienna* (Images ©1991 epo-film).

1.26 Schlingensief's Container, 2000 (Photo: S. Ingram).

1.27 Schlingensief's Container, 2000 (Photo: S. Ingram).

1.28 *The Third Man* (Images ©1949 London Film Productions/British Lion Film Corporation).

1.29 *The Third Man* (Images ©1949 London Film Productions/British Lion Film Corporation).

1.30 *Third Man* tour poster (Photo: S. Ingram).

Part II:

Conclusion:
3.1   Clowning around in the Böhmischer Prater (Photo: M. Reisenleitner).
3.2   Fiaker sunset (Photo: M. Reisenleitner).
3.3   The History of Fashion: Barock (©Mato Johannik Weinper at Idee Konzept Mario Soldo).
3.4   Vienna Tourist Board advertising poster (www.wien.info).
3.5   WIEN JETZT ODER NIE poster in Berlin (Photo: S. Ingram).
3.6   Apple-banana (Photo: S. Ingram).

Preface

The genesis of this book is surprisingly easy to locate and, as one might suspect, it happened in Vienna. We had just finished translating Ackbar Abbas's *Hong Kong: Culture and the Politics of Disappearance* into German (Abbas 1997), and I (Markus) was tracking down a few remaining quotes in the Kafkaesque maze of Vienna's university library system. Figuring out exactly why the Institut für Germanistik has a completely different call number system from the Institut für Romanistik, and exactly which Thursday afternoon the Institut für Komparatistik is open for a couple of hours can be exhausting, and what better thing for somebody interested in popular culture's urban imaginaries to do after a day's worth of detection in the city's labyrinthine libraries than watch a couple of cop shows on television? What happened to be on television when I tuned in (having only a television without cable reception and therefore only access to ORF, the Austrian national broadcaster) were back-to-back broadcasts of recent episodes of *SOKO Donau* and *SOKO Kitzbühel*. I had been vaguely aware of the Munich-based *SOKO 5113 roman policier*-derived cop show that started in 1978 and has for almost 35 years provided a rather low-key, realist and team-focused counterpart to the more spectacular, high-budget and protagonist-oriented *Tatort* series. What I was not aware of – not having been exposed to German-language television for 15 years – was that in the new millennium, *SOKO 5113* had spawned a number of local offshoots in locations ranging from the predictably urban (Leipzig, Cologne, Vienna) to the somewhat less predictable and out-of-the-way – one of the *SOKO*s operates out of Wismar, a Hanseatic town of some tourist appeal and claim to historical heritage.[1] Among the new offshoots of *SOKO 5113* were the shows I had stumbled across, co-produced by the German ZDF and the Austrian ORF.[2] Working on global flows that traverse the portal city of Hong Kong and following Abbas's dissection of issues of spatial framing and distinction, I found the shows remarkable in several ways. The cookie-cutter plots, characters and dialogues were not worse than what can reasonably be expected from the genre, and I admit to being pleasantly surprised at their production value and competent craftsmanship. More unexpected for me were the regional imaginaries that the shows presented. While both shows clearly provide place imaginaries that "brand" their locations and add a seasoning of tourist-board picture-postcard shots that *SOKO*

Kitzbühel's gourmet chef Hannes Kofler would have found quite distasteful, they were not the imaginaries I had anticipated. Clichéd the shows might be, but the clichés of Kitzbühel and Vienna (which is what Donau metonymically stands for) had changed on me over the course of 15 years.

I am offering this anecdote not only as the kind of self-positioning mandated by post-linguistic-turn humanists. If we take a Benjaminian understanding of the historical seriously, then an anecdote provides a methodological tool "of making things present [...] to represent them in our space (not to represent ourselves in their space)" (Benjamin 206 [H2,3]). An anecdote "brings things near to us spatially, lets them enter our life" (Benjamin 545 [S1a,3]). What had entered my personal as well as academic horizon, a horizon ineluctably marked by flows of the global distribution of academic labour and scholarly exchange, was an imaginary that was at odds with what I remembered from growing up in Vienna. The dialectic of moments I experienced made me curious to account for this change and to explore the role that fashion had played in bringing it about. It made the book seem like a natural follow-up to *Berliner Chic*, which was just being finished at the time.

This book is a much more personal one than the Berlin volume and based on friendships in Vienna of great strength and duration; to avoid making anyone feel overly historical, we will refrain from dropping names and simply express the hope that they find themselves well-reflected in what follows. Katrina Sark was invaluable in finding and accessing resources for us. She made extraordinary use of the summer she spent in Vienna and made much more material available for us than could make its way into this work. We also appreciate her taking the time from her own work to go over ours at various stages. Thanks, too, to all those who took time to share their knowledge about Vienna's fashion system with Katrina, in particular Gerda Buxbaum, Monika Kycelt, Regina Karner, Karin Moser, Elizabeth Freiss, Elisabeth Noever-Ginthor, Andreas Oberkanins, Daniel Kalt, Brigitte Winkler, Astrid Weigelt, Isabella Wimmer, Sonja Weinstabel, Birgit Rampula, Anna Aichinger, Cloed Priscilla Baumgartner, Gabriele Rigby, and Maria Steiner, and the helpful staff in the Modebibliothek Schloss Hetzendorf. We were also very lucky to have the enabling research support of Margarete and Eberhard Reisenleitner. The project is all the richer for their tremendous spadework. Our work further benefited from the enthusiastic, insightful students in our Vienna classes at York and the feedback we received after presenting preliminary versions of various parts of it at scholarly gatherings. Special thanks to Helga Mitterbauer, Carrie Prei-Smith, Lora Senechal Carney and Joan Coutu, and the organizers of "Fashion Tales 2012" at ModaCult, Università Cattolica del Sacro Cuore, for organizing very fruitful sessions and to all of the participants in those sessions who helped us to clarify our ideas. We would also like to acknowledge the financial support of York University, the University of Auckland and Siegfried Mattl's Boltzmann Institute in Vienna, as well as Intellect's continued fostering of academic projects on visual and material culture.

Notes

1   *SOKO Leipzig*: 2001; *SOKO Kitzbühel*: 2001; *SOKO Köln*: 2003; *SOKO Wismar*: 2003; *SOKO Donau*: 2005; *SOKO Rhein-Main*: 2006-2008; *SOKO Stuttgart*: 2009.

2   My not even being aware of the existence of these shows is a clear indication of how television, with its basis on serialized mass production and a programming machine that needs to maintain an audience, is still strongly rooted in the regional, linguistic as well as national frameworks of media production that it represents as well as perpetuates (see Morley). One could develop an interesting comparative reading of the circuits of the *SOKO* shows in Europe (according to Wikipedia, *SOKO Donau* is shown in 15 countries, Canada not being one of them – http://de.wikipedia.org/wiki/SOKO_Donau, accessed 6 June 2013) and the flows of Korean, Japanese and Hong Kong television shows in southeast Asia.

Introduction

Vienna's Culture of Appearance

La forme d'une ville/Change plus vite, hélas! que le coeur d'un mortel
The form of a city/Changes more quickly, alas! than the human heart (Baudelaire, "Le Cygne" ("The Swan"))

"[…] fashion to be conceived as a cultural technology that is purpose-built for specific locations" (Craik xi)

As in so many cities, summer is normally construction season in Vienna, but the summer of 2012 saw an unusual amount of activity in the city. Beyond the expected street repairs, there were major redevelopment projects around the city's main transportation hubs in what is arguably the largest planned reconstruction the city has seen since the Ringstrasse was built in the second half of the nineteenth century.[1] At the same time several fashion-oriented developments were trying to give Vienna a makeover and turn it into a fashion- and design-conscious European urban centre worthy of global recognition for its style culture. The Museumsquartier (MQ) declared summer 2012 the "Summer of Fashion" [Figure 0.1, Figure 0.2] and organized a packed four-month program that included fashion shows, exhibitions, public talks and the fourth annual MQ Vienna Fashion Week. The second annual Vienna Fashion Night also took place in the summer of 2012 [Figure 0.3], during which the city's high society was invited to select locations along and around the *Luxusmeile* (luxury mile) in the first district to shop after hours, sip champagne and watch an exclusive fashion show. The luxury mile itself was extended [Figure 0.4],[2] and new insider guides to fashionable consumption have sprouted up, such as Robert Kropf's *Be Inside*,[3] Tina Haslinger's *Guided Vienna* and the Inoperable Urban Culture Gallery's *Urban Guide Vienna*,[4] so that people who want to be in the know can learn about the "in" places to shop, eat, drink and make merry.

In other words, Vienna is changing, and like Baudelaire's Paris, when Vienna changes, it changes dramatically and under public scrutiny. These are cities that are not merely states of mind (Park), ways of life (Wirth) or structures of visibility (Donald 1999), but ones that generate, to appropriate John Berger's meme for the context of urban culture, unique ways of seeing. However, in contrast to the televisuality characteristic of urban post-cultures that create what Ackbar Abbas has termed the urban double-take or *déjà disparu*, in which global cities such as Hong Kong change so rapidly that it produces "the feeling that what is new and unique about the situation is always already gone, and we are left holding a handful of clichés or a cluster of memories of what has never been" (Abbas 25), Vienna's historical substance lends it something we see as a kind of clichéd, mythical visuality, in which nothing

Figure 0.1: MQ Summer of Fashion billboard (Photo: S. Ingram).

Figure 0.2: MQ Summer of Fashion advertising pillar (Photo: S. Ingram).

Figure 0.3: Vienna Fashion Night (Photo: S. Ingram).

Figure 0.4: Luxury Mile during Fashion Night 2012
(Photo: M. Reisenleitner).

appears to have changed even though, or even when, it has, creating a culture of appearance, or *toujours paru*.

Vienna's urban imaginary is predicated on the city being structured by fashionable appearances that misdirect those who are content to project complacently their desires and fears onto them. Like the Litfaßsäule that Orson Welles's Harry Lime escapes through into the sewers in *The Third Man* (Graham Greene, 1949) that guileless viewers and visitors

Figure 0.5: *The Third Man* (Images ©1949 London Film Productions/British Lion Film Corporation).

Figure 0.6: *The Third Man* (Images ©1949 London Film Productions/British Lion Film Corporation).

Figure 0.7: *The Third Man* (Images ©1949 London Film Productions/British Lion Film Corporation).

presume are mere surfaces for advertising [Figures 0.5, 0.6 and 0.7], and like the testament written onto a painting of the Prater in an episode of *Kommissar Rex* (1994–2004)[5] that prevents it from falling into the wrong hands,[6] Vienna is full of palimpsestic objects and spaces that are more than they appear to be.[7]

While Vienna may be just another European city for non-Europeans, a key component of its self-identity is its insistence on its unique qualities, that it is "anders" (other/strange/different/quirky). One of its best-known and long-living advertising and promotional campaigns bore the slogan "Wien ist anders." Associated with its charismatic promoter, Mayor Helmut Zilk (1927–2008; mayor 1984–1994), the slogan formed a catchy counterfoil to the long-standing adage that "Wien bleibt Wien" (Vienna remains Vienna, i.e. no matter what). The purpose of the "Wien ist anders" campaign was to distinguish the city from its European competitors on two counts: first, as a place with an ongoing tradition of art, theatre, music, cabaret and alternative culture vis-à-vis cities whose histories are more industrial, like Berlin's; and, second, as a place with a particular kind of charm, characterized by taste, culture and bonhomie (Musner 14–15). Musner provides the example of a publication prepared for an EU–Latin America summit in May 2006, which maintained:

Vienna simply is different. The city's marketing established that as a slogan years ago. But it's more than an effective saying – because Vienna really is different. Back then no one could quite imagine what the brand 'Vienna is different' stood for. Today one associates it

Figure 0.8: Sign on park bench (Photo: S. Ingram).

Figure 0.9: Sign on garbage truck (Photo: S. Ingram).

with many things – for example, the conviction that in no other city contemporary spirit and tradition are as closely intertwined as here (Musner 14).[8]

Decades later, one still finds "Wien ist anders" signs on park benches [Figure 0.8] and garbage trucks [Figure 0.9], and it is the title of a recent academic monograph on the twentieth-century history of Jewish writers in Austria (H. Herzog).

A key aspect of Vienna's distinctiveness is that it puts a unique wrinkle on the typical attribution of modern to urban centres. Modernity means something quite different, something much more inflected and influenced by the weight of the historical, especially the baroque, in the Viennese context than it does in other modern Euro-American cities, such as London, Paris, Berlin, New York, Chicago and Los Angeles. This underscores both Doreen Massey's argument "that the identity of places in the modern world is constituted as much by their relation with other places as by anything intrinsic to their location" (cited in Driver and Gilbert 4), as well as the necessity of redressing the unfortunate homogenizing effects produced by the otherwise admirable provincializing and de-centring of Europe and the West in scholarship on modernity. If it is true that "the spatial dimensions of modernism [/modernity] have yet to be fully understood" (Kalliney 751), that speaks to the scope of the issue more than any lack of interest in the question. On the contrary, as Susan Stanford Friedman notes in countering Jameson's contention in *A Singular Modernity* that "the only satisfactory semantic meaning of modernity lies in its association with capitalism" (Jameson 12),

> The field [of modernism/modernity studies] abounds in such adjectives for modernity or modernities as multiple, polycentric, early, at large, alternative, other, peripheral, divergent, discrepant, uneven, conjunctural, and recurrent. Each term is its own keyword, with different nuances, particularly in what it suggests about the relation to Western modernities. I like how they suggest a spatial approach to modernity, a necessity for globalizing a concept that has been predominantly temporal (Stanford Friedman 480).

Indeed, since Bruno Latour declared in his 1993 *We Have Never Been Modern* that "[m]odernity comes in as many versions as there are thinkers or journalists, yet all its definitions point, in one way or another, to the passage of time. The adjective 'modern' designates a new regime, an acceleration, a rupture, a revolution in time" (cited in Stanford Friedman 478), an extensive scholarship has developed whose anti-Eurocentrism has encouraged geographical and spatial sensitivity (such as Chakrabarty, Mohanty, Brooker and Thacker, and Huyssen). While there exists an awareness "that the concept of 'the West' is itself deeply centric, repressing the heterogeneities and peripheries within Europe and North America and the degree to which the West has never been and is not 'one'" (Stanford Friedman 477), less common are attempts to revisit the heterogeneities within Europe and North America from the planetary perspective Stanford Friedman champions. Possibly because "where is modernism?" was one of the hoary chestnuts of Eurocentric scholarship, such threads often quickly become meta-textual, evoking "the challenge of simultaneously expanding the field's cultural boundaries while continuing to classify the movement's chief aesthetic attributes" (Kalliney 752).

In contrast to literary scholars such as Stanford Friedman and sociologists such as Anthony Giddens, for us modernity is neither primarily aesthetic nor primarily social but rather cultural-historical, in the sense of E.P. Thompson's "whole way of struggle" (54), and we find fashion a useful heuristic wedge to open up the spatial specificity of the cultural-historical struggle inherent in the modernity of Vienna's urban context, both because of its polysemy and its relation to modernity. Like Eugenia Paulicelli and Hazel Clark in their *Fabric of Cultures* project, we ascribe to the view that "fashion is a privileged lens through which to gain a new understanding of cultures" (Paulicelli and Clark), and we also ascribe to their understanding of fashion as "a cultural system of meanings and an ongoing process of communication [...] acquired through a process of cultural mediation that takes place in a variety of ways, such as film, photography, the internet, publicity, and magazines" (2). While this understanding does not spare us the usual difficulty in Fashion Studies of the "lexical disjuncture between fashion as garments that are worn and fashion as something popular" and the fact that "in the late nineteenth century, corsets were fashionable, in fashion, but so was riding a bicycle and playing tennis" (Bancroft 394, cf. Buxbaum 2009, "Vorwort"), it also does not prevent us from championing an approach like Claudia Ebner's, which embraces both possibilities:

> Whether one speaks of the fashion of the Baroque or of it being fashionable to holiday by the sea in the summer, it is always about a momentary acceptance; that is, it was not the case that it was usual to spend summer holidays by the sea or to dress or build things as they did during the Baroque – therefore, there has been an observable change, which has been accepted by a significant segment of a society (Ebner 143).[9]

For Ebner, what is at stake in fashion is the pleasure derived from change ("Vergnügen am Wechsel" 143), an all-encompassing cultural phenomenon that applies to more than dress or ornamentation (144). Vienna's dreamlike stasis would seem to challenge Ebner's catholic take on fashion, but it also points to other forms of pleasure that are to be had besides those derived from change, specifically, those derived from the lack of change – or the negotiation, and manifestations of articulation, between those opposite poles of how to encounter modernity. Just as one returns to the same places in one's dreams, the structure of Vienna's fashion system reveals loci frozen in the logic of dreamtime, a schizophrenic suspension of temporality. In the cultural phenomena we examine here that are relevant for the formation and awakenings of Vienna's fashion system, we find traces of struggles that work to suspend the impression of time passing and thereby induce a schizophrenic logic of "both and."

Vienna's dual nature is almost as much of a fixture in the city's urban imaginary as its state of being "different" [Figure 0.10]. Typical comments in this vein include Hilde Spiel's Freudian-tinged description of the city's "doubled identifying mark of uncanny sociability,"[10] Bruno Bettelheim's observation that "the modern buildings of the Ringstrasse gave Vienna a double and somewhat contradictory character: that of both an old imperial capital and a center of modern culture" (Bettelheim 70), and Janik and Toulmin's noting "the bitter pill that lay beneath the sugar-coating of hedonistic aestheticism and *Sachertorte*" (Janik and Toulmin 61). The sentiment is echoed in Schwarz's "With the gilded veneer gone, the worm-eaten inside became painfully visible" (Schwarz 51) and assertions like "Vienna films

Figure 0.10: Showdown in front of the Cafe Griensteidl (Photo: M. Reisenleitner).

are always a tale of two cities" (Burri 6). The city remains, as Majorie Perloff sums up with the title of her memoir, very much a paradox, something also true of its fashion scene. As designer Anna Aichinger has noted, "Vienna is not a fashion city but rather a city with a fashion scene. Actually there are two fashion scenes. There are the designers who work here locally (mostly in the 7th district), and those that show internationally."[11] However, this doubled aspect of the city – a great imperial city as well as a breeding ground for violence and political upheaval (Perloff 2003, 228), an intertwining of contemporary spirit and tradition, progressively industrial as well as cozily village-like, global and local – is not unique to Vienna. Rather, it is the hallmark of modernity. As Homi Bhabha details in his analysis of the "'double and split' time of national representation" in *The Location of Culture*:

the failure of the Realistic to completely triumph over the Romantic reveals that there is 'always the distracting presence of another temporality that disturbs the contemporaneity of the national present,' a present which must constantly surmount the ghostly, the terrifying and the unaccountable. Freud, he reminds us, 'associates surmounting with the repressions of a "cultural" unconscious; a liminal, uncertain state of cultural belief when the archaic emerges in the midst of margins of modernity as a result of some psychic ambivalence or intellectual uncertainty' (Ingram 2003, 87).

That a city has also been subject to such doubling and splitting reminds us that the nation does not have a monopoly on (increasingly late) modern experience. And what better cultural phenomenon to get at that experience than one that "directly reflects the mobility and mutability of modernity itself" (Wilson 12), one, moreover, that even shares its etymology (Lehmann 5–19)?

While our approach is grounded in Roland Barthes' (1967) seminal work on the fashion system, which investigates a structure of representation rather than material products, we find a methodological apparatus based on a dichotomy between visual and written representations, like the one Barthes established in distinguishing between "image clothing" and "written clothing," difficult to maintain in the contemporary reality of digital media and global (tele-)visuality, in which "the urban scene – advertising, music, cinema, television, fashion, video clips – exist[s] in the rapid circuits of electronic production/reproduction/ distribution" (Chambers 185). Rather, this situation calls for an approach that does justice to the complex cultural practices situated at the intersection of visuality, narration, performance, and spectacle. We thus go beyond a semiotics of "representation" and "structure" (defined by Barthes, following Hjelmslev, as "an autonomous entity of internal dependencies," 1983, 3) by approaching the nexus between fashion and urbanity as an imaginary, understood "as a constructed landscape of collective aspirations, which is [...] now mediated through the complex prism of modern media" (Appadurai 31), constituting lived experience, material practices, social relations, and public discourse; generating the taken-for-granted; and operating beyond the level of individuals' intentionalities.

In establishing how the nexus of fashion and modern urbanity structures Vienna's contemporary imaginary, we hope to bring together and add to the scholarship on Vienna, fashion, and urban studies. Even though Vienna is generally considered a secondary world city in global city scholarship and is therefore not very present in it (cf. Brenner and Keil), we show that global city issues, such as gentrification and the flows and "scapes" of finance, media and people (cf. Zukin, Sassen, King, and Appadurai), are also very pertinent in the case of Vienna. Vienna is even more absent in the scholarship on fashion cities than it is in the scholarship on world cities, and even more absent than Berlin in that scholarship, garnering, for example, nary a mention in the index of either Breward and Gilbert's *Fashion's World Cities* or Potvin's *Places and Spaces of Fashion 1800–2007*. Further, as we detail in Part I, fashion has not figured in any substantial way in the scholarship on Vienna. In response, we mobilize fashion as a structure of visibility that can direct the critical gaze at revealing aspects of the urban fabric, from façades to festivals. This is to take the material and fashionable dimensions of urban imaginaries seriously and to question with Pheng Cheah "why is it that matter is text-ile or woven?" (Cheah 74). We are not arguing that Vienna is a city of fashion per se (it would be difficult to contradict local fashion luminaries such as Anna Aichinger and Gerda Buxbaum on this point). However, it is home to a fashion system, which implies, first, that material products have always constituted only a small part of a wider cultural phenomenon, and, second, that its urban imaginary exists as a discernible fashion space. Bradley Quinn developed the concept of fashion space to analyse the consistency of the vision informing fashion-designed spaces, such as a label's flagship stores and websites, and as was shown in *Berliner Chic*, there can be a discernible consistency to an urban imaginary that the concept of fashion space can be useful in elucidating.

Fashion, design, architecture, and cinema are all constitutive parts of Vienna's fashion space – multiple cultural practices that negotiate Vienna's form of mythical urban visibility, symptoms of what moulds the city's imaginary in diverse ways. In this book, we offer probes – symptomatic readings of indicative cultural phenomena. In the first part, we delve into the question of how Vienna's urban imaginary came to take the forms it has, and we find that the locations of Vienna's fashion are predominantly social and that useful coordinates are provided by the classes that have been influential in setting the agenda for the forms of cultural production for which the city has become known: first, the aristocrats around, or associated with, the Habsburg dynasty, whose grip on power began to loosen in the mid-nineteenth century with the ascent of the Ringstrasse Liberals, against whom the unruly petty bourgeois and proletarian masses offered increased resistance, and whose place as a threat in the post-war years was increasingly taken over by "foreigners." When Musner writes, "In different historical and political contexts, self-representations of Vienna as a city of music, a city of theatre, a city of the Baroque, a city of architecture, a city of literature and not in the least a city of harmonious and humane everyday life was produced, made permanent through the media and assembled in new collages" (17),[12] he is gesturing towards the same formation,[13] as is De Frantz when she notes that:

> The city's inhabitants and opinion leaders identify themselves strongly with their cultural heritage, including the highly conflictive social and political traditions of: Habsburg imperialism carried by aristocratic elitism and a neo-absolutist bureaucracy; a bourgeois retreat from political emancipation into nineteenth-century Biedermeier culture, culminating in Vienna's turn-of-the-century excellence in arts and sciences; and a strong working-class tradition institutionalized throughout decades of Social Democratic cultural education policy (De Frantz 2005, 52).

What needs to be added is a sense of the relationality among these items, and their relation to fashion and style culture.

One finds a similar constellation in the City of Vienna's latest advertising campaign – *WIEN JETZT ODER NIE* (Vienna, Now or Never), which has been implemented by the Vienna Tourist Board since 2009, the year after Helmut Zilk's death [Figure 0.11]. Five "brand modules" were identified that the Vienna Tourist Board decided would be useful in persuading international tourists to visit Vienna: imperial heritage, profusion of

Figure 0.11: Materials from the Vienna Tourist Board advertising campaign (www.wien.info).

music and culture, savoir vivre, functional efficiency and balance of urban and green areas (Section 1.2 of the brand manual *Vienna Now Or Never*). That this campaign has not yet taken off as a meme, and certainly not in the way "Wien ist anders" did, can be attributed to a number of factors. The relationality of the various parts is not made explicit, and the modules are all rather vague. "Imperial heritage" conflates the absolutist Baroque and Kaiser Franz Joseph's modern Ringstrasse, while "profusion of music and culture" allows the city's extraordinary international reputation for music (cf. Nussbaumer 2007) to be watered down by its strong theatrical and literary traditions, as well as glossing over the variety of music available in the city from opera and waltzes to jazz, musicals, and pop festivals. "Savoir vivre" aims to evoke the city's taste culture but does not reveal what is special about Viennese coffeehouse culture that distinguishes it from that of other European cities. "Functional efficiency" does the same for the city's impressive public transportation system but does not make a point of stressing the city's relatively small size vis-à-vis comparable cities such as Paris, Berlin and Milan, and "balance of urban and green areas" conflates the forested hills that surround the city and make for lovely weekend outings with the central park areas and the Prater. In short, the brand modules do not capture the essence of the

Figure 0.12: Eissalon Schwedenplatz (Photo: K. Sark).

city's uniqueness and how it exists as a fashion space the way "Wien ist anders" does, and "poor but sexy" does for Berlin.

Additionally, for a place that can boast of being *the* city of music, "Now or Never" does not work to harmonize the five brand modules but rather only muddies already murky waters. Based on "O Sole Mio," a popular Neapolitan song, it was a chart-topper for Elvis Presley in 1960 and "is commonly heard playing from ice cream vans all over Europe."[14] While Vienna does have wonderful Italian ice cream in the summer, it is not one of the city's main tourist attractors [Figure 0.12]. Nor is Elvis's reputation and style of rock n roll any more in keeping with Vienna's style culture than Neapolitan ice cream. In that respect, east coast North American singer-songwriters of Jewish descent who are temperamentally more in tune with the city and have actually written songs about it, such as Billy Joel ("Vienna Waits For You") and Leonard Cohen ("Take This Waltz"), might have been much more appropriate choices.

The Chics

Instead of modules, we propose in the first part of the study a series of four "chics" that work together to capture, and help us to locate, the city's multifaceted appeal: Baroque Chic, Ringstrasse Chic, Prolo Chic and *Ausländer* Chic. There are various ways one could theorize these chics, the first being as fashion-oriented memes. Richard Dawkins coined the term 'meme' in *The Selfish Gene* to help account for the spread of cultural phenomena and ideas in evolutionary terms. For Dawkins, memes are "items that are reproduced by imitation rather than reproduced genetically" (Millikan 16). Further, a meme acts as a unit for carrying cultural ideas, symbols or practices, which can be transmitted from one mind to another through writing, speech, gestures, rituals or other imitable phenomena. Supporters of the concept regard memes as cultural analogues to genes in that they self-replicate, mutate and respond to selective pressures (ibid.).

Dawkins' examples of memes include melodies, catchphrases, fashion, and the technology of building arches.[15] If one is interested in the transmission of the chics, then it can be useful to conceptualize them as visually transmitted memes that are based on modernity's groundedness in cinematic perception.

We understand cinematic perception in Kara Keeling's sense as "involved in the production and reproduction of reality itself," processes that "order, orchestrate, produce, and reproduce social reality and sociality" (Keeling 11). Cinematic perception is based on what Keeling, following Bergson and Deleuze, calls cinematic clichés, which "will come to predominate perceptions under conditions wherein one's set of memory-images is already a set of clichés or, speaking more broadly, when that set consists of collective images, experiences, traditions, knowledges, and so on" (12). Keeling explicitly links this concept to Benjamin's notion that film prepares the senses for life in modernity, and to Gramsci's notion of hegemony, which establishes common sense as "a radically historical category" (22) that records a group's historical becoming and reveals moments of resistance and change: "When common sense (as memory-image) and a present perception are incommensurate and the present image cannot be recognized so that an arrested movement can continue, something has become too strong in the image [...] Common sense explodes" (23). When that happens, as we see in the case of Vienna, the image changes, forming a new meme or cliché with the potential to become hegemonic, as "Vienna 1900" did in the 1980s when it replaced the "Vienna as baroque" cliché that had reigned up until that time [Figure 0.13]. Exemplary of what a commonplace the baroque cliché was before it was overtaken by the cliché of *fin-de-siècle* Vienna is the 1980 *The Imperial Style: Fashions of the Hapsburg Era* catalogue:

It all sounds baroque – extravagant, bizarre, flamboyant – but Vienna remains a baroque city. 'Vienna reached its cultural zenith during the Baroque, and remained baroque in its strangest and finest expressions of life,' wrote Egon Friedell, who was himself a baroque mixture of essayist, philosopher, cultural historian, and actor. In Vienna the Baroque became a state of mind (Cone 22).

Understanding chic as a subset of cinematic perception with rotating clichés achieving hegemony establishes an explicit link between fashion, style, and modernity (Breward and Evans 2005). It points to the profoundly visual nature of the work we are investigating, and the intimate connection of cinematic apparatus with fashion and style.

It would also be possible to think of our chics in terms of imagoes, a concept that emerges from Jacques Lacan's understanding of the three psychic registers: the Imaginary, the Symbolic and the Real. As Jane Gallop cogently outlines:

Figure 0.13: Baroque splendour (Photo: M. Reisenleitner).

The imaginary is made up of *imagoes*. An imago is an unconscious image or cliché 'which preferentially orients the way in which the subject apprehends other people.' In the imaginary mode, one's understanding of other people is shaped by one's own imagoes. The perceived other is actually, at least in part, a projection. Psychoanalysis is an attempt to recognize the subject's imagoes in order to ascertain their deforming effect upon the subject's understanding of her relationships. The point is not to give up the imagoes (an impossible task) or to create better ones (any static image will deform the perception of the dynamics of intersubjectivity). But, in the symbolic register, the subject understands these imagoes as structuring projections (Gallop 271–272).

It is not only people's understanding of other people that is shaped by their own imagoes, but also, as we show here, their understanding of places.

Structuring projections are what our analyses aim to understand the chics as, but we do so with an awareness of the historical components involved, that they do not come out of nowhere but rather reflect aspects of a historical trajectory that needs to be understood so that one can see the extent to which the projections have altered or departed from historical precedent, rupturing the common sense of historical lineage. Our goal, like that of psychoanalysis, is to reveal the mirror upon which unconscious clichés have been projected, and in doing so expose the process of their formation.

One will notice that the historical trajectory of Baroque Chic, Ringstrasse Chic, Prolo Chic and *Ausländer* Chic mirrors the phases Gilles Lipovetsky has shown are central to the development of fashion. Seeking "to understand the emergence of fashion in the late Middle Ages and its principal lines of evolution over the centuries," Lipovetsky identifies an initial "artisanal and aristocratic stage of fashion," which "held sway for five hundred years" and was followed by "the first phase of the history of modern fashion, its sublime, heroic moment," which had Parisian haute couture as its epicentre and lasted until "the point in the 1960s when the system began to crack" and *prêt-a-porter* became ever more dominant (Lipovetsky 5, 17, 55). Writing in the mid-1980s (the original *L'Empire de l'éphémère: La mode et son destin dans les sociétés modernes* appeared in 1987, with Catherine Porter's English translation following in 1994), Lipovetsky did not include the more contemporary street style in his narrative. Nevertheless, that our chics so nicely map onto Lipovetsky's history of the fashion system "as an exceptional process inseparable from the origin and development of the modern West" (15) demonstrates that fashion implicitly underlies the development of Vienna's urban imaginary.

The term "chic" also has its own history in Vienna [Figure 0.14].[16] In the twelfth issue of the Austro-Hungarian magazine *Das Blatt der Hausfrau!* (*The Housewife's Magazine!*,

Figure 0.14: Wiener Chic shop (Photo: W. Fischer).

the issue from the beginning of October 1901 to the end of September 1902), an editorial addressing the question "What is chic?" defines it as "the customizing of the prevailing fashion in a matter advantageous to the wearer" (870).[17] What makes one "chic" as opposed to simply fashionable is the ability to reconcile one's own individual tastes with those of one's time. In other words, "chic" in this sense presupposes that one has developed a style of one's own and is not dictated to by the latest trends, but also that one does not reject those trends wholesale. Chic is to be found in the crowd, like the object of desire in Edgar Allan Poe's "The Man of the Crowd," and the challenge is to keep that object in sight without losing oneself by being swallowed up. As one of the characters in *The Moderns* (Alan Rudolph, 1988) puts it, it is to be "among the throng but not of the throng." The editorial in *The Housewife's Magazine!* warns, "But only a slight emphasis of what counts as a characteristic outline. Every exaggeration excludes chic, puts caricature in its place" (870).[18] The greatest errors committed in not being chic involve colour, according to the editorialist, who finds it odd "how uncritical our ladies are in that regard. Whether they are dressed in a fashionable colour, whether they make a pretentious blot in the landscape, or whether they go around for years in a 1901 or 1902 model, seems not to matter at all. It is fashion, one wears it" (ibid.).[19] To appear chic in Vienna is to walk a fine line; Wiener Chic is a stylistic tightrope between the Scylla of convention and the Charybdis of ridicule.

After we elaborate the trajectory of Baroque Chic, Ringstrasse Chic, Prolo Chic and *Ausländer* Chic in the first part of the study and demonstrate their ongoing relevance and reach with examples from films from the 1990s, the period when Vienna began to go global in reacting to the fall of the Wall and the opening of the Iron Curtain, we then turn in the second part of the study to the impact fashion has had on the city in establishing unique structures and cultures of visibility. We first explore the offerings of the three museums responsible for maintaining fashion collections and staging fashion exhibitions and events – the Wien Museum, the Museum of Applied Arts (MAK, Museum für angewandte Kunst), and the Museumsquartier (MQ) – and then turn our attention to designers such as Helmut Lang who have helped to give Wiener Chic a recognizable international style, characterized by an elegant minimalism and independence of spirit.

What we find again and again is a city that has found ways to render itself seemingly immobile and dreamlike, a city that is charting its global future while carefully conserving its past. Vienna, we find, is like the poster for a Seurat exhibition that the French young woman in *Before Sunrise* (Richard Linklater, 1995) admires because it depicts an environment that is stronger than the people who inhabit it and can make them fade into its pointillist background [Figure 0.15].

Like the Ferris wheel on the Prater and the Ringstrasse that encircles the inner district, Vienna has a magical, ironically anti-modern way of appearing to bring people back to where they started. However, its seeming to prevent forward progress will be shown to be the secret to its successfully parlaying its predominantly historical heritage into an environmentally sustainable, multicultural and liveable urban space that seems to offer a viable third way between musealizing its urban environment (à la European cities like Prague and Florence) and

Figure 0.15: *Before Sunrise* (Images ©1995 Detour Filmproduction/F.I.L.M.H.A.U.S. Wien/Sunrise Production/Castle Rock Entertainment).

relentlessly disappearing its past (à la Asian cities like Hong Kong and Beijing). While Vienna may appear to some in Austrian Studies to have gone from being a "vibrant metropolis (and capital of sexology) at the beginning of the twentieth century to a conservative museum-city trapped in the amber of tourism at century's end" (McEwen 2006, 132), we show that its urban texture continues to be characterized by tensions, conflicts and compromises that, as we move deeper into the twenty-first century, the city's fashion system is working to open up to competing global influences in an ongoing dialogue with the pressures tradition exerts. By outlining how fashion and style have contributed to the development of Vienna's culture of appearance and structure of visibility, it will become apparent how the "chic" of a particular city is never simply the result of branding or the formation of a unique "identity." Rather, it is, as we show, a complex process at the intersection of histories manifest in the material shape of a city, which generate specific and singular visualities, global connectivities, and institutional and political choices that result in unique, contingent and highly fluid "mixes."[20] The following probes attempt to identify and analyse this mix, and to unravel the key strands that weave the texture of Wiener Chic.

Notes

1   A new terminal at the airport opened on 5 June 2012; the area around Wien Mitte, site of the CAT rail link to the airport, was being overhauled; the old Südbahnhof was torn down and is set to become the new Hauptbahnhof; and not only was the U-Bahn network being

expanded and one central line overhauled, but the area around the Schwedenplatz, one of the main central stops, was set to be revamped (https://schwedenplatz.wien.gv.at/ppr19/schwedenplatz/, accessed 7 June 2013).

2 As of the end of summer 2012, the luxury shops now located in and around the Kohlmarkt included: Vivienne Westwood, Valentino, Chopard, Tiffany & Co., Diesel, Dolce and Gabbana, Louis Vuitton, Ferragamo, Chanel, Akris, Burberry, Gucci, Giorgio Armani, Emporio Armani, Cartier, Hermès, Jil Sander, Agent Provocateur, Prada, Versace, Gianfranco Ferré, Missoni, Philipp Plein, and Stephen Webster (cf. http://www.wien.info/en/vienna-for/luxurious-vienna/flagshipstores, accessed 7 June 2013).

3 Kropf also runs a website, "Insidereicom: Local Heros, weltweit, ganz persönlich" ("local heroes, across the globe, up close and personal"), that would seem to have aspirations of competing with Wallpaper in searching out global style culture: http://www.insiderei.com/start-content/, accessed 7 June 2013.

4 It is available on their website: http://www.inoperable.at/, accessed 7 June 2013.

5 The second most successful television series after *Baywatch*, the Austrian cop show *Kommissar Rex* is the most successful television detective series of all time, featuring a police dog as its eponymous protagonist and playing to an international audience relishing its humorous takes on Viennese stereotypes.

6 The episode is called "Das Testament" and is in season 5 (episode 10).

7 The stolen letter left prominently on display not once but twice in Edgar Allan Poe's "The Purloined Letter" provides an apposite metaphor to better understand the ongoing interest that people who live in and with Vienna have in cultural practices such as façades and exteriors, and the pressing need Freud felt to find out what was behind them.

8 All translations of quotes from the German are ours unless otherwise noted, and the originals are included so that readers who know German may form their own impression: "Wien ist eben anders. Das hat das Stadtmarketing schon vor Jahren als Slogan positioniert. Dahinter steht aber mehr als ein werbewirksamer Spruch – weil Wien ja tatsächlich anders ist. Damals hat man sich unter der Marke 'Wien ist anders' noch nichts vorstellen können. [...] Heute verbindet man viele Assoziationen mit dem Spruch 'Wien ist anders' – zum Beispiel die Überzeugung, dass sich in keiner anderen Stadt Zeitgeist und Tradition so eng aneinander schmieden wie hier."

9 "Ob man von der Mode der Barockzeit spricht, oder von der Mode, im Sommer an den See zu fahren, immer geht es um die momentane Akzeptanz, das heisst, es war nicht immer üblich, im Sommer an den See zu fahren bzw. sich so zu kleiden oder zu bauen, wie es sich in der Barockzeit geschah – also liegt ein offensichtlicher Wandel vor, der von einer signifikanten Menge einer Gesellschaft akzeptiert wird" (143).

10 "Doppelsignatur unheimlicher Gemütlichkeit," cited in Musner 202.

11 "Daher ist Wien keine Modestadt, aber eher eine Stadt mit einer Modeszene. Eigentlich gibt es zwei Modeszenen. Es gibt die Designer, die lokal hier (die meisten im 7. Bezirk) arbeiten, und die, die international präsentieren" (in communication with Katrina Sark). Aichinger, one should note, belongs to the latter of the two categories she mentions and shows in Paris.

12 "In unterschiedlichen zeitgeschichtlichen und politischen Kontexten wurden nämlich Selbstbilder von Wien als Musikstadt, als Theaterstadt, als Barockstadt, als Architekturstadt,

als Literaturstadt und nicht zuletzt als Stadt einer harmonischen und menschengerechten Alltagskultur produziert, medial verstetigt und in immer neuen Collagen miteinander vermischt."

13 As Lutter makes clear in her review, "Musner's point is exactly not to tell a story of the city's singularities" because his view is the commonplace one in Vienna that "behind this slogan of the 1980s expressing Vienna's self-image, lurks the 'typically Viennese' as a symbolically differentiating feature in the tradition of Lueger's imagined community of the Viennese petit bourgeoisie" (469). While that may have been true of the 1980s, by the 1990s, as we show in Part I, "Vienna is different" had come in film to mean that Vienna was full of quirky, colourful characters that were able to register globally as chic and that involved lifestyle choices that have an ethical as well as an aesthetic dimension.

14 http://en.wikipedia.org/wiki/%27O_Sole_Mio, accessed 7 June 2013.

15 http://en.wikipedia.org/wiki/Meme, accessed 7 June 2013.

16 As one can tell from the lettering of the shop sign, this shop was used as a backdrop for the postcard image upon which our cover is based. It is a costumer in the Schönbrunnerstraße, whose website is at: www.wienerchic.com.

17 "das Anpassen an die herrschende Mode auf eine für die Trägerin [sic] vortheilhafte Art."

18 "Aber doch nur ein leichtes Hervorheben der charakteristischen Umrisse des eben Giltigen. Jedes Übertreiben schließt den Chic aus, setzt die Carikatur an seine Stelle."

19 "wie kritiklos unsere Damen ihr gegenüberstehen. Ob eine Modefarbe sie kleidet, ob sie einen pretensiösen großen Klex in die Natur macht, ob man mit so einer auffallenden Nuance noch jahrelang als Modell 1901 oder 1902 herumgeht, scheint ganz gleichgiltig zu sein. Es ist Mode – man trägt es."

20 We are grateful to Alan Blum for sharing his recently developed concept of "the mix" with us. We have found that it captures the dynamics of Vienna's urban imaginary in ways that other concepts, such as "scene," do not.

PART I

Chic Formations: The Cinematically Historical Underpinnings
of Vienna's Urban Imaginary

In his introduction to *World Film Locations: Vienna*, Robert Dassanovsky claims that "Vienna, much like Paris, is a film city obsessed with love" (5). More accurate would have been to note that this obsession is with obsession itself, something he would seem to acknowledge in the qualification that follows, that "this attitude presents a somewhat thornier prospect in the city of Freud, as the recent *A Dangerous Method* (David Cronenberg, 2011) aptly underscores" (5). In this vein, when asked to name traditional Viennese designers for a new publication on "what's in" in Vienna, the newly appointed Director of the Museumsquartier, Christian Strasser, responded: "One such brand is *Tiberius* for sure, which is celebrating its 20 year anniversary this year [2012] and has become a benchmark for the Viennese fashion scene in the past few years" (Kropf 20). That a fashion designer known for bringing fetish-wear into the twenty-first century would be singled out for his influence is not unrelated to the image of Vienna that emerges when one turns to films associated with the city. Not coincidentally, Tiberius's lifestyle concept store, located in a Biedermeier building in the 7th district and designed by BEHF Architekten, is described as being "a set right out of a David Cronenberg film."[1] From the *Kinopioniere* collection of material from the years 1908–18, which opens with "Das eitle Stubenmädchen" (The Vain Parlourmaid) disrobing and comparing herself with a sculpture, to Cronenberg's biopic about Sabina Spielrein's role in the development of psychoanalysis, the red thread running through films associated with Vienna is a weave of eros and thanatos that underscores the challenge of establishing gratifying relationships given the difficulties, desires, and impermanence inherent in the human condition: the parlourmaid flees from her employer, who eagerly follows her out of the room, while Spielrein returned to the Soviet Union, where in 1942 she was among the Jewish victims of the SS.

What we offer in this section is not a broad survey of the kind done by film scholars such as Dassanovsky and those associated with the 2010 "Wien im Film" exhibition at the Wien Museum, which ably deal with the twisted relations, *Weltekel* (disgust with the world) and *Fremdschämen* (feeling embarrassed for others) so predominant in the larger entities of Austrian cinema and culture. As Lutter notes, "this ambivalent imagery of Vienna – nostalgically glorified on the one hand, *critically morbid* on the other – has a long tradition in its own right that starts neither with Thomas Bernhard nor with the biting comments of Karl Kraus more than half a century earlier" (471, italics added). Rather, we are interested in this section in how the cinematic has contributed to making Vienna chic, and to that end we have identified a series of chics (Baroque Chic, Ringstrasse Chic, Prolo Chic and *Ausländer* Chic) that allow us to account for the various facets that have come to dominate Vienna's urban imaginary. In charting the distance between this imaginary's historical underpinnings and films that have drawn on these underpinnings to "chicify" the city for the twenty-first century, our analyses necessarily involve the emergence of globalization.

Defined by Roland Robertson as "the compression of the world and the intensification of the consciousness of the world as a whole" (Robertson 8), the globalization that followed upon the fall of the Wall, the ensuing demise of the Warsaw Pact and the enlargements of the EU irrevocably re-situated Vienna in the minds of filmgoers. While Vienna has never shaken the "fantasy imperial image… [that began] with operetta themes in silent film, which were popular in export" (Moser 8–9) and continued on both at home, most prominently by Willi Forst before and during the Nazi era, and in Hollywood by expats like Erich von Stroheim (*The Wedding March*, 1928) and Billy Wilder (*The Emperor Waltz*, 1948), that fantasy was re-spatialized and re-historicized with the effects of globalization, something our readings of *Before Sunrise* (Richard Linklater, 1995) and *Eyes Wide Shut* (Stanley Kubrick, 1999) bring out. We then show a parallel internal development in Prolo Chic and *Ausländer* Chic by analysing *Blutrausch* (Thomas Roth, 1997) and *I Love Vienna* (Houchang Allahyari, 1991). Given that the Baroque and Ringstrasse varieties of chic seem to have had much more of a global impact than the more local Prolo and *Ausländer* ones, one can see an overall conformity to the "global-local" expectations of globality, which in this case can more accurately be termed "glurbanity" to draw attention to the fact that we are dealing with a decidedly *urban* imaginary. After first providing the historical background which underpins the memes/clichés/imag[o]es in question, we then turn in each of the following four chapters in this part to the fashioning they have undergone in film.

Note

1   From the write-up in the "Unlike" guide: http://unlike.net/vienna/shop/tiberius, accessed 7 June 2013.

Chapter 1

Baroque Chic: Fashioning Courtly Spaces

The Habsburgs come to town: Establishing Vienna's baroque imaginary

"When I walk along the Ring I always get the feeling that a modern Potemkin has wanted to create, in the visitor to Vienna, the impression of a city exclusively inhabited by nobles."

(Adolf Loos, cited in Stewart 78)

Vienna's global imaginary might be shaped by the imperial grandeur that is part of its baroque legacy, but Vienna was not always a court city. Nor has it ever been a court city like any other. As the seat of the Holy Roman Emperor, it hosted, for several centuries, the largest court in the European realm (Kauffmann 31), and that court determined the city's character more intensively and for a longer period of time than is true of other European court cities, whether London, Paris, St. Petersburg, or Madrid; only in the Istanbul of the Ottomans do we find something of comparable length and impact. The Habsburg legacy in Vienna is complex and motivates our decision to translate the designation *Residenzstadt* as court city rather than imperial city. The Driver and Gilbert edited collection *Imperial Cities*, which explores "the role of imperialism in the cultural history of the modern European metropolis" (Driver and Gilbert 3), is indicative of the tendency in contemporary, especially postcolonial, scholarship to focus on the colonial empires of the modern period rather than their ancient, medieval or early modern predecessors. Vienna's Habsburg heritage seamlessly bridges the city's pre-modern and modern pasts and requires a designation that sidesteps the danger of reducing that heritage to its baroque glory. One can see this tendency to blend the pre-modern and modern in the exhibition that Diana Vreeland spearheaded at the Metropolitan Museum of Art from December 1979 to August 1980 on "Fashions of the Hapsburg [sic] Era: Austria-Hungary." The catalogue of the exhibition opens with an essay by Joseph Wechsberg on the "Glory of Vienna" that, in turn, opens with "[t]he oldest known relic, a small figure of a woman, known as 'Venus of Willendorf' [that] was found northwest of Vienna [… and] is believed to date from the Old Stone Age, from about 20,000 BC [sic]" (Cone 21). Wechsberg proceeds to rattle off the city's accomplishments but soon finds himself caught up in the city's legendary taste culture. Vienna's past becomes a blur of music and bonhomie à la Musner: "Even in those days the Viennese liked music and celebrations. The city became known as a place for good living. Many nobles 'stayed much longer than their affairs demanded.' Same as today" (21). The days in question refer to Ottokar II's occupation of the city in the thirteenth century, but one sees how easily the city's courtly traditions can be dehistoricized and used to reduce past and present to a dreamlike fantasy of the splendiferous style that has come to be associated with the Habsburgs.

Although Vienna was first settled by the Celts in 500 BCE and called "Vindobona" by the Romans, for whom the Danube served as the northeastern border of their empire, it was not until the late Middle Ages that Vienna began to acquire the accoutrements that later became determinative for its urban mythology (ibid.). During the Early and High Middle Ages the predecessors of the Habsburgs as Austrian rulers, the Babenberg family, held itinerant courts, as was customary for the period, with Vienna being just one among other, equally important, central places of residence such as Innsbruck and Wiener Neustadt.[1] Only in the late Middle Ages under the newly established dynasty of the Habsburgs did Vienna emerge as the most important city in this territory. The power vacuum created when the last Babenberger, the appositely named Friedrich *der Streitbare* (the Quarrelsome) who fell in battle with the Hungarians in 1246, was filled first by Ottokar II of Bohemia and then challenged by Rudolph I of Habsburg. Ottokar is credited with rebuilding the city after it was devastated twice by fire and with moving the court from Am Hof to the Hofburg (Lehne and Johnson 15), while Rudolph, who deposed him after a five-week siege in 1276, established what ended up being over 600 years of more or less uninterrupted Habsburg presence in the city, something that got off to a rather rocky start with further destructive fires and bouts of the Black Death. The rivalry that developed in the second half of the fourteenth century between the archduke Rudolph IV, who was withheld the honour of becoming an Elector in the Holy Roman Empire, and his father-in-law in Prague, the Wittelsbacher Holy Roman Emperor Karl IV, and the concomitant vying for prestige of the two powerful dynasties, left its impact on Vienna's urban fabric in the form of the Stephansdom and the founding of the university, the "Alma Mater Rudolphina 1365" (Vocelka 2001, 14), offsetting Prague's hegemonic status as a centre. Subsequently, the practice of the Habsburgs dividing their lands among their heirs led to political turmoil, factionalism, and a generally confusing situation during the late Middle Ages, with Graz and Innsbruck competing with Vienna as residences of branches of the Habsburgs, and the citizens of Vienna demonstrating their independence and political weight. This situation did not altogether change with the unification of the lands under Maximilian I (1493–1519), for whom Vienna was again just one among other places of residence, with Innsbruck his favourite. By 1510, all Vienna had become was the permanent place of assembly of the diets of what is now Lower Austria (Vocelka 2001, 15).

The situation changed when the Bohemian Crown and a smaller part of the Hungarian lands fell to the Habsburgs through the death of Louis Jagiello in 1526 at the important Battle of Mohács, which in many respects was far more influential for future Central European developments than the (vastly overrated) Peace of Westphalia of 1648. Maximilian's successor Ferdinand I (1522–64) became the ruler over a multinational empire (in 1556 he was also elected emperor of the Reich, establishing a tradition that would last until 1806), with centralized institutions and a constantly increasing imperial household and opportunities for the nobility to gain status and wealth by "being around." Vienna was the logical choice as court centre for Ferdinand, and during the sixteenth century the central agencies of the

Austrian lands as well as the Reich were moved there. Ferdinand had already broken any political resistance on the part of Vienna's citizenry in 1522 (the *Blutgericht* – bloody court), and, after the successful defence against an Ottoman siege in 1529, he set up the Habsburg court there in 1533 and began fortifying the inner city with bastions to replace the heavily damaged medieval walls that Suleiman the Magnificent and his troops had left behind, the expense of which contributed to the paucity of Renaissance architecture in Vienna (Lehne and Johnson 27). The lasting threat from the Ottomans, firmly established in the greater part of Hungary, with constant border skirmishes interrupted by a few full-fledged wars, greatly damaged the reputation of Vienna and made Prague an obvious and much less dangerous alternative. In 1583, Rudolf II (1576–1612) moved the court to Prague, and Vienna was reduced to a fairly provincial status for the next decades.

It was only after the defeat of the Bohemian estates in the battle of White Mountain in 1620 that the importance of Prague was curtailed and Vienna became the undisputed court centre of the Habsburg Empire. The ultra-catholic Ferdinand II (1578–1637) permanently moved his court to Vienna, a city that had turned to Protestantism at the outset of the Thirty Years War. Spearheading the Counter-Reformation, Ferdinand II, together with supporters such as the Viennese Mayor Daniel Moser and Bishop Melchior Khlesl, forced upon the city a "monastery offensive," which visibly changed the city's complexion: "between 1603 and 1638 13 Catholic orders competed in an ecclesiastical building boom of monasteries and churches [… in a] style of triumphant Catholicism which turned churches into palaces: Baroque" (Lehne and Johnson 29). By the time the Ottomans returned for their second siege of the city in 1683, and were again sent packing, this time with the help of the Polish-Lithuanian Commonwealth and the much improved city fortifications, the Habsburgs had given up their residences in Prague and Graz, made Vienna their own and started a breathless land-grab of territories previously held by the sultan, while the Ottoman Empire started its rapid decline. With the centralization of power around court centres that is characteristic of the early modern period, where royal power was consolidated by creating a centralized bureaucracy, a hierarchical state apparatus, and processes of decision-making that required nobility to be in the vicinity of the emperor, the Habsburgs permeated Viennese society with the pomp and theatricality of their absolutist courtly presence. The consequent establishment of the Habsburg Empire as a major European power in the late seventeenth and eighteenth centuries was mirrored in the splendour and size of the Habsburg court in Vienna, which now became renowned for its festivities, cultural activities, and court ceremonial, and grew from a size of about 500 under Ferdinand I to well over 2000 under Karl VI (1711–40).

Vienna then underwent a baroque building boom that led to dramatic growth and a change in the inner city's fabric and also that of its surroundings. Architects Johann Bernhard Fischer von Erlach, his son Joseph Emanuel Fischer von Erlach and Lukas von Hildebrandt led the way in erecting palaces around the Habsburg's Hofburg[2] as well as aristocratic summer residences beyond the city's gates, beginning with one for the Habsburgs at Schönbrunn [Figure 1.1], while a preliminary form of public sphere in the form of a lively coffeehouse culture – in later periods one of the signature images of the city – began to flourish [Figure 1.2].[3]

Figure 1.1: The Gloriette at Schönbrunn (Photo: M. Reisenleitner).

Figure 1.2: "Zu den blauen Flaschen" (The Blue Bottles), Old Vienna coffeehouse scene (anon., courtesy of Creative Commons).

Figure 1.3: Haas Haus (Photo: M. Reisenleitner).

Figure 1.4: Loos Haus (Photo: M. Reisenleitner).

Figure 1.5: Panoramic view from the Belvedere (Photo: M. Reisenleitner).

Despite being born out of the Habsburgs' suppression of Vienna's civic independence and Protestant leanings and being imposed on Vienna by an autocratic dynasty and its noble elites (which during and after the Counter-Reformation were frequently recruited from other parts of Europe), the churches and palaces as well as the pomp and pageantry of the court provided Vienna's central districts with an enduring baroque legacy in its historical architecture that a majority of the city's inhabitants still cares strongly about and has fought hard to maintain, as Musner reveals in detailing contemporary struggles over the development at the Südbahnhof and the failed attempt to build a reading tower during the redesigning of the Museumsquartier (Musner 59–64). In both instances baroque elements in the city's image were seen to be threatened by the "modernity" of contemporary architects' signature projects, offending additions were denied, and the architects reprimanded that the "historical substance" not be damaged by the rebuilding (62). Unlike the shiny reconstructed Haas Haus across from the Stephansdom, which opened in 1990 [Figure 1.3], not to mention the modernist green marble facade of the Loos Haus across from the Hofburg on the Michaelerplatz [Figure 1.4], both of which were allowed to proceed despite the controversy they created, the Museumsquartier and Südbahnhof developments were judged to be too visible and the proposed changes too radical a departure from the view of the city from the Upper Belevedere made canonical by a veduta Bernardo Bellotto painted for Maria Theresia in 1759 or 1760 (65). For the powers-that-be who decided on the final look of the Südbahnhof and Museumsquartier projects, it was vital that Vienna be associated specifically with the baroque. It was that particular component of its history, and that particular panorama [Figure 1.5] which was seen to be of value for Vienna's image – and not the "Alt-Wien" of Biedermeier nostalgia.

One cannot know what role, if any, a film by an independent American film-maker played in this decision-making; however, as we show next, *Before Sunrise* did much to establish Vienna as a European capital of romance in the global cinematic imaginary by associating it with baroque tropes that carried on into modernist art and on into the present, tingeing that present with courtly grandeur and an awareness of life's fleetingness.

After the Wall is before…the Enlightenment: Linklater's refashioning of Vienna's baroque imaginary

"If you wish it, it is no fairy tale […] If you don't wish it, it is a fairy tale and will remain one" (Herzl, cited in Schorske 164).

In 1995, Richard Linklater won the Silver Bear for Best Director at the Berlinale for his third feature-length film, *Before Sunrise*, which tells the story of two twenty-somethings – the male American (played by Ethan Hawke) and the female French (played by Julie Delpy) – who meet on a train headed from Budapest to Paris and spontaneously decide to disembark in Vienna and spend the day and night together. The film's thematics were already set, as were the types of characters that would wander through the city talking and falling in love, before Vienna was chosen as the film's location. While Weixlgartner and Zeilmann would have us believe that a screening of *Dazed and Confused* at the Viennale occasioned Linklater's decision to set *Before Sunrise* in Vienna,[4] according to the Viennale archives, the film was never screened there.[5] Whatever the circumstances of Linklater's first encounter with Vienna, what is of interest here is his intuition that the city was the ideal place to set and shoot this film. Critics have commented on Linklater's "very exact sense of history, in terms of both [his] own personal place in it and observing things culturally with a high degree of accuracy" (B. Thompson 21); as will be shown here, that sense carried over to aesthetics. Examination of the paintings, music and literature Linklater chose to include in *Before Sunrise* reveals a fascination with the baroque echoes in modernity that result in a uniquely historical recoding of the neo-baroque.

Linklater's sensitivity to the influence of environment on aesthetics is demonstrated unequivocally in one of the scenes in *Before Sunrise*. After Céline has her palm read at the Kleines Café and has been told by the fortune-teller that she is on her way to becoming the kind of strong and creative woman she admires, she and Jesse wander past a poster for an exhibition at the Kunsthaus Wien and, unexpectedly, it is not of Klimt, Kokoschka, Schiele or any of the other painters that are usually associated with Vienna but rather, as noted in the Introduction, one of the French neo-impressionist painter Georges Seurat. Standing in front of the poster, Céline recounts having seen this early drawing, entitled *La Voie Ferrée* (*Railway Tracks*, 1881–82), in a museum and having been so transfixed by it that she must have spent at least 45 minutes in front of it; in other words, it made time stop for her, at least temporarily. What she particularly loves about Seurat's paintings, she tells Jesse, is the way "the people seem to be dissolving into the background [...] It's like the environments are stronger than the people." She is attracted to Seurat's human figures, she tells Jesse, because they "are always so transitory," and she stops to check that she has the right word in English, drawing the audience's attention to it.

This exhibition, it turns out, never took place. In fact, according to the archive of its exhibitions available online, it seems that there has never been a Seurat exhibition at the Kunsthaus Wien, which opened on 9 April 1991.[6] Moreover, when *Before Sunrise* was being filmed in Vienna in the summer of 1994, what was showing at the Kunsthaus was an exhibition of works by the American sculptor John De Andrea. Why would Linklater substitute early Seurat drawings for the De Andrea exhibition that was actually on? De Andrea is known for his hyperreal depictions of female nudes and for the controversy that the exhibition of one of his photos at Documenta V in Kassel in 1972 caused. One of the curators of the "Hyper Real" exhibition at the Ludwig Forum in Aachen in 2011, which included a controversial De Andrea sculpture, sums up the point of the pieces as follows:

> The exhibit at Documenta, which depicted a couple that had obviously just finished having intercourse, caused considerable consternation. The meaning of this work actually is not to be found in its provocation as such or in its unveiled representation of sexuality, but in the obvious and equally outspoken human problems of the couple. The work induces feelings of misfortune, misery and pity.
>
> This alienation between the lovers and their incurable misfortune becomes even clearer with the work shown in Aachen. The man is not only fully dressed and the woman naked, but she clings to him, while he touches her only minimally, in order to not induce an open rejection.[7]

Clearly misery and pity were not the kind of emotions Linklater wanted his couple to be reminded of after their romantic kiss on the Ferris wheel and encounter with the palm-reader, who left them with the invocation that they were stardust. Rather, he chose to have them contemplate the relatively unknown and atypical early drawings of a painter known for his pointillist ability to translate emotion into colour, who:

> in a celebrated letter to Maurice Beaubourg [...] spoke of creating a style of art that could harmonize opposites. For [Seurat], it was about the transferring of oppositions and paradoxes into a new harmony that was the privilege of art. 'Art is harmony. Harmony is the analogy of opposites, the analogy of like things.' So Seurat himself saw his art under the sign of harmonizing apparent opposites (Franz and Growe 10).[8]

One can understand Linklater's finding the work of an artist whose style is characterized by the "harmony of contrasts" (cf. Herbert 22) apposite for his love story about transatlantic opposites who attract. Given that Seurat was very much in the air in the early 1990s, with major retrospectives at the Galeries Nationales du Grand Palais Paris (9 April–12 August 1991) and the Metropolitan Museum of Art in New York (24 September 1991–12 January 1992) and the publication of the English translation of Zimmermann's major monograph, *Seurat and the Art Theory of his Time*, it is not inconceivable that Linklater would have had reason to delve into Seurat's aesthetics. One can further imagine him to have been very taken to have discovered an artist who "[q]uite clearly [...] was at first looking for a style and themes that could reflect the technological and social development of the newly established liberal democracy" (Zimmermann 449), an artist who recognized that the liberalism that emerged in the second half of the nineteenth century "proved to be artistically sterile as soon as it was established as a system" (ibid.) and who therefore developed a new artistic method to represent the dominant mood in the 1880s, namely: "[t]he Baudelairean suffering under modern existence, which saw every redemption as a living dream and every aspiration as an illusion" (447). The discussion of Seurat's art theory that Linklater has his characters carry out is done in such a way as to draw attention to the way Seurat's drawings reflect on modernity and call its basic premises into question: first, by rejecting the modern emphasis on the individual, and second, through the transitory nature of his figures and their ability to suspend time, with *transitoire* being both one of the trademarks of Baudelaire's *modernité* as well as part of the *carpe diem* mentality of the baroque.

Linklater's fascination with the baroque echoes in modernity also helps explain the decision to feature Seurat's early drawings and not the pointillist paintings. The drawings reveal the inspiration Seurat derived from the Dutch masters Vermeer and Rembrandt (Herbert 57–58), which Herbert notes goes beyond their use of baroque chiaroscuro and conception of three-dimensional mass to the very form of the drawings themselves: "Several of them depart from Seurat's customary predilection for the planar and show the model in a three-quarter Baroque diagonal" (58). Moreover, for art historians, the drawings, and not the better-known paintings, are the markers of Seurat's artistic gift: "Although Seurat's drawings can be logically situated within major currents of French art of the 1880s, the particular resonance of his works in black and white, especially his figure compositions, remains unique. What makes these drawings immediately identifiable as his creations, and no one else's, is the way their stately, simple shapes arise from an interlace of light and dark from which they cannot be separated" (21). Insofar as something similar could be maintained of Linklater's films – that they are logically situated within the major currents of American independent film-making yet with a unique approach to perspective – one could suspect that Seurat was something of a role model for Linklater.

The Seurat drawing whose title Cécile mentions in the original, *La Voie Ferrée*, is of further significance, in that it subtly alludes to and acknowledges Linklater's debt to cinematic depictions of modernity. Train tracks structure the title sequence of *Before Sunrise*, hearkening back to the beginnings of cinema (the Lumières' famous 1895 *L'Arrivée d'un train en gare de La Ciotat*), as well as to the canonical German-language city film, *Berlin: Symphonie der Großstadt* (Walther Ruttmann, 1927) and *The Third Man* (Carol Reed, 1949),

38

which opens with Joseph Cotton's character arriving at Vienna's Westbahnhof. Linklater's characters not only arrive at the Westbahnof; it is also where they take leave of each other, and while the European female leaves by train, the American male is last seen taking a bus to the airport – two modes of public transportation more in keeping with his nationality. Here we can see Linklater reflecting on whether and how the modern tradition he has inherited still obtains and realizing the need for geographical refinement.[9]

On the topic of transportation and moving through the city, one can also note that Linklater's couple mostly walks. There are only two instances they do not, and both involve touristy, modern conveniences that work against the forward, linear progress of modernity by returning people who travel with them back to where they started, namely, the Ferris wheel at the Prater and the streetcar that travels around the Ring (as a matter of fact, they are shown as going along the same stretch of the Ring several times).

In walking, Linklater's characters offer a further instance of rethinking modernity, namely by forcing us to reflect on that *Urtyp* of the *Moderne*, the flaneur: not on his gender, but rather on his monadic status. Had Jesse gotten off the train in Vienna alone, as was his original plan, he would have been a flaneur, a lone male wandering aimlessly through the crowds of the metropolis. In providing him with a European companion who can introduce him to places such as the *Friedhof der Namenlosen*, the cemetery of the nameless that she knows from a childhood visit, Linklater encourages us to reflect on how Old Worldly the figure of the flaneur is, and how different from it both the models of masculinity that developed in the US are, and the modes of contemporary sociality among young people.

That the baroque is central to Linklater's romantic rethinking of modernity is evident in the fact that the film's thematics are inspired by the baroque sensibility for the transitory, dreamlike nature of life. The couple decides to leave it up to *fortuna* whether they meet again, while the first of the quirky locals they encounter invite them to an updated version of a pastoral (a key genre for the baroque). Religious power appears as a strong background presence both by day and at night, while crucial dialogues about life's meaning occur in a cemetery and a church. The most apparent baroque presence in the film, however, is its musical frame. The opening sequence, with a train arriving in Vienna, is set to Purcell's overture to *Dido and Aeneas*, one of the great tragic love stories, while the final sequence also has a baroque accompaniment. After the two have parted and begin to head in their own separate directions, the strings of a Bach sonata start up as the camera returns us to some of the quintessentially Central European way-stations the two have enjoyed together during their stopover. The most graphic musical demonstration of Linklater's blending of the baroque and the modern has to be in the morning scene, after the park, where Jessie and Céline stop by an open window to listen to a harpsichordist practising the Goldberg Variations and then, in a lovely cinematic moment, briefly attempt to waltz to it. Given the contemporary popularity of Glenn Gould's piano version of Bach, the film can be seen to be offering a significant reworking of the piece by having it performed on the original instrument.[10]

The scene following the harpsichordist waltz, which contains the one major literary allusion in the film and serves as a final climactic scene before the farewell at the Westbahnhof, is also exemplary of the intricate modernist-baroque pas de deux Linklater orchestrates in *Before Sunrise*. Having returned to the lookout on the Albertina, Jesse wistfully remarks, out of the blue, that: "Years shall run like rabbits." When questioned by Céline, he explains that he has a recording of Dylan Thomas reading this W.H. Auden poem.[11] His appreciation of Auden's "As I Walked Out One Evening" parallels Céline's of Seurat's *La Voie Ferrée*, and the sections of the poems he recites are precisely the ones most tinged with baroque sentiments. He does not recite the passages in which the speaker overhears "a lover sing[ing]/Under an arch of the railway" but rather the ones that counter the lover's exuberance with a reminder of life's transitory nature:

> But all the clocks in the city
> Began to whirr and chime:
> O let not Time deceive you,
> You cannot conquer Time.
> […]
> In headaches and in worry
> Vaguely life leaks away,
> And Time will have his fancy
> To-morrow or to-day.

Linklater seems to have known that Auden's brand of baroque pragmatism would come to be recognized as an antidote to lovesickness among Generation Xers and Yers.[12]

What does Dylan Thomas add to the mix? Why would Linklater include him as a filter? Thomas is known to have championed Auden and to have considered his poetry:

> as a hygiene, a knowledge and practice, based on a brilliantly prejudiced analysis of contemporary disorders, relating to the preservation and promotion of health, a sanitary science and a flusher of melancholia. I sometimes think of his poetry as a great war, admire intensely the mature, religious and logical fighter, and deprecate the boy bushranger (Haffenden 270).

Thomas himself never managed to transcend the boy bushranger. It is often commented on that "Thomas was indulged like a child and he was, in fact, still a teenager when he published many of the poems he would become famous for."[13] He also kept a series of notebooks between 1930 and 1934 (i.e. when he was 16 to 20), which "reveal the young poet's struggle with a number of personal crises, the origins of which are rather obscure. In his 1965 *Dylan Thomas*, Jacob Korg describes them as 'related to love affairs, to industrial civilization, and to the youthful problems of finding one's identity.'"[14] Having Jesse imitate Thomas's recitation adds to viewers' impression of him as the less mature of the pair, but also implicitly underscores what a formative experience he has undergone in the film.

Baroque vs neo-baroque

What we need to note in moving this section in the direction of a conclusion is that it is not a case of Linklater playing up Vienna's baroque heritage per se, but rather extracting elements from its legacy in order to mobilize, and reconstitute, the cinematic perception of the city's presence in and for the 1990s. After all, while the Karlskirche may have been chosen by a marketing team for the film's poster, neither it nor any of the city's other main baroque attractions feature in the film – not Schönbrunn, not the Belvedere, not the Pestsäule on the Graben, and none of the baroque churches. It is not a historical architectural baroque imaginary that is on display in *Before Sunrise* but rather Linklater's art-house Texan imaginary of one. In this imaginary, the power of images prevails over historical verities, something we see in the Habsburg enlightenment empress, Maria Theresia, being depicted as a "beautiful" benevolent fairy godmother.

Neither, however, is it a neo-baroque imaginary of the kind associated with the postmodern in the early 1990s. As Angela Ndalianis points out in *Neo-Baroque Aesthetics and Contemporary Entertainment*, "Omar Calabrese (1992), Peter Wollen (1993), Mario Perniola (1995), and Christina Degli-Esposti (1996a, 1996b, 1996c) have evaluated (from different perspectives) the affinities that exist between the baroque – *or, rather, the neo-baroque* – and the postmodern" (Ndalianis 12, italics added). The slippage that occurs here between baroque and neo-baroque is indicative of a spate of work on neo-baroque visual practices in contemporary culture, in which the baroque is understood not as a limited period of artistic production, but rather as a trans-historical countermovement that erodes and displaces established visual practices. The baroque is read as what Martin Jay has termed an ocular regime, the subterranean presence of which has long accompanied the dominant but not fully homogeneous "scientific or 'rationalized' visual order" as an uncanny double (Jay 1993, 45). Having been liberated by Jay from its historical confines by showing that "the inherent 'madness of vision' associated with the baroque was present in the nineteenth-century romantic movement and early-twentieth-century surrealist art [...] the word 'baroque' is being adopted by historians and theorists who recognize the modernist and abstract qualities inherent in the baroque; the baroque becomes a tool critical to understanding the nature of these early modernist artistic movements" (Ndalianis 9).

Linklater's filmic practice in *Before Sunrise* was thus part of a much larger trend of exploring the relationship of modernism and the baroque. His instinctive feeling that Vienna was the ideal setting for his film and his choices of filming locations in the city show, however, that he came to a somewhat different understanding of the neo-baroque than the one promulgated by Visual Studies scholars in Jay's wake. Linklater was struggling in the early 1990s to make sense of the end of the Cold War, "the end of history" and the impact that a new zeitgeist was having on the young people who were coming of age during it. His first two feature films, *Slacker* (1991) and *Dazed and Confused* (1993), deal with the young people he was most familiar with, those in Austin, Texas. By *Before Sunrise*, he was ready to go at least somewhat global (somewhat because Ethan Hawke is from Austin). What going global ended up entailing for Linklater was a re-historicizing of the neo-baroque, not by drawing on Vienna's baroque sites but rather by working with aspects of the baroque that lived on in modern aesthetics. For him, it was not "a permanent, if often repressed, visual possibility" (Jay 1988, 16) as much as an attitude, a sensibility and personal ethos, for which the work of Seurat, Auden, and Thomas all served as guides, and which, as Lipovetsky draws our attention to, was conditioned by fashion:

> The influence of the spirit of play dominating the courtly imagination gave rise to an optics of theatricality, an imperious need for effect, a propensity for emphasis, excess, and the picturesque that are particularly characteristic of fashion; this courtly art remained dominated by the baroque spirit at least until the purist and modernist ruptures of the twentieth century (Lipovetsky 50).

While one could argue that Linklater does favour neo-baroque vision understood as "the product of new optical models of perception that suggest worlds of infinity that lose the sense of a center" (Ndalianis 28), the form his version of that vision takes is far from the typical ones "explored in the quadratura and science fiction genres" (ibid.). That does not mean that his characters are not adventurers and seekers (the fortune-teller who reads Céline's palm declares that to be precisely what she is, while Linklater admitted to Ben Thompson in an interview that the film is "actually all about the mindset of travel"), but it also means that their sensibility, in which a playful, excessive baroque theatricality is tempered by modern seriousness, can be understood as a very specific variation of the neo-baroque.

Spatially, Linklater's neo-baroque vision is equally idiosyncratic. Ndalianis has suggested that

> (neo-)baroque spectacle strategically makes ambiguous the boundaries that distinguish reality from illusion. With unabashed virtuosity, the (neo-)baroque complicates classical spatial relations through the illusion of the collapse of the frame; rather than relying on static, stable viewpoints that are controlled and enclosed by the limits of the frame, (neo-)baroque perceptions of space dynamically engage the audience in what Deleuze (1993) has characterized as 'architectures of vision' (Ndalianis 28).

Setting *Before Sunrise* in Vienna made it possible for Linklater to get the city and its history to generate a neo-baroque spectacle for him, in a similar way to his use of rotoscoping (an animation technique in which animators trace over live-action film movement frame by frame) in *Waking Life* (2001) and *A Scanner Darkly* (2006). In both cases, the boundaries between reality and illusion blur.

Linklater's highly formalist, almost flirtatious aesthetic approach to the neo-baroque helps explain his decision to make the 2004 sequel *Before Sunset* not in Vienna but in Paris. Taken together, the two films are a definite departure from the rest of his oeuvre, which, with the exception of the UK production *Me and Orson Welles* and the most recent sequel *Before Midnight*, were all made and set in the United States (mostly Texas, California and

New York), and concern themselves with American issues like high school, baseball and fast food. It is striking that in deciding to make another film in Europe, Linklater went for the only other city with a baroque-modernist heritage comparable to Vienna's. No other European cities were subject to the same kind of massive re-engineering in the second half of the nineteenth century as occurred with Vienna's Ringstrasse and the Haussmannization of Paris. Both cities saw their medieval centres swept away and replaced with a system of wide, radial roadways that encouraged the baroque lines of sight that Linklater's camera seems naturally to gravitate towards in these two films. Put differently, both cities have a unique confusion of historical signifiers, modernist incisions motivated by baroque visions of grandeur tempered by medieval accoutrements and a river. The resulting mélange has come to represent the ultimate in romantic Old World urbanity, and it is this meme that Linklater recognized as the ideal setting for the timeless love story he wanted to tell, and he also used the structuring principles of its formation – the interplay of the baroque and modernism – to provide thematics and generate content.

To conclude, for Linklater, Vienna in the early 1990s appeared to be an enchanted, neo-baroque playground, a safe, timeless space that was the ideal setting for the playing out of romantic fantasies against the background of a specific architecture and visuality that remains intimately connected to the narrative he constructed. A very different take on the city's cultured legacy than historical dramas such as the extremely popular *Sissi* trilogy (1955, 1956, 1957), *Amadeus* (Milos Forman, 1984) and *Immortal Beloved* (Bernard Rose, 1994), it is also one of the rare films to attend specifically to the city's baroque cultural legacy (the beginning of Sofia Coppola's 2006 *Marie Antoinette* and Bond film *The Living Daylights* (John Glen, 1987) being exceptions that prove the rule). That this cinematic imaginary was to prove far more popular in both Europe and Asia than on its American home turf indicates the limited place of art-house in American society as well as the generational gap between him and his a-historically, non-aesthetically inclined compatriot Generation Yers, for whom Prague, and not Vienna, was the destination of choice in the 1990s.[15]

Notes

1 The following account is a modified version of Reisenleitner 2009.
2 At the beginning of the eighteenth century, fully a quarter of all of the buildings inside the city's fortifications were palaces (Lehne and Johnson 38).
3 Viennese coffeehouse culture was added to the UNESCO list of intangible cultural heritage in 2011 (http://immaterielleskulturerbe.unesco.at/cgi-bin/unesco/element.pl?eid=71&lang=en, accessed 7 June 2013).
4 "Der Groschen fiel, als Linklater im Herbst 1994 auf der Viennale seinen zweiten Film präsentierte. 'Schon als wir ankamen, wussten wir, dass es Wien werden würde, obwohl wir nicht genau sagen konnten, warum,' erinnert sich die Produzentin Anne Walker-McBay" (147); "The penny dropped when Linklater presented his second film at the Viennale in the fall of 1994 [something that would in any case not have been possible as the film was shot in

Vienna in the summer of 1994]. 'As soon as we arrived we knew Vienna was going to be it, although we couldn't say exactly why,' remembers producer Anne Walker-McBay."

5   According to the online archive (http://www.viennale.at/en/archiv/), only three Linklater films have been shown at the Viennale: *Waking Life, A Scanner Darkly*, and *Fast Food Nation*.

6   http://www.kunsthauswien.com/en/exhibitions/archive/47-1991, accessed on 24 April 2012.

7   "Die Ausstellung eines Liebespaars auf der Documenta, das offensichtlich gerade seinen Höhepunkt hinter sich hatte, erregte erhebliches Aufsehen. Die Bedeutung dieses Werkes liegt aber nicht in der Provokation an sich oder in der unverhüllten Darstellung von Sexualität, sondern in der mindestens ebenso offensichtlichen menschlichen Problematik des Paares, das nach dem Liebesakt keineswegs von überströmenden liebevollen, glückseligen Gefühlen erfüllt ist, vielmehr wird eine Verwirrung und Entfremdung deutlich, die eher an Unglück gemahnt. Bei dem in Aachen ausgestellten Werk wird diese Entfremdung zwischen dem Liebespaar und das unheilbare Unglück noch deutlicher. Nicht nur ist der Mann angezogen und die Frau nackt, sondern sie schmiegt sich verlangend an ihn, während er sie nur soweit berührt, wie es der Anstand verlangt, ohne dass daraus direkt eine Zurückweisung wird." John De Andrea at Ludwig Forum für internationale Kunst, Aachen, Germany: http://en.wikipedia.org/wiki/John_De_Andrea, accessed 7 June 2013.

8   "Dans sa célèbre lettre à Maurice Beaubourg, Seurat lui-même a parlé de créer un art par l'harmonisation des contraires. Pour lui, il s'agissait de transférer oppositions et paradoxes dans une nouvelle harmonie, privilège de l'art. 'L'art c'est l'harmonie. L'harmonie, c'est l'analogie des contraires, l'analogie des semblables.' Ainsi, pour Seurat lui-même, son art se place déjà sous le signe de l'harmonisation d'éléments apparemment incompatibles."

9   One cannot doubt that the film-maker who started up the Austin Film Society in 1985, helping that city to become a hub of independent film-making, a film-maker who named his film production company Detour as an homage to Edgar Ulmer's 1945 film noir by that name, and who has a film called *Me and Orson Welles* (2009) to his credit, was familiar with the locations in *The Third Man*.

10 Our thanks to musicologist Maurizio Corbella for sharing his expertise on this matter with us.

11 This recording is available online at: http://www.dailymotion.com/video/xf9ocv_w-h-auden-as-i-walked-out-one-eveni_creation, accessed 7 June 2013.

12 In the 22 December 2010 issue of *Slate*, for example, Julia Felsenthal offered "Procrastinate Better" readers the following cultural pick: "A friend recently prescribed me some W.H. Auden poems to contend with a broken heart. Reading the poet's words in my own head helped some, but the feeling of catharsis really came once another friend alerted me to this recording of Dylan Thomas reading Auden's 'As I Walked Out One Evening.'" Interestingly, Felsenthal is struck by, and includes, different verses from the poem: "In Thomas's tremulous, hellfire brogue, Auden's allegorical verse sounds like both a sermon and a song. Thomas's driving voice, rising in intensity and in pitch, builds marvelously towards the moment of reckoning in Auden's climactic pair of stanzas:

O look, look in the mirror,
O look in your distress:

Life remains a blessing
Although you cannot bless

O stand, stand at the window
As the tears scald and start;
You shall love your crooked neighbor
With your crooked heart"

She concludes that "It's hard not to feel small against the scope of this poem, and it's also hard not to listen again and again."

13 http://en.wikipedia.org/wiki/Dylan_Thomas, accessed 7 June 2013.
14 http://www.poetryfoundation.org/bio/dylan-thomas, accessed 7 June 2013.
15 Our thanks to Sarah McGaughey for sharing her insightful ideas about this with us.

Chapter 2

Ringstrasse Chic: Vienna Moderns

"Modern man: one 'condemned to re-create his own universe'" (Oskar Kokoschka, cited in Schorske xxix) [Figure 1.6]

It will not have eluded viewers of Richard Linklater's *Before Sunrise* that the modernist artistic references discussed in the previous section are all distinctly non-Viennese. To encounter Seurat and Auden when one expects Schiele and Altenberg is jarring, and the reason it is jarring provides the startingpoint for this chapter.

By 1995, *fin-de-siècle* Vienna had achieved a certain clichéd status thanks in no small part to Schorske's magisterial 1981 monograph and the "Traum und Wirklichkeit" (Dream and Reality) exhibition that opened in Vienna's Künstlerhaus in 1985 (before moving on to the Centre Georges Pompidou in Paris and the Museum of Modern Art (MoMA) in New York) and that made Vienna, as the exhibition's designer, Hans Hollein, laconically summed up, "in" (Jahn 6D). Schorske's book and the exhibition did not popularize the city per se. Rather, it helped to make hegemonic a facet of Viennese cultural history that has come to be known by the name of the MoMA catalogue: "Vienna 1900." As Varnedoe warned in his introduction to it:

> To the extent that this success of Viennese art is linked to Vienna's new place in the historical imagination, it is a perilous success, precisely because the new idea of Vienna is such a powerful and potentially deforming myth. That lost world, seen through the compound lens of late twentieth-century hindsight, has come to seem the classic fusion of decadence and genius: on the one hand, the guilty pleasures of *fin-de-monde* opulence and sensuality; and on the other, the familiar morality tale of an embattled modernist avant-garde steeled to challenge official order and tradition. 'Secession-style,' in the art of Klimt and Hoffmann and the other young Viennese artists who banded together against the establishment in 1898, has often been made to mean both things simultaneously. And a subcurrent of lurking, inexorable fate – the retrospective knowledge that all this would be short-lived and end tragically – lends a Romantic savour to the sensuality, and pathos to the struggle for the new (Varnedoe 17–18).

While Varnedoe recognized that "[t]hese are the elements of folklore, or more bluntly of cliché. Part Athens, part Babylon, Vienna before World War I has become a modern archetype of a doomed society" (18), this knowledge in no way dispelled but rather seemed to add to the power of the cliché, providing welcome stability in light of the tendency Schorske claimed in his introduction motivated his work: "the very multiplicity of analytic

Figure 1.6: Wiener Chic (Alphonse Mucha).

categories by which modern movements defined themselves had become, to use Arnold Schoenberg's term, 'a death-dance of principles'" (xix). While there is much overlap among them, Vienna 1900 is not exactly Vienna, City of Music, is not exactly *Jung-Wien*, is not exactly *fin-de-siècle* Vienna, is not exactly Ringstrasse Vienna, and none, when done in period style, is exactly chic. Vienna 1900 tends to refer to the visual arts and design associated with the secession and the Wiener Werkstätte, Gustav Klimt, Oscar Kokoschka, and Egon Schiele; the City of Music to composers, musicians and their critics, from Mozart, Beethoven, and Schubert, to Brahms, Mahler and, of course, Johann Strauss; *Jung-Wien* to the literary circle of that name (led by Hermann Bahr and Arthur Schnitzler, the group comprised Hugo von Hofmannsthal, Peter Altenberg, Richard Beer-Hofmann, and Felix Salten),[1] *fin-de-siècle* Vienna to all those imagined to have commingled in the city's coffeehouses, and Ringstrasse

Vienna, to the larger society from the Emperor Franz Joseph and his much beloved Empress Elisabeth, better known as Sisi, to the officers and *süße Mädl* (cf. Seibel) who spent their Sundays at the Prater. What they all share, however, is a modernity that was, as Varnedoe reminds us, always already cliché, something confirmed by tributes written to Arthur Schnitzler in 1922 on the occasion of his sixtieth birthday (cf. Ingram 2001).

This bundle of myths has in the meantime been revisited by European and Anglo-American scholars dissatisfied with "the tendency to ontologize the *fin de siècle* as the sum of its intellectual and artistic achievements and thus to stylize it as a treasure chest of the most precious objects of high culture" (Maderthaner and Musner, 1, cf. Lutter).[2] While many have added key characters and components to the terrain overlooked by previous scholarship,[3] the Ringstrasse Chic meme has nonetheless endured as "a major cottage industry" for English-language "writers, scholars, cultural historians, art historians, and museum curators alike" (Jones), with the "Vienna: Art and Design: Klimt, Schiele, Hoffmann, Loos" exhibition at Melbourne's National Gallery of Victoria in 2011 proving the progenitor's ongoing fecundity [Figure 1.7].

Figure 1.7: Vienna 1900 exhibition posters in the Wien Museum (Photo: S. Ingram).

Film has also actively participated in the propagation of the Ringstrasse Chic meme in all its varieties. Late imperial Vienna and the tragic fate of Sisi have proven a popular subject on the silver screen, featuring actresses such as Romy Schneider in *Sissi* (1955), *Sissi – die junge Kaiserin* (*The Young Empress*, 1956), and *Sissi – Schicksalsjahre einer Kaiserin* (*Fateful Years of an Empress*,1957, all directed by Ernst Marischka); Audrey Hepburn (*Mayerling*, Anatole Litvak, 1957) and Catherine Deneuve (*Mayerling*, Terence Young, 1968). As the latter two titles indicate, there has also been a plethora of films about Sisi's son Rudolph's *Liebestod* suicide.[4] One sees that late imperial Vienna was very much a city of music in titles such as *The Wedding March* (Erich von Stroheim, 1928); Willi Forst's *Leise flehen meine Lieder* (*Unfinished Symphony*, 1933), *Maskerade* (1934), *Operette* (1940) and *Wien, Du Stadt meiner Träume* (*Vienna, You City of My Dreams*, 1957); *The Emperor Waltz* (Billy Wilder, 1948); *Wiener Walzer* (*Vienna Waltz*, Emil E. Reinert, 1951); and *Song Without End* (Charles Vidor and George Sukor, 1960). The Ringstrasse itself figured prominently in *Burgtheater* (Willi Forst, 1936), while the Prater featured in the *fin-de-siècle* stories of *Merry-Go-Round* (Erich von Stroheim, 1923), *Pratermizzi* (Gustav Ucicky, 1927), and *Letter from an Unknown Woman* (Max Ophüls, 1948) (cf. T. Herzog). *Jung-Wien* has featured cinematically primarily through the adaptations of works by Freud-doppelgänger Arthur Schnitzler (imdb.com lists 91, most of which are TV movies), while biopics have enjoyed a renaissance as one sees from *Bride of the Wind* (Bruce Beresford, 2001), *Klimt* (Raoul Ruiz, 2006), and *A Dangerous Method* (David Cronenberg, 2011). Far less common is Linklater's contemporary approach of trying to figure out what the meme has come to mean. Nicholas Roeg's 1980 *Bad Timing: A Sensual Obsession* darkly does something similar, with Klimt's paintings serving to guide a Cold War couple through the underground passageways of the city's mythologies. But it is from the extent of Stanley Kubrick's chic revisioning of Vienna in *Eyes Wide Shut* that we can best appreciate the pastness that has come to encapsulate the Vienna of the turn of the century. After a brief outline of the historical contours upon which the image is based, we will proceed to the film itself.

The birth of the modern from the spirit of revolution

If the Habsburgs' coming to Vienna precipitated Baroque Chic, then the impetus for Ringstrasse Chic can be located in the modernist crucible that added to Vienna's cityscape what is arguably today its most prominent dimension. The year-long revolutions of 1848 swept the 18-year-old Franz Joseph onto the throne, where he remained for 68 years, but much of the neo-absolutist agenda legitimized by religion that accompanied the defeat of the revolution eroded quickly during the two decades following it. Franz Joseph presided over the replacement of the city's fortifications with a large boulevard designed with military, representational and financial purposes in mind, with a program of urban renewal that reflected the somewhat disparate agendas of the city's shapers. While the wide streets, laid out in a radial pattern, were originally designed "to maximize mobility for troops and to minimize barricading opportunities for potential rebels" (Schorske 30–31), the new *Prachtbauten* – the

Stock Exchange, Votivkirche, University, City Hall, Burgtheater, Parliament, the Museums of Art History and Natural History, State Opera House, and Austrian Museum for Art and Industry – celebrated "the triumph of constitutional *Recht* over imperial *Macht*, of secular culture over religious faith" (31) in the centre of an empire that had, by 1867, turned into a constitutional monarchy. However, as Schorske also notes, the extraordinary array of these monumental buildings "can easily obscure the fact that large apartment houses occupied most of the building space" along the new Ring (46), a combination of political, financial, and military interests that converged seamlessly in the emerging capitalist system.

Among those who initially invested most heavily in this new housing in the 1860s were the textile manufacturers. As Schorske has detailed, they "composed the largest group of resident owners concentrated in a single neighbourhood, occupationally defined. What the Schwarzenberg Quarter was for the aristocracy, the Textile Quarter was for the bourgeoisie: an area of visible pre-eminence" (56). The reason for their dominance has been attributed to the fact that:

> The textile industry was well into the process of modernization in the sixties when the Ringstrasse development began. Yet it had strong ties with the past. Until the twentieth century, textile firms in Austria were not anonymous corporations, but family firms headed by individual entrepreneurs. While manufacturing was carried on largely in the provinces especially in Bohemia and Moravia, management remained centred in the capital. The ancient clothmakers' quarter of the inner city simply spilled over into the northeast sector of the Ringstrasse to become the new Textile Quarter. There the textile entrepreneurs built houses which united residence and workplace in the customary way (56–58).

These entrepreneurs are indicative of the ascendency of the Liberals, whose party dominated city council from 1861 to 1895 and governed according to the guiding principles of economic progress: *Besitz* and *Bildung*, property and education (Lehne and Johnson 77).

While there is now general agreement that Schorske's narrative overstates the oedipal dimension of the revolt embarked on by the modernist artists, writers, composers, thinkers, and scientists, who stemmed primarily from such backgrounds, the lasting influence of this small stratum of society on the city's image is as unquestionable as the ongoing primacy of its baroque theatrical tradition. During the final phase of the Habsburg monarchy, which Stefan Zweig, whose father was a highly successful textile manufacturer,[5] recalls in loving detail in *Die Welt von Gestern* (*The World of Yesterday*), the Viennese "fanaticism for art, and for the art of the theater in particular, touched all classes" in the city and could rightly be considered a kind of "theatromania" that invited mocking (Zweig 17, 18):

> It was not the military, nor the political, nor the commercial, that was predominant in the life of the individual and of the masses. The first glance of the Viennese into his [sic] morning paper was not at the events of parliament or world affairs, but at the repertoire of the theatre, which assumed so important a role in public life as hardly was possible in any other city. [...] The stage, instead of being merely a place of entertainment, was a spoken

and plastic guide of good behavior and correct pronunciation, and a nimbus of respect encircled like a halo everything that had even the faintest connection with the Imperial theater. The Minister-President or the richest magnate could walk the streets of Vienna without anyone's turning around, but a court actor or an opera singer was recognized by every salesgirl and every cabdriver. Proudly we boys told one another when we had seen one of them pass by (everyone collected their pictures and autographs); and this almost religious cult went so far that it even attached itself to the world around them. Sonnenthal's barber, Josef Kainz's cabdriver were persons to be respected and secretly envied, and elegant youths were proud to have their clothes made by an actor's tailor (Zweig 14–15).

Unlike the typical modern Western theatre depicted by Barthes in *Empire of Signs,* whose function was "essentially to manifest what is supposed to be secret ('feeling', 'situations', 'conflicts'), while concealing the very artifice of such manifestation (machinery, painting, makeup, the sources of light)" (61), the artifice of the Viennese stage was not concealed but revelled in – not the theological space of a lie or a sin, but rather a compensatory, commodified one of adoration and emulation.[6]

This early form of celebrity culture meant that in Vienna, unlike in the Paris of Baudelaire's "Painter of Modern Life," it was not just the streets that were trendsetting. Rather, what one saw there was presumed to have come from an imagined elsewhere, from an influential, fantasy and spectacle-producing space that deserves recognition as a precursor to Hollywood. The way Daniel Boorstin, whose aphorism "the celebrity is a person who is well-known for their well-knownness" is practically as well known as the phenomenon he is defining (58), describes celebrity culture, applies equally well to both Hollywood and Ringstrasse Vienna. Intending to critique contemporary American popular culture for its inauthenticity à la Adorno and Horkheimer's culture industry, Boorstin describes "a culture impelled by its fascination with the image, the simulation, and losing its grounding in substance or reality" (Turner 8). The descent of Vienna into fantasy and delusion in this period is a firmly established part of its myth.

The way the beginnings of celebrity culture have traditionally been identified reflects the presentist, heavily Anglo-American focus of much of the work done under the Cultural Studies banner. According to Graeme Turner's valuable synopsis:

It is overwhelmingly the standard view that the growth of celebrity is attached to the spread of the mass media (particularly the visual media). Increasingly, it is also connected to the invention of public relations and the growth of the promotions and publicity industries from the beginning of the twentieth century. In fact, the development of these industries made celebrity a necessary invention:

'[D]uring the period – roughly 1895–1920 – when the first blocks of the modern celebrity system were sliding into place everything was improvisatory, primitive. Something more was needed, something that could, on a fairly regular basis, provide the public with a reliable supply of sensations together with an equally steady, glamorous, and easy-to-follow real-life serial adventure. Something that could, as well, allow the press to return to a slightly more passive role in gathering and presenting the news of these creatures, not force it constantly to risk its reputation in prodigies of invention' (Schickel, 1985: 33–34).

Richard Schickel is perhaps most categoric in his claim that 'there was no such thing as celebrity prior to the beginning of the twentieth century' (ibid. 21). Before that, he suggests, we had people who were successful and therefore famous. That changed on 24 June, 1916, when Mary Pickford signed the first million dollar film contract with Adolph Zukor (13).

Mary Pickford may have been the first American celebrity, but by World War I, there was already a well-developed continental tradition of the kind of celebrity Alberoni has classified as exercised by social elites (23). This trend has been acknowledged in the more recent *Constructing Charisma: Celebrity, Fame and Power in Nineteenth-Century Europe*, in which Edward Berenson and Eva Giloi demonstrate that while "[t]he famous and celebrated constituted a tiny elite" in the aftermath of the French Revolution, celebrity "exploded" into the kind of phenomenon we now know with the emergence, beginning in the 1850s, of new technologies such as "steam-powered rotary presses, automatic paper folders, linotype machines, railroads, telegraphs, and soon telephones, and innovative photographic techniques" as well as the first mass media (Berenson and Giloi 2). The volume's taking its cues from Weber's writings on charisma leads it to concentrate on stars of the Parisian and London scenes, such as Sarah Bernhardt, Franz Liszt, and explorers such as Henry Morton Stanley; the only Viennese who comes in for comment is the "populist demagogue" and anti-Semitic mayor, Karl Lueger (7). However, much of what is identified as initiating the shift in American celebrity culture from "traditional, 'larger than life' heroes to cultural icons" is also true of the changes Vienna underwent in the nineteenth century (Henderson 49). It, too, experienced "the vast cultural changes wrought by the communications revolution of the late nineteenth and early twentieth centuries, and by the rise of immigration and urbanization" (ibid.); it, too, struggled with the resulting need for a self-definition adequate to the new circumstances; and, as we will see in the following two chapters, it, too, "felt threatened by 'a new universe of strangers' who bristled with 'anarchic change' and the specter of social fragmentation. […] As Lawrence Levine has argued in his discussions on 'highbrow/lowbrow' culture, upper and middle class Americans felt threatened" by these changes and "[t]o overcome these fears, the culture tilted inward, away from 'character' toward 'personality'" (Henderson 50). Therefore, the rise of celebrity-based culture is in part to be attributed to the "changeover from a producing to a consuming society" (ibid.), something true not only of nineteenth-century America and its Viennese counterpart, but also of other parts of the modernizing world. Any city capable of staging a world exhibition in the nineteenth century did so to establish itself as part of this changeover, as one of the new metropolitan centres in which entrepreneurial bourgeois elites were beginning to usurp the ruling powers.

Viewing Ringstrasse Vienna through the lens of celebrity brings out some of its fundamental mechanisms. Marshall, for example, has shown how celebrity works to construct and maintain "the discursive linkages between consumer capitalism, democracy and individualism" by providing "a very powerful form of legitimation of capitalism's models of exchange and value by demonstrating that the individual has a commercial as well as a cultural value" (Turner 26–27). Certainly the Burgtheater represented an exemplary model of social mobility in imperial Vienna. Its stars suddenly had access to the monarchy, which would otherwise have been unthinkable and which translated into material as well as cultural forms of capital for them; and its audience was given the opportunity to at least be in the same space as the emperor and his family, a prerogative of nobility in any other setting. Indicative of the special status of actors in Vienna, and in the Burgtheater in particular, is that institution's *Ehrengalerie* (Gallery of Honour), a unique collection of portraits that dates back to 1786.[7] As we have already seen with Zweig, it was also true of Vienna that "[i]ncreasingly, established leaders […] had to operate within the new culture of celebrity, which forced them to compete for the recognition they had long taken for granted" (Berenson and Giloi 2). As we will see next, the film director who most clearly saw through turn-of-the-century Vienna's supposedly high-culture spectacle and who understood both that it was powered by celebrity and what consequences and conclusions could be drawn from this, was Stanley Kubrick, whose work – precisely because it is not set in Vienna – can shed light on the forms in which this imaginary continues to live on.

Eyes Wide Shut and the pastness of the fin-de-siècle[8]

S.K. What's the problem? F.R. Underlying assumptions. Which are dated, aren't they? About marriage, husbands and wives, the nature of jealousy. Sex. Things have changed a lot between men and women since Schnitzler's time. S.K. Have they? I don't think they have. F.R. (After thought) Neither do I. (Raphael 26)

Stanley Kubrick's much anticipated cinematic spectacle *Eyes Wide Shut*, an adaptation of Schnitzler's 1926 *Traumnovelle*, was released in the summer following his death on 7 March 1999, at age 70, of a massive heart attack, a few days after he had delivered the final print to Warner Bros. and a few weeks after David Hare's *The Blue Room* (an adaptation of Schnitzler's 1903 play *Der Reigen*) had closed after phenomenally successful runs in London's West End and on Broadway. Unlike previous adaptations of Schnitzler's works, such as Jacques Feyder's *Daybreak* (1931),[9] Max Ophüls's nostalgic *Liebelei* (1933) and *La Ronde* (1950), Roger Vadim's seductive version of *La ronde* (1964), and Tom Stoppard's more hard-boiled *Undiscovered Country* (1979) and *Dalliance* (1986), these two adaptations recouped some of the shocking impact that Schnitzler's originals had on their audiences, in no small part due to the scintillating presence of Nicole Kidman, who starred (and disrobed) in both. Kubrick, in particular, was keen to have his lead roles played by a celebrity couple, and the Kidman-Cruise dynamic added a rather definitive layer to the narrative's thematics of artistic and marital fidelity and transgression (they married on Christmas Eve 1990 and divorced in 2001).[10]

Another reason *The Blue Room* and *Eyes Wide Shut* generated the controversy they did is that both directors insisted on not only freely adapting but also contemporizing Schnitzler's stories. Hare noted that Schnitzler wrote *Reigen* in 1900 to be read among friends and that its eventual premières in Vienna and Berlin in 1921 were subject to police persecution. To achieve a similar impact as the original, he set *The Blue Room* not in Schnitzler's Vienna, but rather "in one of the great cities of the world, in present day" and updated the characters that encounter each other in the sexual daisy chain. As a world-weary critic for *Time* put it in a review bearing the headline "Room for Improvement":

> Hare updates the play in predictable ways – the soldier becomes a taxi driver; the 'young miss' a miniskirted model – and has all the parts played by the two stars. The casting gimmick, along with the chicly impersonal production (a semiabstract set framed in neon), makes the vignettes seem more facile and obvious: Schnitzler's acid portrayal of sex as the great leveler on a climb up the social ladder now looks more like *Love, American Style* (Zoglin 184).

In their screenplay of *Eyes Wide Shut*, Stanley Kubrick and Frederic Raphael took similar liberties with Schnitzler's *Traumnovelle*. During one of their initial discussions on the collaboration, Raphael remembers asking Kubrick: "F.R.: Are you thinking of doing it in period? S.K.: Period? *No*. In New York. Today. In the present, I shoulda said. What do you think?" (Raphael 25, italics in original). In addition to transposing the setting to present-day Manhattan, they shifted the time from the end of Carnival to Christmas, chopped much of the lengthy husband–wife exchanges of fantasies and dreams, and added a decisive character, a surrogate father/director figure by the name of Victor Ziegler, who frames the film – it is his party to which the husband and wife, Bill and Alice Harford, are invited at the opening of the film, and to him that Bill returns at the end for the answers that Schnitzler's Fridolin finds in his wife.

Kubrick and Hare were by no means the first to tamper with Schnitzler's work. Ophüls added to his 1950 *La Ronde* an emcee who narrated the merry-go-round goings-on, while screenwriter Jean Anouilh transposed Roger Vadim's 1964 version to art-nouveau Paris. Both, however, and the vast majority of the treatments of Schnitzler's work leave the stories in the mythical *fin-de-siècle*. Is there something about Schnitzler's work that resists being brought into the present? And why was Kubrick so insistent that it be contemporized?

It took Kubrick more than two decades to find a way to adapt the *Traumnovelle*.[11] Some of that difficulty might be surmised to have lain in his coming to terms with his desire for Schnitzler's part of the world. His second wife, Ruth Sobotka, with whom he was married from 1955 to 1958, was Viennese (she died in 1967), while his third wife, Christiane (née Harlan), for whom he left Ruth and to whom he remained married until his death, was German. Kubrick's decision to set *Eyes Wide Shut* in contemporary New York could have something to do with this. Patrick Webster calls our attention to the parallels between *Eyes Wide Shut* and Kubrick's second film, *Killer's Kiss*. In addition to them being the only two in Kubrick's not very large oeuvre (of thirteen feature films) to be set in New York,[12]

> *Killer's Kiss* and *Eyes Wide Shut* share a number of intriguing similarities: for example, each film has a narrative duration of three days. Also, each film has similar beginnings – in each a couple, a man and a woman in New York apartments – are depicted as preparing to go out for the evening. [...] In addition, the narrative detail that Nick Nightingale is from Seattle, and has supposedly returned from there, provided a clear correspondence to Davy; in *Killer's Kiss*, Davy is making just the same journey: escaping New York for Seattle (Webster 161–162).

Given that *Killer's Kiss* is the only Kubrick film Ruth appeared in (she had a bit part playing a ballet dancer), one is indeed tempted to attribute some significance to this early work in establishing a New York–Vienna axis in Kubrick's erotic economy.

There is, however, a more obvious reason for *Eyes Wide Shut* having been set in Manhattan, although it was generally overlooked in the backlash against the film upon its release. As Tim Kreider perceptively noted in chastising his fellow critics on their prudery: "*Eyes Wide Shut* is not about 'sex.' The real pornography in this film is in its lingering, overlit depiction of the shameless, naked wealth of end-of-the-millennium Manhattan, and of the obscene effect of that wealth on the human soul, and on society" (Kreider 41). While Herbert J. Gans concurs with this assessment in reading the film as "a Marxist analysis of sex in society," he does not attend, as Kreider does, to the specificity of "Kubrick's world" in which, he notes, "sex is freely – and very freely available – only to the ruling class" (Gans 60). Kreider, on the other hand, makes a point of the geo-aesthetic implications of Kubrick's final film:

> to focus exclusively on the Harfords' unexamined inner lives is to remain blind to the profoundly visual filmic world that Kubrick devoted a career's labours to creating. The slice of that world he tried to show us in his last – and, he believed, his best – work, the capital of the American Empire at the end of the millennium, is one in which the wealthy, powerful, and privileged use the rest of us like throwaway products, covering up their crimes with shiny surfaces and murder, ultimately dooming their own children to servitude and whoredom (Kreider 48).

What Kreider, in turn, does not underscore, is that Kubrick is thereby subtly reminding us that at the turn of the previous century Vienna used to be this kind of decadent capital, a capital of capital, with the unstated implication that it is no longer, at least in the global cinematic imaginary that the film addressed. This is not to say that abusive wealth and privilege no longer exist there; that they do, notwithstanding this imaginary, is made clear in the work of the New Austrian Cinema. However, as we see in the next chapters, Vienna had become by the end of the millennium a very different place from Manhattan, which is why Ringstrasse Vienna lends itself to nostalgic historical re-enactment, rather than the reality check Kubrick is exposing his audience to. Not only is his final film in keeping with the fantasy element of the period's nascent celebrity culture, the transposition of the film's setting reminds us that a key part of Vienna's imaginary has been unceremoniously relegated to the past. The *süße Mädl* of yesteryear, that is, the sweet, young, working-class girls who were invariably seduced and then abandoned to their shameful lots in the works of Schnitzler and his contemporaries now inhabit the city's *Nordrand* (*Northern Skirts*, Barbara Albert, 1999) and in the process have tapped into global "Grrl power" and gained access to safe abortions. In light of the Austro-Marxism that became a force in the intervening period and brought to the fore the plight of the proletarians, who in the interceding century turned into "the rest of us" and who are discussed in the next chapter, Viennese elites' eyes can no longer remain as wide shut to their plight as their *fin-de-siècle* counterparts were. That New York's elites still could be in 1999 continues to have dramatic consequences.

Notes

1   Salten, a lesser-known figure in the group, created what is arguably one of the group's best-known literary creations (although not one usually associated with Vienna) when in 1923, he published *Bambi – Eine Lebensgeschichte aus dem Wald* (*Bambi – A Life in the Woods*), which in 1942 became a famous children's film thanks to Walt Disney Productions.

2   All quotes from Maderthaner and Musner are from the excellent English translation.

3   Key additions to the scholarship include le Rider 1990, Rotenberg 1995, Maderthaner and Musner 1999, Horak et al. 2000, Stewart 2000, Beller 2001, Csendes and Opll 2001, Janik 2001, Bunzl 2004, Rose 2008, Musner 2009, Parsons 2009, H. Herzog 2011, and McEwan 2012.

4   These include *Tragödie im Hause Habsburg* (Alexander Korda, 1924), *Mayerling* (Anatole Litvak, 1936), *De Mayerling à Sarajevo* (Max Ophüls, 1940), *Le Secret de Mayerling* (Jean Delannoy, 1949), *Vizi privati, pubbliche virtù* (Miklós Jancsó, 1975). One can also add the 1945 operetta *Marinka* with music by Emmerich Kalman, Kenneth MacMillan's 1978 ballet *Mayerling*, and the 1992 musical *Elisabeth*.

5   That this tradition was temporally limited to Zweig's generation is indicated by the fact that Marjorie Perloff, who was born Gabriele Mintz in Vienna in 1931, notes in her memoir that "both of [her] Jewish *grandfathers* (Sigmund Schüller and Emil Rosenthal) were textile manufacturers, the former in Brünn (Brno), the latter in Hohenems (near the Swiss border)" (Perloff 2003, 222, italics added).

6   Barthes claims in the fragment entitled "Inside/Outside" that: "The [Western] stage since the Renaissance is the space of this lie: here everything occurs in an interior surreptitiously open, surprised, spied on, savored by a spectator crouching in the shadows. This space is theological – it is the space of Sin: on one side, in a light which he pretends to ignore, the actor, i.e., the gesture and the word; on the other, in the darkness, the public, i.e., consciousness" (61).

7   It was the subject of the "Burg Stars: 200 Jahre Theaterkult" exhibition at the Hermesvilla (30 March to 4 November 2012).

8   This section draws substantially from Ingram 2001 and Whitinger and Ingram 2003.

9   *Daybreak* is not, as indicated in *World Film Locations: Vienna*, based on Schnitzler's *Traumnovelle* (8) but rather on *Spiel im Morgengrauen*, a novella published the following year (1927).

10   Another couple on Kubrick's wish list was Alec Baldwin and Kim Basinger, who married in 1993, separated in 2000 and divorced in 2002.

11   When Raphael began working on the project, he remarked: "I did not know at the time that he had been trying to find a way of making a movie out of this particular novella for more than twenty years" (23). In the meantime, Kate McQuiston has found evidence in the Kubrick archives that Kubrick had contact with Schnitzler's grandson Peter in 1959, pointing to a deeper web of connections that remains to be unearthed.

12   Webster claims *Killer's Kiss* is "the only other Kubrick film to be shot in his birthplace" (161). While an intriguing point, it is not quite true as *Eyes Wide Shut* was famously *not* shot in New York. Rather the sets were recreated in England, where Kubrick had total control over the signage, colour schemes, etc. of the street scenes.

Chapter 3

Prolo Chic

"Vienna must be the only metropolis that doesn't have a 'City,' that doesn't have a district where people live; rather, it is a hodgepodge of villas, luxury apartments, palaces, tenements, houses that are falling apart, shanties, accommodation for the poor. In one and the same street one can find millionaires and proletarians, small, stone-old houses with gardens and swank, five-storey palaces out of fake gold with elevators and steam-heating, palais from the seventeenth century and abominable modern apartment buildings with one- and two-room apartments for simple folk."

(Hugo Bettauer, *Die freudlose Gasse. Ein Wiener Roman aus unseren Tagen.*
Wien, Leipzig, 1925, 1, cited in Vana 134)[1]

Class and political conflict have been a staple of modern Viennese history, from the imperial army retaking the city in October 1848 and the uprising in Ottakring on 17 September 1911 (cf. Maderthaner and Musner) to the riots in July 1927, during which the Palace of Justice was set on fire. While scholarship on Viennese working-class culture has been playing catch-up with that on its aristocratic and artistic elites, the proletarian character of the city has become a recognized, even respected, entity.

The formation of the city's proletarian imaginary can be traced back to the migratory flows that have provided the city with the workers it has needed since the early modern period:

Artisans, journeymen, and apprentices, a particularly mobile group, formed the major part of the foreigners in Vienna in the pre-industrial era. Aside from this artisanal migration during the seventeenth and eighteenth centuries, the Habsburg Monarchy recruited labourers from other areas of the empire or from abroad, particularly those skilled in luxury crafts and textile production. Over the course of the nineteenth century, these were followed by industrial pioneers and workers (Hahn 308).

As Hahn notes, the shift in type of migrant brought about by the onset of industrialization was accompanied by a shift in their geographical origin:

Until the beginning of the nineteenth century, migration was predominantly from the area of southern and central Germany – moving from west to east. Over the course of the nineteenth century, however, migration to Vienna was primarily from Bohemia, Moravia, and Silesia as well as from the eastern Habsburg lands of Galicia, Bukovina, and

Hungary. Thus the migratory current shifted in the nineteenth century to a north-south and east-west flow (313).

More to the point, this new stream was literally from the Habsburg *lands*: "[t]he village proletariat, village poverty and the rural 'surplus population' became the main reservoir for a colossal flow of migration within the Habsburg territories, which supplied the monarchy's few industrialized enclaves, above all its rapidly expanding and booming capital, Vienna" (Maderthaner and Musner 24). Maderthaner and Musner underscore the mutual influence the metropolis and its hinterland had on one another in the nineteenth century, quoting from Karl Renner's observations on the "penetration of capital into the village" and the resulting social differentiation and proletarianization:

the 'relation between the peasant and his helpers' came to be completely 'stripped of personal friendship and frequently acquired a quite hostile form.' The old 'honorary distinction of rank' was replaced by 'the antagonism of two classes' and the formerly 'peaceful and friendly coexistence' was transformed into 'an unpleasant and hateful antagonism' (ibid.).

These antagonistic relations were to characterize the Viennese milieu these workers moved to as well, which was undergoing enormous changes on account of the massive expansion it was experiencing. The industrialization process was an uneven one:

the boom of the early Gründerzeit years was followed by a long phase, from 1857 to 1866, of stagnation, and the dynamic period of industrial expansion in the main Gründerzeit years of 1867 to 1873 ended with a 'big crash,' which ushered in a depression that lasted for more than two decades (Ehmer 139).[2]

At the time of the census taken in 1754, Vienna had approximately 175,000 inhabitants. [...] As a result of administrative measures, which incorporated outlying communities into the city, Vienna reached the million mark in 1890. The population continued to climb to around two million by 1910, whereby 53 per cent of the growth was attributable to net migration (immigration minus emigration) and 47 per cent was due to the excess of births over deaths (Hahn 313).

When the population increased by around 40 per cent between 1830 and 1850 and housing only increased about 10 per cent, social strains quickly became untenable (Maderthaner and Musner 32). As might be expected from what we saw in the Ringstrasse chapter, the priorities of the Liberals, who governed from 1861 to 1895, encouraged the demand for housing to be met by private investors, who erected huge, inhumane apartment buildings called *Zinskaserne* (rent barracks), and the demand for transportation to be met by a privately owned horse-drawn tramway system.[3] As both proved inadequate and high rents made the old commercial suburbs unaffordable for a large part of the lower-class population, who needed to be within a manageable distance from their work, the outer districts saw "disproportionate growth and massive concentration in building and population" (34). Maderthaner and Musner give the example of Neulerchenfeld, where in the mid-1880s "more than twice the population lived jammed together in only two-thirds of a square kilometre than there was in the square kilometre of the inner city" (34). They further explain that "not the least reason for this being that the western suburbs on both sides of the Mariahilferstraße continued to form, as they always had, the centre of the most labor-intensive branch of Viennese industry, the garment trade" (34). J. Robert Wegs reminds us of both these workers' migrant backgrounds and their relatively high status: "Immediately before World War I, 28 per cent of the Czech-speaking immigrants worked in the clothing industry. Still associated with tailoring in popular consciousness, many of these immigrants settled in the better districts of Vienna, or at least the better-off sections of the working-class districts" (Wegs 7). Moreover, he shows with the example of the garment industry the extreme differences in income and status often disguised by occupational designations:

> For example, in the Austrian putting-out system (*Verlag*) that was widespread in the late nineteenth and early twentieth centuries, a shoemaker-master might employ scores of small shop-masters who produced shoes or parts of shoes for him. The small shop-masters might produce only a portion of a product for the larger master. Obviously, the income and living conditions of these artisan-masters would be very different. A 1901 study of tailors showed that about 15 per cent earned above 2,600 kronen a year, while 33 per cent earned 1,040 or less. Shoemakers earned even less; in a 1906 study 70 per cent of the masters and 94 per cent of the journeymen earned 1,040 or less a year. By comparison, the study of 119 families (70 per cent skilled workers) in 1912-14 revealed an average income of 1,945 kroner a year. In the clothing industry a large number of women, called *Zwischenmeisterinnen*, worked on contract for larger masters. Their income was much higher than the two to five artisans they employed in their home or the many home-workers they hired [... and] artisans tended to put more emphasis on secondary school than did skilled workers. The larger numbers of artisans who continued to produce goods independently in competition with factories or who had switched to repair functions could normally not support a family on their earnings (Wegs 29).

However, even for the better paid, housing remained inadequate and unaffordable:

> Up until World War One, 85 per cent of housing units in the outer districts were the smallest possible size (consisting of one room, or two including a kitchen). Four-fifths of the population here lived in this 'poorest housing category.' Even for the most wretched accommodation in cellars, outbuildings, and attics, rents were demanded that were higher per square meter than those for apartments on the Ringstraße. The exorbitant level of rents led to overcrowding, subletting and bed-letting, and by 1900, only 4 per cent of the inhabitants of Ottakring had a room of their own (Maderthaner and Musner 43).[4]

Given these conditions, it is perhaps not surprising that two of the most important characteristics of the proletarian plight in Ringstrasse Vienna for its further development were its politicization and spatialization, something revealed in Zweig's description of the first May Day demonstrations in Vienna, which were part of the international Social Democratic commemorations of the 1886 Haymarket Affair in Chicago:

> On 1 May 1890, the first workers' marches took place in Vienna, demonstrating to the world 'how proletarian festivals should be celebrated.' [...] The workers, in order to demonstrate *visibly for the first time* their strength and numbers [...] had decided to march in closed ranks in the Prater, in the main avenue of which, a lovely, broad, chestnut-lined boulevard, usually only the carriages and equipages of the aristocracy and the wealthy middle-classes appeared. This announcement paralysed the good liberal classes with fright. Socialists! the word had a peculiar taste of blood and terror in the Germany and Austria of those days (Zweig 56, quoted in Stewart 150, italics added).

As Janet Stewart notes, the liberal reaction reveals that, contrary to its reputation, the Prater was not a place where the various classes co-mingled but rather "a microcosm of Vienna itself, mirroring and geographically articulating the social difference that characterized the city at the turn of the century" (150). Also clear is the fact that, for those in Zweig's milieu, the working class were usually invisible, a "striking contrast to the situation in other European metropolises" (Maderthaner and Musner 44). Unlike Manchester and London, they had no Sir Kay-Shuttleworth or Charles Dickens to champion their cause; unlike Paris, they had no Eugène Sue to chronicle and fictionalize their experiences or Eugène Atget to photograph their milieu; unlike Berlin, they had no Heinrich Zille to cutesify them in sketches. Rather, the pre-World War I Viennese working classes were absent in the works of the bourgeois writers and remained in the dangerous, alluring darkness of the suburban streets.

This Viennese microcosm found itself vastly altered with the dissolution of the monarchy at the end of World War I. In 1920, the city became a province as well as a municipality, giving the city council the status of a provincial government and putting the mayor on an equal footing with the premiers of the provinces, the only mayor in Austria to have such a status (cf. Hampel-Fuchs 6). The introduction of universal male and female suffrage brought about elections in which the Socialists won 60 per cent of the vote, which proved trendsetting for both the city's administrative trajectory and its imaginary: "Vienna was the first major city in the world to have a socialist administration, and since 1919 every freely elected *Bürgermeister* (mayor) and the majority of the City Council have been socialist" (Lehne and Johnson 108). These administrations have since garnered an international reputation for their health, welfare, education and housing programs. For example, between 1925 and 1934, 337 humane apartment complexes with about 64,000 apartments were built with low rents, access to green space, and toilets inside the apartment and not, as in the case of the rent barracks, at the end of the corridor (Vocelka 2000, 285). While such steps did help to ameliorate some of the misère, the aftermath of the war plus the inadequacies of the existing infrastructure meant that these efforts were, as the German expression has it, drops of water on hot stone. Vienna's reputation in the interwar period can be gauged from the fact that the Greta Garbo vehicle *Die freudlose Gasse* (*Joyless Streets*, G.W. Pabst, 1925) was set in Vienna, although the film itself was made in Berlin.[5] The crass living conditions depicted in the film help us to understand the rise of the Austro-Marxism that the city is also known for producing. Taking place in Vienna's Melchiorgasse in 1921, as the crazy, post-war inflation reached its height, the plot follows a rich butcher, who provides the district's female inhabitants with meat in exchange for sexual favours and is in the end slaughtered by one of the women.

While Red Vienna was officially brought to an end with the imposition of the *Ständestaat* (corporate state) in 1934, the cultural legacy of an activist, socially aware, and politically progressive city administration in a staid, socially and culturally conservative Catholic country continued to reverberate. In the post-war *Wiederaufbau*, Austria's socialist party (SPÖ), whose cadres had a stronghold in the city and whose elites often progressed through the ranks via Vienna's city administration, adopted a patriarchal, hierarchical, and socially rather conservative stance (one section of Fischer's article is "Der paternalistische Utilitarismus der 1960er" – the paternalist utilitarianism of the 1960s); their focus on economic reconstruction and providing social welfare from above is most notably associated with the Social Democrat Bruno Kreisky, who served as Chancellor from 1970 to 1983 and initiated a plethora of reforms, beginning with free school books.[6] Artists, in contrast, drew on the stroppier cultural legacies of the city's left after the "tame revolution" of 1968 (cf. Ebner and Vocelka) and breathed more creative life into the city than it had had in the interwar period or in the twenty years immediately following the war. Eventually they made inroads into the SPÖ at both the local and federal levels, but, more importantly, they established a genuinely Viennese style of artistic and popular culture that reworked proletarian traditions in creative and unique ways.

In 1976, the intriguingly named "Politrock" group the *Schmetterlinge* (Butterflies) [Figure 1.8] debuted for the *Wiener Festwochen* a theater-spectacle called the *Proletenpassion*, a two-and-a-half hour Marxist musical journey through the modern history of revolt.[7] From the peasant wars in the wake of Luther's Reformation to the need to resist contemporary consumer culture, the piece was understood by the collective who created it as a political secularization of J.S. Bach's passions, something one can see from contemporary reviews was greatly appreciated by progressively minded audiences.

> Seldom enough does dynamite get snuck into the saccharine factories of the entertainment industry [...] With great effort and attention to detail, the five musicians and the lyricist Unger have produced a timely oratorio about the struggles of the simple folk, who never figure in the great chronicles or only in the numbers of the lost and victims [...] A well-wrought, almost too-perfect opus, which is rather unique in its field.[8]
>
> Unger has a gift for words and a radical attitude [...] He gets the folk-song tone, the soldierly tone, the Eisler and Brecht tone; he can do doggerel verse and hammer out

Figure 1.8: The Schmettlerlinge.

ballads à la Biermann; as a Viennese he's learned from Karl Kraus how to turn quotations into boomerangs.[9]

Indeed, the *Proletenpassion* became such a touchstone among the Viennese left that unions there made it part of the training that apprentices underwent. The Schmetterlings' political engagement can also be seen in their 1979 record *Herbstreise* (Autumn Trip), an allusion both to Heine's similarly political *Winterreise* as well as to the extreme action by the RAF (*Rote Armee Fraktion*/Red Army Fraction) in the fall of 1977, considered one of the most severe crises Germany has ever experienced and subsequently known as the *Deutscher Herbst* (German Autumn).

One of the Schmetterlinge went on to apply this level of socio-political engagement specifically to Vienna by developing a style of music called the "Favoriten n Blues," translating rock n roll hits into the dialect of the working-class district of Favoriten.[10] Despite the fact that he was a Burgenland-Croatian who had grown up speaking Croatian and studied English and Sports at the University of Vienna, Willi Resetarits was able to so convincingly embody the musical personality of "Ostbahn Kurti" that the character quickly became a cult hero.

Also known as Dr Kurt Ostbahn, this literary character made its first appearance as a cameo in Günter Brödl's 1979 play *Wem gehört der Rock n Roll* (*Who Does Rock n Roll Belong To?*). Brödl was so taken with his creation that he created an entire, and entirely fictitious, biography for Ostbahn.[11] Graffiti claiming that "Kurt Ostbahn lebt!" (Kurt Ostbahn is alive!) began appearing on overpasses, an interview with Ostbahn was broadcast on Brödl's *Musicbox* show on Ö3,[12] and a sold-out concert of Ostbahn and his band, the

Figure 1.9: *Blutrausch* (Images ©1997 Dor Film Produktionsgesellschaft/Österreichischer Runkfunk ORF).

Chefpartie, was organized for 1 April 1983 (the date should have been a warning). In that year, Brödl met Resetarits, and the character sprang to life [Figure 1.9]. With Brödl providing lyrics in working-class Viennese dialect to songs like "Sharp-Dressed Man," "I Heard it on the Grapevine," and "I've Got a Rock n Roll Heart" and with Resetarits in his Wayfarers, well-patinated leather jacket, and slicked-back hair acting appropriately *lässig* (nonchalantly cool), the band created its own scene. Their first concert in March 1985 in the Schutzhaus on the Schafberg and the ensuing album were both great successes, and by the time Ostbahn started broadcasting his *Trost und Rat* (*Comfort and Advice*) show on Radio Wien in 1995, he was a bona fide cult star.[13] Brödl's death of a heart attack in 2000 brought their successful cooperation to a sudden halt, and in 2003 Resetarits formally retired the character he had been playing for twenty years.

However, this did not mean a retirement from performing. On the contrary [Figure 1.10]. Resetarits has a busier concert schedule than Bruce Springsteen, the cover to whose "Fire" first propelled him to cult status in the 1980s. He regularly plays Stubnblues, and has even begun performing again with the Schmetterlinge.[14] All the while, as one can read on his website:

Political and social engagement have always been important to Willi Resetarits. He helped to found 'Asyl in Not' and 'SOS Mitmensch' and is head of the 'Projekt Integrationshaus' association. His inexhaustible commitment to the needs of those socially weaker and with politically radical ideas has brought him both great honours, such as the Austrian Bruno Kreisky Prize for Human Rights [1997] and the German Josef Felder Prize for General Well-Being and Civil Courage [2000], as well as a criminal conviction for 'inciting the rejection of military service.'[15]

Figure 1.10: Willi Resetarits and Ernst Molden in the Kunstzone-Karlsplatz (Photo: Manfred Werner, courtesy of Creative Commons).

Resetarits has also been awarded the Karl Renner prize (2003), which acknowledges exceptional contributions to Vienna and Austria's cultural and economic interests, and the Fritz Greinecker prize for Civic Courage (2008).

Blutrausch: Real Prolo Chic wears leather

"Dezenz ist Schwäche" ("Decency is weakness," Taxidriver in *Blutrausch*).

At the time of his death, Brödl had written six Ostbahn Kurti novels, the first of which, *Blutrausch* (1995), was made into a film that is the epitome of Prolo chic on the silver screen. *Blutrausch* (*A Vienna Murder Mystery*, Thomas Roth, 1997), the one film Resetarits has thus far starred in, is a detective thriller about the smuggling of pirated Whitney Houston CDs. Riffing on the question "Was macht der Musikant, wenn er nicht musiziert?" ("What does the musician do when he's not making music?"), the plot features the Dr Kurt Ostbahn character as an amateur detective who comes across the dead body of a neighbourhood punk and, when the circumstantial evidence points to Ostbahn himself, has to find the real killer. The action shifts from his local *Beisl*/sportsbar hangout [Figure 1.11], where he first encounters the soon-to-be victim, whose smuggling activities

Figure 1.11: *Blutrausch* (Images ©1997 Dor Film Produktionsgesellschaft/Österreichischer Runkfunk ORF).

have gotten him into trouble; to a pricy hotel room, in which he rendezvouses with the beautiful woman who strayed into his *Beisl* [Figure 1.12]; to the swank *Altbau* apartment of an alternative band's dominatrix lead singer from Berlin [Figure 1.13], where he barely escapes being attacked in the elevator; to her band's concert in the legendary Arena [Figure 1.14];[16] to a villa in the hills west of the city, where Ostbahn is taken by the singer's psychotic lover, who also happens to be the son of the beautiful woman he met in the *Beisl*. There he is tied up in bondage gear courtesy of Tiberius [Figure 1.15] and almost filleted before freeing himself just in time for the crusty female detective, with whom he has shared many cigarettes and shots over the course of the investigation [Figure 1.17] to show up for his unneeded rescue.

Blutrausch was clearly made with Ostbahn Kurti's local fan base in mind; the soundtrack proved as popular as the film. However, while the film did not go global in the same way *Lola Rennt* (*Run Lola Run*, Tom Tykwer, 1998) did the following year, something not unrelated to its selective use of practically impenetrable (if stylized, rather than "authentic") dialect, it was nevertheless a similarly glurban phenomenon, showing how Vienna was developing into a global city traversed by flows of both contraband and capital, a central node in globally networked alternative scenes. Ostbahn's love-interest in the film is the wife of a Canadian hotelier, who had become acquainted with the Californian S&M scene when she was young. She is played by Uschi Obermaier, who "was and, many would say, still is the beautiful, albeit surgically improved, face of Germany's chaotic 1960s era of student rebellion" (Paterson). In his review of the docudrama *Das wilde Leben* (*Eight Miles High*, Achim Bornhak, 2007)

Figure 1.12: *Blutrausch* (Images ©1997 Dor Film Produktionsgesellschaft/Österreichischer Runkfunk ORF).

Figure 1.13: *Blutrausch* (Images ©1997 Dor Film Produktionsgesellschaft/Österreichischer Runkfunk ORF).

Figure 1.14: *Blutrausch* (Images ©1997 Dor Film Produktionsgesellschaft/Österreichischer Runkfunk ORF).

Figure 1.15: *Blutrausch* (Images ©1997 Dor Film Produktionsgesellschaft/Österreichischer Runkfunk ORF).

Figure 1.16: *Blutrausch* (Images ©1997 Dor Film Produktionsgesellschaft/Österreichischer Runkfunk ORF).

based on her autobiography of that name (which was translated as *High Times*), Roger Ebert introduces Obermaier as:

> Germany's uber-groupie, a provincial Bavarian girl who lucked her way onto a magazine cover, became a famous model, slept with Jimi Hendrix and Mick Jagger, and had something a little more than that with Keith Richards. Along the way, she was also involved with a radical commune, was on the cover of *Playboy*, traveled the world with a playboy in the bus he constructed for her and gave a face to the word Eurotrash (Ebert).

Unlike Veruschka, the German supermodel who made her breakthrough in *Blow Up* (Michelangelo Antonioni, 1966) and would have been far too sophisticated a figure to pair up with Ostbahn, Uschi Obermaier's counter-culture credentials contribute to the *Lässigkeit*, the particular kind of coolness, that *Blutrausch* aims at, and indeed exudes.

The international character Obermaier plays in *Blutrausch* also offers an instructive counterpoint to the other two female figures in the film: the relatively young dominatrix lead singer of Mom & Dead, Donna, and Police Commissioner Sedlacek. The former is played by the German Inga Busch, resulting in the two most upscale settings in the film being associated with foreign (i.e. non-Austrian) women involved in alternative scenes. Playing the police commissioner is Viennese-born Silvia Fenz, who trained at the prestigious Max Reinhardt Seminar in Vienna and has enjoyed a distinguished career both on stage and screen. Both Fenz and Busch are familiar faces to TV viewers of detective shows like *Tatort*, *Kommissar Rex* and the *SOKO* series.

Blutrausch offers a glurbanized take on the hard-boiled detective genre that recuperates and stylizes the city's proletarian lineage. While anglophone genre conventions dictate that the detective/private eye is a lower-middle class loner, Ostbahn Kurti is very much a person of the working-class hood, with a local *Beisl*/ watering hole at its centre. He indulges in ritualized forms of Viennese repartee that are irreverent, defy authority and evoke an ethos situated somewhere on the social scale between blue collar and the lumpen. While the historical and social references can be accused of inauthentically glorifying proletarian values, they are presented as immunizing its protagonists against both the corruptions of global capital and the puritanical value system of the middle classes that Karl Kraus had railed against in his day. Sexuality is taken in stride, leather fetish-wear is visually related to the everyday outfits of Vienna's outer districts, and crime is the result of personal trauma and aberration, rather than linked to a moralizing discourse of "evil." The Viennese take on the hard-boiled genre thus acquires, via its stylistic markers, an almost quaint liberal-humanitarian, but also libertarian character rare in contemporary global popular culture.[17]

Blutrausch's specific character and style also manifest themselves in a more recent update of a related genre, the *roman policier*, in television: *SOKO Donau/Wien*,[18] which has since 2005 been co-produced by the German television station ZDF and the Austrian television station ORF and which, as mentioned in the Preface, was something of an impetus to this study. The series constructs imaginary urban geographies that articulate Vienna, both its metonymic sites and its materialized histories, to the popular imagination of the early twenty-first century. While the solitary detective of the novel is replaced by a team of specialists (a hearkening back to *roman policier* traditions that at the same time acknowledge the institutionalized foundation and multiplicity of expertise required to police the contemporary metropolis), the show clearly focuses on the flows and fashions that have traversed Vienna since the beginning of the new millennium, while in some ways continuing the style and ethos associated with Ostbahn Kurti.

The fictional headquarters of the team in what is in reality the headquarters of the Danube cruise ship company DDSG (on Handelskai 265) metonymically situates – anchors – the team's police work in a very contemporary, and very corporate, architectural space located in the 2nd district; for those in the know, it is next to the Mexikoplatz, a socially indeterminate part of the city with a large population of *Ausländer* (foreigners) but also clear gentrification potential. This setting is a marked contrast to the inner-city locations and posh villas of the earlier *Kommissar Rex* series (cf. 7 in this study). Much more compliant with Vienna's 1990s brand of being *anders*, *Kommissar Rex* was high-culture oriented, quirky, and likably old-fashioned in the same way the Vienna in the 1995 *Before Sunrise* is, with a palm-reader and local actors, one of whom makes a point of telling the visitors that he plays a cow in a local theatre production they are invited to attend. *SOKO Donau* works to disrupt this kind of quirkiness. More relevant than its shifting from the 1st to the 2nd district, from traditional and more or less stable to contemporary and contested urban space, is how the river signifies

Figure 1.17: *SOKO Donau* (Images ©2008 ZDF and ORF).

the flows and connections that characterize the metropolis's status of connectedness in the new millennium. Perpetrators and victims in *SOKO Donau* are drawn from across the class spectrum of the city as well as the regions that the city is most connected to; corrupt sports coaches from Mödling, business tycoons who own villas on the slopes of the Kahlenberg, and gang leaders from Floridsdorf cross paths with Russian mobsters, German embezzlers and Serbian war criminals in locations that range from the non-places of international glass-and-steel corporate headquarters to the *Schrebergärten* (allotment gardens) on the Danube's flood planes.

The detectives move effortlessly across these imaginary spaces and know how to read them correctly, but only as a team. They are decidedly typecast and rooted in their locality, but they can also, like the good detectives that they are, make themselves at home in any of the milieux that constitute the city's imaginary. Their style, however, their particular brand of Prolo Chic – ratty leather jackets, longish retro hair styles, stubble and Aviators – are updated versions of Ostbahn [Figure 1.17], which makes the *Miami Vice*-like shots of them cutting across the waves in a motorboat as much ironic as iconic [Figure 1.18]. The buddy team is made up of a rather pudgy comedian from the Austrian provinces, who knows how to talk to both those who clean and those who own villas, and a German Kosovo veteran, who speaks the languages of the Balkans. Both are proud of their authority- and rules-defying proletarian common-guy ethos, something they share with their female partner, the leather jacket-sporting daughter from a good family on Vienna's outskirts. The trio are supported by their irascible yet unfailingly supportive "Chef," who wears Wayfarers and has the mannerisms,

Figure 1.18: *SOKO Donau* (Images ©2008 ZDF and ORF).

diction and suits of a Viennese bureaucrat and a heart of gold, and a team that further fleshes out Vienna's social spectrum (and wardrobe choices). All share a core set of liberal values.

Is *SOKO Donau* simply a reflection of Vienna's current status as a wanna-be global city? What is important to note is that it is not the global connectivity signified by airports that is at the core of *SOKO Donau*'s imaginary. Rather, it is the Danube – the waterway that connects Germany and Austria to what used to be known as "the East" (Hungary, Serbia, Croatia, Bulgaria, Moldova, Ukraine and Romania). It is tempting to enlist the Thames in the opening section of Joseph Conrad's *Heart of Darkness* as a parallel to the role of the Danube in the show and provide a postcolonial reading of *SOKO Donau*; however, apart from our misgivings about the usefulness of postcolonial theory for questions relating to Central and Eastern Europe,[19] there is simply not a trace of centrality attributed to the old metropolis in its relation to the east. Habsburgian hegemonies, pre-1989 dichotomies between Communism and democracy, and post-1989 imagined Central European commonalities seem to no longer obtain or be relevant for the show's imaginary.

That does not mean, however, that the histories that converge in and around Vienna no longer matter. What the show helps us imagine is a city at the crossroads of borders that have become undone, permeable but not completely open, a city struggling to integrate into its texture the violence that gave rise to the twenty-first century's flows of people and capital. In the wake of the Balkan wars, the flows of drugs that make athletes internationally competitive and that incapacitate others, and the human misery caused by the greed of finance speculation, the contours of histories that come together in contemporary Vienna are delineated and re-imagined as "a momentary coexistence of trajectories, a configuration of a multiplicity of histories all in the process of being made" (Massey 229). While this imaginary is still very specific to Vienna, it has successfully dispensed with the nostalgic longing for a single, simple past, while showing the resilience of a proletarian ethos with a history of being able to deal with the fallouts of capitalism.

Notes

1. "Wien ist wohl die einzige Großstadt, die keine City, kein Wohnviertel hat, sondern ein Kunterbunt von Villen, Luxusbauten, Palästen, Mietskasernen, verfallenen Häusern, Baracken, Armeleutequartieren bildet. In ein und derselben Straße hausen Millionäre und Proletarier, stehen uralte niedrige Häuser mit Gärten und protzige fünfstöckige Talmipaläste mit Lift und Dampfheizung, Palais aus dem siebzehnten Jahrhundert und abscheulich moderne Mietshäuser mit ein- und zweizimmerigen Wohnungen für kleine Leute."

2. "Die Hochkonjunktur der frühen Gründerjahre wurde von einer langen Stagnationsphase von 1857 bis 1866 abgelöst, und die dynamische industrielle Expansionsperiode der Hochgründerjahre von 1867 bis 1873 endete im 'großen Krach,' der eine mehr als zwei Jahrzehnte dauernde Depression einleitete."

3. Details of the horrendous working conditions at the Vienna Tramway Company and the resulting strike of 1888 can be found in Chapter 11 of Maderthaner and Musner.

4. This situation seems to have replicated itself in the preparations in London for the 2012 Olympics. Unlike in Beijing, where the local population that was in the way was simply relocated, those in London, as those in Vienna a century earlier, were rather put in the position of having to find places in the city where they could make do: "The result will be empty construction sites and voids in the city – temporarily secured and fenced at public expense. Such predictions of inactivity might seem pessimistic when situated in a part of London that is experiencing severe housing shortages. To unravel this paradox a basic question must be addressed: housing for whom exactly? Local boroughs of Hackney, Tower Hamlets and Newham contain some of the poorest wards in the city, with many residents forced to rely on the sharp end of the private rental market due to the lack of social housing provision. Stories abound of multiple families crowded into decaying houses, with modern day slumlords renting out garden sheds and even commercial fridges. There is no need to study the promotional images of the London Legacy Development Corporation (LLDC), with their luminous greensward, tropical skies and happy photo-shoppers, to realise that low-income residents of the Olympic boroughs are not the target market for these developments. The actual definition of the much-touted affordable rented housing is also open to question, as affordability has been defined as 80% of market rates that are already far beyond the reach of most locals" (Comerford).

5. On the differences between Hugo Bettauer's novel and G.W. Pabst's film, see the Loacker volume.

6 See Moser's documentary *Die Ära Kreisky* for interviews with many of the key figures around Kreisky, who offer their views on his contribution to Austrian society.

7 The information in this section is based on the German Wikipedia entry: http://de.wikipedia. org/wiki/Proletenpassion, accessed 9 June 2013.

8 "Selten genug schleicht sich in die verzuckerten Fabriken der Unterhaltungsindustrie Sprengstoff [...] In mühevoller Kleinarbeit produzierten die fünf Musiker und der Textdichter Unger ein zeitgemäßes Oratorium über die Kämpfe der kleinen Leute, die in den großen Chroniken namentlich nie und sonst nur in den Ziffern von Verlusten und Opfern Platz finden [...] Heraus kam ein geschliffenes, beinahe überperfektes Opus, das ziemlich einzigartig in der Branche dasteht [...]."

9 "Unger ist ein sprachbegabter Mann von radikaler Gesinnung [...] Er trifft den Volksliedton, den Landsknechtston, den Eisler- und Brecht-Ton, er kann Knittelverse schnitzen und Balladen à la Biermann hämmern, er hat als Wiener von Karl Kraus gelernt, wie man Zitate zu Bumerangs macht [...]."

10 Contrary to what many guidebooks on Vienna advise, there is not just one *Wiener Dialekt* but several, which are class- and location-based. Given the city's clear social stratification and the resulting reluctance on the part of inhabitants to move into strange, far-flung districts, it is relatively easy for locals to be able to place the accents of their fellow inhabitants in specific districts of the city.

11 Two versions of it are available on the Ostbahn website. The first is in the section "Kurtologie" and offers a chronology of the band's music. It claims that Kurt and his pals began playing in 1973 in Vienna's Simmering district and quickly established their reputation as Vienna's most merciless r&b band (erspielen sich Kurt und seine Kumpanen bald ihre Reputation als Wiens gnadenloseste Rhythm & Blues-Band – http://www.ostbahn.at/archiv.html, accessed 9 June 2013). The second also traces the first iteration of the band back to 1973 and takes the form of a family tree (http://www.ostbahn.at/chefpartie/fahrplan.html, accessed 9 June 2013).

12 Ö3 was launched in 1967 by the ORF to cater to the growing youth demographic, and *Die Music-Box* was one of its most popular programs (see Ebner and Vocelka 92–94). The future director of the Wien Museum, Wolfgang Kos, participated in Ö3's formation in the late 1960s and took over the production of the show in 1980, just in time for the introduction of the Dr Ostbahn character. That the Wien Museum and the RadioKulturhaus of the ÖRF were sponsors of the recent Schmetterlinge revival, and that Resetarits performed "Jesus & seine Hawara" at the Wien Museum on 15 September 2012 is an indication of the intricate historical weave of Vienna's cultural scene (http://www.akzent.at/home/spielplan/415/Die-Schmetterlinge-in-Originalbesetzung; http://radiokulturhaus.orf.at/radiokulturhaus/artikel/310850, both accessed 9 June 2013).

13 The radio show ran from 1995 to 1998 and was revived in 2006 as *Trost und Rat mit Willi Resetarits* for 200 episodes. See the "ausführliche Biographie" section of http://www.williresetarits.at/ and the archive of http://www.trostundrat.at/sys/ for more details (both accessed 9 June 2013).

14 His concert schedule is available at: http://www.espressorosi.at/konzert_kal.html and under "Neues" on http://www.williresetarits.at/, accessed 9 June 2013.

15 From the "Ausführliche Biographie" on http://www.williresetarits.at/: "Politisches und soziales Engagement war Willi Resetarits stets wichtig. Er fungierte als Mitbegründer von 'Asyl in Not' und 'SOS Mitmensch' und Obmann des Vereins 'Projekt Integrationshaus'. Sein unermüdlicher Einsatz für die Belange sozial Schwacher und politisch Andersdenkender brachte ihm sowohl hohe Auszeichnungen wie den Bruno-Kreisky-Preis für Menschenrechte (Ö) und den Josef-Felder-Preis für Gemeinwohl und Zivilcourage (D) als auch eine Verurteilung wegen 'Aufrufs zur Wehrdienstverweigerung' ein."

16 The old slaughterhouse became legendary as the scene of performances and happenings in the early 1970s, and when it was threatened with being torn down in 1976, was occupied for three months. It now houses the fashion wholesaler, MGC Fashion Park (http://www.mgcwien.at/, accessed 9 June 2013).

17 If one compares the new *Hawaii Five-O* with the original series that starred Jack Lord and aired from 1968 to 1980, one finds that the villains in the old series were portrayed with more empathy and understanding for the plights they had gotten themselves into. In the new series, the "bad guys" are hard-core cartel members and the like, whose business is crime and who are beyond rehabilitation. The criminals in *Blutrausch* and *SOKO Donau* are much more like those in the original *Hawaii 5-O*, people who have fallen afoul with the law for a variety of reasons usually related to personal issues and/or societal hardship.

18 We refer to the series by its Austrian name: *SOKO Donau*. In Germany, the series is known as *SOKO Wien*, presumably because the Danube has different connotations for Germans and Austrians.

19 We are not convinced that the region, with its traditions of nationalism, education, and modernization, is comparable to postcolonial situations in non-European parts of the world.

Chapter 4

Ausländer Chic

How the *Gastarbeiter* made foreigners out of strangers

"The one-syllable name of the capital and imperial residence always had a rousing effect, even in the furthest, most isolated corner of the Monarchy."

(Manes Sperber, cited in Hahn 308)

As we saw in the previous chapter, Vienna has long been a city of "foreigners." Sylvia Hahn reminds us that a common theme in eighteenth- and nineteenth-century travel fiction about the city was that it was "crowded with foreigners" (ibid.):

In 1784, for example, Johann Pezzl – a German writer of the Enlightenment era who lived most of his life in Vienna – noticed that 'every day people from all nationalities, languages and religions come together in this city.' In the early nineteenth century, when the German musician and critic Johann Friedrich Reichardt visited Vienna, he wrote that he found it 'full to bursting with foreigners.' Even at the numerous social events that revolved around the city's artistic circles he repeatedly met fellow Germans as well as many other men and women from foreign countries. About 50 years later, in the 1860s, the Viennese essayist Friedrich Schlögl pointed out, 'Vienna doesn't belong to the Viennese people any longer' (ibid.).

There are, however, many different understandings of foreignness, and this earlier understanding was of "Fremde," strangers, that is, people who are strange to a place because they come from somewhere else. As we saw in the historical component of the chapter on Prolo Chic, the people who moved to Vienna did so because they were looking for work and a betterment in their life chances. There was a geographical shift in this influx with the onset of industrialization, which coincided with the dissolution of the Holy Roman Empire in 1806 and refocused attention on the Habsburg lands themselves, and then another with World War I. "While immigrants comprised an important part of the working-class in the period before World War I, the collapse of the Habsburg Monarchy and the poor Viennese economic conditions in the interwar period sharply reduced the percentage of migrant families" (Wegs 7). In the aftermath of World War II, the terrain again shifted. Austria became a "Transitland," a country of transit, with about 1.4 million foreigners in the country at the end of the war, over a third of whom were displaced persons; some 650,000 people passed through Austria on their way to the West between 1945 and 1990 (Bauer 4).

When it became clear that extra labour power would be needed to help rebuild Germany and Austria after the destruction wreaked on them during World War II, the West German government led the way in 1955 by signing the first bilateral labour-recruitment agreement; it was with Italy and involved 100,000 labourers in Rome. "By 1960 'some 686,000 foreign workers, mostly from Italy, live[d] in West Germany,' making up 1.2 per cent of the population, and West Germany went on to sign bilateral recruitment agreements with Spain and Greece" (Göktürk et al. 497). Austria followed on 18 December 1961 with the Raab/Olah Agreement, signed by Julius Raab, President of the *Bundeswirtschaftskammer* (Federal Economic Chamber), and Franz Olah, President of the ÖGB (*Österreichischer Gewerkschaftsbund*, Austrian Trade Union Association), which allowed foreign workers to be admitted to the workforce. In 1966 it was decided to rename these workers "*Gastarbeiter*" (literally: guest workers) because of the unfortunate associations "*Fremdarbeiter*" (translated literally: alien workers, or workers from abroad) had from the Nazi era. In 1963, there were about 21,000 of these workers in Austria. By 1973 the amount had climbed to 227,000, while ten years later it sank back to 145,000. In contrast to other European cities such as Berlin, in which the foreign workers tended to congregate in particular areas that then became ethnic ghettos, the Viennese urban space accommodated the *Gastarbeiter* and their families in the same way it had the earlier waves of immigrants from the Habsburg lands. The newcomers again gravitated towards the cheapest rental markets in the areas around the Gürtel in the 15th, 16th and 17th districts as well as parts of the 2nd, 5th, 10th and 20th, that is, areas with unrenovated *Altbau* apartments from the *Gründerzeit* with one or two rooms and shared toilets at the end of the hallway (Payer 4–6).

Because of the extreme need at the beginning of the 1970s for female labour, especially in the textile and service sectors, and because it had become obvious that the initial plan for the workers to only stay temporarily and then return to their home countries was not working, more attention came to be given to the needs of families and education, and an increasing number of *Hausmeister* positions (caretakers of buildings) were filled by foreigners. By 1973, there were already 6000, something which eased the way for immigrants to settle in their buildings (Payer 6, 12). The foreign workers also contributed to a renaissance in the Viennese street market scene, in the first instance the more central Naschmarkt, but also those in the outer districts: the Brunnenmarkt, Viktor Adler Markt, Hannovermarkt, Schlingermarkt, Volkertmarkt, Simmeringer Markt and Meidlinger Markt (Payer 9). Their most noticeable presence, however, was in the 2nd district:

Mexikoplatz became for many foreign workers the first stop. Nowhere else in the city were they as present: on the street one had the impression of having been transported to a southern country, such a picturesque scene was offered to the observer and so little German could the ear find. Groups of thin, dark-skinned men stand together, wildly gesturing and speaking in dialects in which the consonants resound off one another in rapid procession. At a respectful distance are their wives, of whom even the younger have strangely old faces, wearing clothes very much like the ones on offer, all in a style that was fashionable years ago (cited in Payer 10).

From this description, which originally appeared in the *A–Z Journal* in 1974, one can see the cultural distance that existed between institutions that developed for the working class and the newly arrived additions to it.

The opening of the Iron Curtain, the toppling of the Ceauşescu regime in Romania, and the Balkan wars in the 1990s complicated the situation, bringing waves of refugees to Vienna, many of whom counted only as "de facto" refugees and not refugees according to the Geneva Convention, and therefore did not qualify for the humane treatment provided for by the Convention. Between 1994 and 1997, an average of 700 refugees per year were granted Geneva Convention status from an application pool ten times that size (Bauer 7).

One of those refugees was Tereza Barta, a Romanian film-maker who had worked as a writer and director at the Romanian National Film Board in Bucharest for 12 years before deciding to flee her country. Shortly afterwards the regime fell, but by then Barta was in Austria's notorious Traiskirchen refugee camp, just south of Vienna. Showing the same initiative that had gotten her out of Romania, and would soon get her to Canada, she established contact with the *Österreichischer Rundfunk* (ORF) and made the half-hour documentary *Mit Ihren Augen* (*Through Their/Your Eyes*), which played on the Ö1 program *Zwischenruf* (*Interjection*) in the early 1990s. The purpose of the documentary was to explain to Austrian viewers how Austria appeared to someone in her position and how dehumanizing it was to be forced into the category of refugee – hence the ambiguity of the title, which plays with the fact that in German the formal form of the second-person pronoun is the same as the third-person plural. Juxtaposing scenes from a Viennese Christmas market with a "shadow" market in Bucharest, in which people stood in line for hours to buy whatever products happened to be available, and intersplicing these scenes with interviews with a range of Austrians, who express increasingly hostile attitudes towards foreigners, with old newsreels of Austrians helping the Hungarians in 1956, with scenes from the harsh unchanging everyday existence in Traiskirchen, and with the ongoing political and social struggles in a grey and foggy Bucharest, Barta makes palpable for viewers why they should value their life in freedom and not begrudge it to those who do not happen to have been born into it. The show ends with her son's elementary school-age classmates, who reveal that they have not yet been infected with the racist discourse of the adult interviewees. One defines an *Ausländer* as "a nice person, who doesn't speak German but instead can speak other languages." A second explains that "They are people who come because they can't live well at home and so they look for work here," something he finds good while at the same time recognizing that "some people don't think so, they find them in the way." Finally, a boy of foreign origin comments in German, and corrects his grammar as he goes along, that he does not understand why everyone speaks about "*Ausländer*," why newspapers say that they should leave, because he likes it in school. The show then concludes with the most hateful, petty bourgeois, adult Austrian interviewee, explaining why foreigners should be sent back to where they came from.

Barta's film succinctly condenses a discourse that has become increasingly hegemonic in Austria. As Peter Payer makes a point of underscoring, the discourse surrounding the *Gastarbeiter* was almost exclusively one of problems:

It was always about the 'Gastarbeiter problematic,' the 'problems of the work-immigrants,' the 'problems of what work to give foreign workers,' etc. The equation of Gastarbeiter and problem, which one can confirm, was the overarching societal perception for a long time. Hans Stotzka, head of the Institute for Depth Psychology and Psychotherapy at the University of Vienna, diagnosed in 1977: No other social question is as burning for Central European industrial countries as the Gastarbeiter question. Nowhere are economic needs on both sides, the host country and the foreign workers, so closely bound up with individual and collective problems (Payer 3–4).

Despite governmental campaigns to encourage tolerance and acceptance among its citizenship outlined in Payer's section on "Countermovements: Struggle Against Discrimination and 'Slavery,'" such as the 1973 "Aktion Mitmensch" and its now legendary posters with a young boy saying to an immigrant: "I haaß Kolaric, du haaßt Kolaric. Warum sogns' zu dir Tschusch" ("My name is Kolaric, your name is Kolaric. Why do they call you a 'Tschusch' [an insulting name for foreigners]?" (Payer 14–15, see also Fassmann and Reeger 77–86, Fischer, Hemetek, and Rathkolb 22) [Figure 1.19], the "problem" discourse seamlessly transferred from the *Gastarbeiter* to the increasingly dominant category of *Ausländer*, which also encompassed the refugees, not in the least because of the overlap in country of origin. At the peak of the intake of *Gastarbeiter* in 1973, 78.5 per cent were Yugoslav citizens and 11.8 per cent Turks. In response to the perceived refugee problem, the Austrian government replaced the *Gastarbeiter* system in 1992–93 with a quota system that provided 159,000 spots for foreign workers from 1993 to 2001 (Bauer 6–8).

The Austrian election in 1999 did nothing to improve matters as it brought about the possibility of having in the government the extreme-right populist Freedom Party (FPÖ), which was on record as favouring restrictions to immigration. The party's support had grown since 1986 from 5 to 27 per cent mainly due to its charismatic leader, Jörg Haider. When the ÖVP-FPÖ coalition was officially announced in February 2000, the other 14 EU member-states agreed to bar Austrian officials from bilateral meetings until the FPÖ was removed from the government, which happened in September 2000. That summer, German bad-boy Christoph Schlingensief was invited to the Wiener Festwochen to stage a multimedia event entitled *Ausländer raus! Schlingensiefs Container* (*Foreigners Out! Schlingensief's Container*):[1]

From June 11 until June 17, 2000, a container was set up on the centrally located Herbert-von-Karajan-Platz adjacent to the [State Opera House]. Just like in the Dutch TV-show *Big Brother*... [which began airing in 1999 and was immensely popular

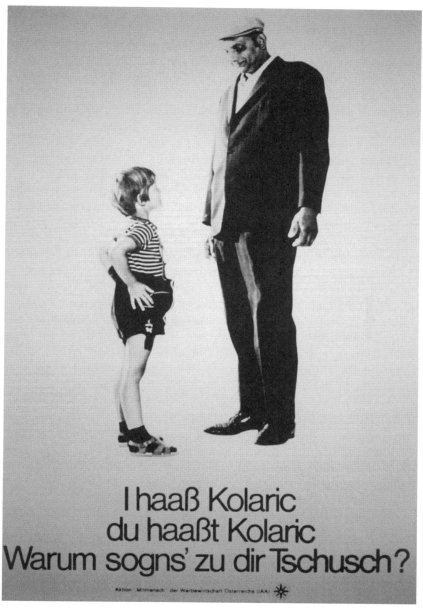

Figure 1.19: Kolaric poster (Initiative Minderheiten).

in Germany and Austria], twelve persons identified as refugees that had applied for political asylum in Austria were asked to live in the container for a week. What happened inside of the container was aired around the clock on an Internet TV channel [www.auslaenderraus3.at]. As in the television show *Big Brother*, the audience could call in daily and place their vote for the two candidates they would most like to see deported from the country. The last refugee to stay in the container was promised a prize of 30,000 Austrian Schillings [about $3,000 CAD] and marriage to an Austrian citizen through which the refugee would attain the status of a legal resident (Weiss 1–2).

The spectacle tapped into the surge in popularity of reality TV and the Internet, while at the same time activating nationally based, regional hostilities. The interaction between Schlingensief and the local populace in Paul Poet's 2002 documentary of the spectacle is characterized by mutual antagonism. Schlingensief goads the crowd gathered around the container with a bullhorn in a display of German arrogance similar to the condescending attitude Ulrike Ottinger displays towards the exotic, difficult to understand Viennese who work in the Prater and make their way into her 2007 documentary, while the elderly woman captured by Poet's camera shrieking "Ausländer rein, Piefkes raus!" ("Foreigners in, Piefkes out," with Piefkes being a derogatory Austrian term for Germans), clearly expresses her disapproval of the cultural imperialism she senses is behind Schlingensief's show.

As the "foreigners" went from being regarded as *Gastarbeiter* to *Ausländer*, they themselves underwent a generational shift. If the first generation of foreign workers felt excluded and alone, the next generation was no longer as willing to be victimized. Growing up in Vienna, they began to understand themselves as part of an increasingly cosmopolitan urban society and were better able to establish themselves in it (Payer 18). One sees this shift occurring in *I Love Vienna* (Houchang Allahyari, 1991). Its director may not be a typical "foreign worker," having immigrated to Vienna from Tehran in 1960 to study theatre and medicine, and then making a career there as a psychiatrist in penal institutions and teaching himself how to make films, in the first instance to use them for therapeutic purposes. However, just as Willi Resetarits did not need to be from Favoriten to be able to create a believable character from that district, neither did Allahyari need to be a *Gastarbeiter* to create a cinematic hit that demonstrates a sensitivity to the shifting challenges that those in Vienna with *Migrationshintergrund* (migrational backgrounds), as they have come to be known in German, face.

I Love Vienna's accented thresholds

At the beginning of *I Love Vienna*, which was the Austrian entry in the Academy Awards in 1992 (Riemer 94), a strict Iranian German teacher, Ali Mohammed (who is a great Sisi fan and claims to have seen the Romy Schneider trilogy seven times), Ali's sister and fifteen-year-old son arrive at Vienna's crowded, noisy Südbahnhof and are confronted with the task of re-imagining their future in a wintery city that clashes with both their expectations and customs [Figure 1.20]. Fortunately, they are not on their own. They are met by Ali's nephew and the nephew's Polish friend and taken to a hotel in the 2nd district that mainly houses Romanian asylum seekers. Confined to claustrophobic, rigidly controlled spaces that stand in stark contrast to the baroque expanses of the city's architectural heritage, the newcomers find ways to negotiate cultural differences with quirky inhabitants who defy the cultural stereotypes projected by well-known sites such as Schönbrunn and the Prater (cf. Ingram and Reisenleitner 2012).

Allahyari pulls no punches about the difficulties all of his characters face, and his casting of the film reveals much about the incommensurable worlds that the film shows interacting. Both the sister and son are played by Allahyari's own relatives, while Allahyari amuses himself in the cameo role of a carpet salesman. The role of Ali's nephew was the film debut of Michael Niavarani, the son of an Iranian and a Viennese, who has won back-to-back awards as most popular cabaret artist on Austrian television. The woman who plays Ali's love-interest is an actress who has also enjoyed success in Viennese cabaret and theatre, while the lawyer Ali visits for advice about emigrating to America is played by the well-known Austrian film director Niki List. There is no record of the actor who plays the Polish friend ever appearing again on screen, while the fate of the actor who plays Ali is unexpectedly shocking. A year

Figure 1.20: *I Love Vienna* (Images ©1991 epo-film).

after the film was released, "[o]n August 9, 1992, Fereydoun Farrokhzad, a well-known singer and opposition figure, was stabbed by an assassin at his home in Bonn. Three days later his body was found lying in a pool of blood with his dog whimpering beside him" (Kadivar). With this slaying of the outspoken younger brother of one of the leading Iranian modernist poets, Forough Farrokhzad, who had died in a car crash in 1967 at the age of 32, Iranian political realities brutally intruded on the film's reception, offering a sobering reminder of the strength of the networks that those who leave authoritarian countries like Iran can be imbricated in. While potentially easing the transition to new places, they can also render not only return a non-option, but also the possibility of a quiet life anywhere else. That the majority of the film's cast members are settled immigrants who have established themselves as part of the city's creative class shows how far along the generational shift among foreign workers was by 1991.

Allahyari's Vienna is not as incommensurable as the worlds his characters represent but rather much more hybrid. Both the wintery exteriors and overheated interiors are grimy and nominally under patriarchal control, with the traffic cop writing out tickets to cars parked in front of the train station a match for the promiscuous owner of the budget hotel near the Praterstern that Ali's family first stay at. It is underscored that Schönbrunn, the site of an enjoyable snowy outing, was the Emperor's summer palace; when Ali excitedly describes the balcony to his companions, he shows how much he has internalized patriarchal norms in stating: "here is where Franz Joseph stood, and Sisi was next to him" ("Hier stand der Franz Joseph und die Sisi daneben") [Figure 1.21].

In the case of each of these three sites, it is the act of crossing its threshold, and specifically his leaving of it, that brings Ali into a confrontational situation from which he must learn new coping strategies. When he first arrives with his sister and son, and his nephew brings them to the car that has been left in front of the train station, they find a traffic cop in the process of writing out a ticket (police are also shown in the station as they are on their way out, removing a man sleeping on a bench and someone sitting on the floor in front of it). Ali's nephew and his Polish friend, familiar with the somewhat peculiar norms of the situation, argue with the cop in proper Viennese style and dialect to give their companions time to load the luggage. Ali, on the other hand, misreads the situation [Figure 1.22] and tries to offer the cop a bribe, an act so unexpected that it creates complete confusion, during which they manage to snatch the money back and drive off. The first time Ali emerges from the hotel, he is accosted by the prostitutes who work in the building across the street and innocently responds to their conversation instead of simply walking past, as the other hotel residents do [Figure 1.23]. A heated exchange ensues, which ends with them snickering at his correcting their German and telling them they should get a proper education.[2] At the end of the outing to Schönbrunn, with sunset prayers approaching, Ali tells the Polish friend, who during the outing has expressed his interest in the sister and inquired what would be necessary to win her affections, that in addition to converting to Muslim and adopting a Muslim name like Abdullah, he must also be circumcised [Figure 1.24]. In each of these situations, the authority Ali is used to exercising proves comically ineffectual, and he is forced to adapt.

Figure 1.21: *I Love Vienna* (Images ©1991 epo-film)

Figure 1.22: *I Love Vienna* (Images ©1991 epo-film).

Figure 1.23: *I Love Vienna* (Images ©1991 epo-film).

Figure 1.24: *I Love Vienna* (Images ©1991 epo-film).

I Love Vienna very much belongs to the category of accented cinema identified by Hamid Naficy. Naficy compares the accented style to Raymond Williams's notion of a structure of feeling, insofar as it encodes responses to a particular, material social experience (Martin), and specifies that: "the accented style continually grapples with the politicized immediacy of films and with their collective enunciation and reception – that is, with the manner in which politics infuses all aspects of their existence" (Naficy 6). Allahyari is a diasporic film-maker who brings to his films a highly developed sensitivity to alterity and what it means to live in a hostile culture, and indeed, one of Allahyari's slightly later films, the 1994 *Höhenangst* (*Fear of Heights*), which won the Max Ophüls Prize in 1995, is briefly treated in *Accented Cinema* (207). Naficy identifies that film's main theme as fear, which is able to be overcome by being shared in precarious circumstances. *Fear of Heights* "ends dramatically on top of a very tall factory smokestack where [the protagonist] Mario and the farm girl are finally able to name and to face their fears, thereby freeing themselves" (207), and *I Love Vienna* has a similarly metaphorical ending. Like Fassbinder's Ali, who suffers a perforated ulcer from the fear that eats at his soul, Allahyari's Ali has an appendicitis attack, and neither he nor his nephew can afford the necessary medical treatment. The fear eating at Allahyari's Ali's insides is of letting go of control. There is much he has to come to terms with: his sister insisting on marrying the Pole; his son learning to fend for himself on Vienna's mean streets, which eventually gets him into trouble with the law; and his love-interest, who sells her share of the hotel to finance his operation. In the penultimate scene, when Ali is recovering and asks her to marry him, she tersely reminds him that he is not a Franz Joseph, she is not a Sisi, and that she will only marry him, at least for three days, when he is no longer in pain.

The film ends with a short final scene in which an elderly woman in a smoky bar performs a jaunty number about love in an English enunciated in cosmopolitan style, in the same spirit as the off-beat performances that used to be held just off the Linke Wienzeile by operetta singers whose glory had long faded [Figure 1.25]. By having Friederike Wilder-Okladek play the singer, Allahyari ends the film by re-situating it in Vienna's larger migrational history. In 1977, Wilder-Okladek completed a dissertation at the University of Vienna on "General and Jewish Migration after the Second World War, with attention to Vienna's Jews" (*Allgemeine und jüdische Migration nach dem Zweiten Weltkrieg. Mit Berücksichtigung der Juden Wiens*), in which she coined the concept of "part-remigration":

A phenomenon repeatedly described is that of part-remigration. Those who have been displaced and who either cannot or do not want to leave their new home to return to their old one often began to develop an increasing distance or a kind of 'reconciliation' with their fate of wandering back and forth between their lifeworlds. Partly this condition has been described as being 'at home' neither here nor there. Every type of attachment has been severed. Friederike Wilder-Okladek coined this concept in her study of Jewish remigration: 'Between the departure and the return is a period of time, and the emigrant comes back different. Often this being different is directed at the fatherland so that he [sic] no longer feels at home there, because when the decision to return is made, the fatherland is idealized so that every further attempt to adapt fails. Then he is properly stateless, an individual that hangs between two worlds: the world

Figure 1.25: *I Love Vienna* (Images ©1991 epo-film).

of immigration, which he fails to connect to, and the old world, which he has partly outgrown' (Holzheu).

Allahyari's Ali may not be a returnee, but he finds it similarly challenging to connect to his new Viennese reality, and the only other possible destination mentioned is the US. Returning to Iran is unsurprisingly never presented as an option.

In subtly evoking the difficult history of the Holocaust, Allahyari also demonstrates a sensitivity to, and the courage to speak out about, the situation of the Viennese in ways that echo Wilder-Okladek's work. For her, as a Jew, there were clear differences between German and Austrian Nazis:

> The typical Austrian is a racial mixture which is at the root of the whole complex situation, much more than the German Nazi whose Germanisation is at least a few generations old. Thus, the Austrian nature of the problem leads to a continuous conflict situation in the would-be Nazi. He [sic] is completely incapable of conforming to the laws of 'Germanic racial purity,' feels inferior and develops profound sentiments of inferiority [...] Thus the Austrian forms extreme variations of Nationalist and National-Socialist activity just because he is unable to come to terms with *the typical Austrian situation of diversity* and his inability to be a 'pure German' (Mitten 262, italics added).

Coming of age just as World War II broke out (she was born in 1921 and grew up in the Lessinggasse in Vienna's 2nd district, not far from the Praterstern hotel that features in

I Love Vienna), Wilder-Okladek had occasion to become familiar with the various national varieties of National Socialism over the course of the war. She "experienced this time consciously as a Jew," as she notes in her memoir (Girtler and Okladek 19).[3] Her unpolitical parents, and her German-national grandmother in particular, were caught off-guard by the welcome Hitler received when he marched into Austria in 1938. Her grandparents, who were of "eastern" origins and had been in Vienna since 1903, were the first the family sent to an aunt in Holland.[4] Friederike followed a few months later and lived in a training camp for Jewish young people to prepare for a new life in Palestine before the Germans invaded Holland and she became involved, first, with the "Joodsche Raad" (the Jewish Council) and then, in Paris, with the French Resistance. Eventually her situation became too precarious, and she managed to escape to Spain in an arduous guided hike over the Pyrenees similar to the one Walter Benjamin was not able to manage. Meanwhile, her parents were allowed to emigrate from Vienna in August 1939 thanks to a relative who arranged positions for them as farm hands ("Diener [...] auf einem Gutshof") in southern England (50).

What is striking about Wilder-Okladek's account of her travails to survive in Nazi Europe, as she recounted them in the early 1990s, is that as soon as she left Vienna, she understood herself to be a refugee. The first thing she did after arriving at her grandmother's in Den Haag was to search out a synagogue, and she explained her difficulties in dealing with this new identity as follows: "I could have introduced myself to the leader of the prayer service and said to him: 'I am a *refugee!*' But no, I didn't. Rather I convinced myself that I now had to be independent" (44, italics added).[5] Similarly, as soon as the group she escaped from France with crossed into Spain, she once again describes her status with this term:

After about five hours hike, always along the stream, we stood in front of a shepherd's hut, where a man was tending sheep [...] He had noticed immediately that we were *refugees* and let us know that people in the village were accustomed to looking after *refugees* (175, italics added).[6]

In using the same vocabulary for the Jews persecuted by the Nazis and the foreigners in Vienna who were the contemporary target of the FPÖ's xenophobic campaigns (Landa 95), Wilder-Okladek is making a strong political commentary about the long-standing nature of prejudice in Austria. The question underlying her text is a frustrated: Has really nothing been learned?

Allahyari's empathetic advocacy of Wilder-Okladek's take on "the typical Austrian situation of diversity" and her efforts to overcome contemporary Vienna's "foreigner problems" by re-signifying *Ausländer* as *Flüchtlinge* could well explain his decision to settle in cosmopolitan Vienna, and not anywhere in Germany. His accented oeuvre is replete with works in which foreigners face enormous social hurdles and Viennese men are confronted with the ridiculousness of their prejudices. In the popular 1999 *Geboren in Absurdistan* (*Born in Absurdistan*), for example, the new-born babies of a Turkish migrant couple and a small-minded Austrian immigration officer are mixed up in the hospital, and after a series of misadventures surrounding the Turkish couple's subsequent deportation, the fathers both come to the realization that DNA is not as determinative as the attachments they have already made to "their" sons and refuse to undergo the tests that would conclusively establish paternity, preferring to bring the boys up together as friends. More recently, Allahyari spent two years following "refugee helper" Ute Bock around and documenting the work she and her association Flüchtlingsprojekt Ute Bock do in support of refugees. Two documentaries championing Bock have thus far resulted: *Bock for President* (2009) and *Die verrückte Welt der Ute Bock* (*The Crazy World of Ute Bock*, 2010). The office of Bock's association at the time the documentaries were made was only blocks away from both the hotel where Ali and his family first stay in *I Love Vienna* and the apartment in which Wilder-Okladek grew up, and in the summer of 2012, she moved to the Zohmanngasse in Ostbahn Kurti's Favoriten (see Brickner), where she had worked for many years in a dormitory for apprentices (*Gesellenheim*). These locations are characteristic of the way Vienna's urban space continues to apportion its newcomers.

Also of note is the fact that Ute Bock won the Bruno Kreisky prize for services to human rights five years after Willi Resetarits did, and that both were awarded the Karl Renner prize in 2003.[7] This speaks to the activist concerns that coalesce under the Wiener Chic rubric. There is not only a recognition of the repercussions that inhumane politics have on society and especially its less fortunate members, but also a willingness to do something to make things at least a little better, a little more manageable. For Schlingensief, it was enough to stage a spectacle that made apparent the extremity of Austria's historical legacy of mistreating those considered foreign. For the young Viennese protesters who stormed his container, tore down the "Ausländer raus" sign and freed the supposed refugees, on the other hand, effective action trumped the show [Figure 1.26, 1.27]. That sense of meaningful intervention seems to be a crucial component of Wiener Chic, as though in response to the bleaker and crueller elements that have also gone into its making.

To recap the first part of this study: what we have discovered in tracing the formation of the four key socio-cultural groups that have been influential for Wiener Chic – the Habsburgs on Baroque Chic, the Liberals on Ringstrasse Chic, the working class on Prolo Chic, and foreigners on *Ausländer* Chic – is that the sense of dreamlike stasis that helps to make Vienna a romantic, neo-baroque playground is counterbalanced by an underbelly of nightmarish, even murderous fantasy. In Wiener Chic, *eros* meets *thanatos*, but whether either is a foreigner or female, and the extent to which either is exoticized or orientalized changes according to circumstance. Baroque Chic paved the way for the expression and understanding of passion and of suffering. Ringstrasse Chic put capital in charge, which restructured the city and expedited the pace of change. Prolo Chic and *Ausländer* Chic both participated in and responded to this change, mitigating its tendency to mythologize elites. Taken together, they provide a unique composite that fashion has had to grapple with in trying to make inroads into the Viennese urban imaginary. We trace those attempts in the next part.

Before we do, however, we need to address the matter of two memes that our socio-cultural ordering of this part precluded: *Alt-Wien* (Old Vienna) and *noir*. As Musner has convincingly shown in the case of the former, "the nostalgic image of Vienna projected back

Figure 1.26: Schlingensief's container, 2000 (Photo: S. Ingram).

Figure 1.27: Schlingensief's container, 2000 (Photo: S. Ingram).

into the past is […] an invention of the early nineteenth century and was repeatedly brought up and newly interpreted in different social and economic contexts" (83). This imaginary "of an originary Vienna as a rabbit-warren of streets, old houses, Gothic neighbourhoods and medieval religious buildings" (ibid.) came into being just as the city was beginning to modernize and create anxiety in its populace that it would have to adjust and keep up. While *Alt-Wien* has been the subject of local academic and museal attention (in German, cf. Sommer, Kos), it has not been as successful at providing images associated with the city as either the baroque or the Ringstrasse, in no small part due to the uncanniness of its heritage. Rather, as Musner makes clear, it has only been mobilized internally and then only "when social and cultural crises together with incisive urban waves of modernization have been felt to be threatening" (Musner 83).[8]

Like *Alt-Wien,* the nostalgically tinged noir image of Vienna in ruins popularized by *The Third Man* (Carol Reed, 1949) never managed to stick to Vienna. Such cinematic ruins are more often associated with Berlin. Films like *Die Mörder sind unter uns* (*The Murderers are Among Us*, Wolfgang Staudte, 1946), *Razzia* (Werner Klinger, 1947), *A Foreign Affair* (Billy Wilder, 1948), *Germania anno zero* (*Germany Year Zero,* Roberto Rossellini, 1948), *Berlin Express* (Jacques Tourneur, 1948) and *Berliner Ballade* (R.A. Stemmle, 1948) provided indelible images of Berlin in ruins that were reactivated following the fall of the Wall, when heaps of rubble once again filled the streets (cf. Sark 2012 "Baustelle Berlin"). In the case of Vienna, however, there is simply too much competing interference. As popular as *The Third Man* has become, it failed to permanently establish a place image for Vienna that could begin to challenge its status as the capital of music and the home of baroque and Ringstrasse glories.[9]

Also, the Vienna in *The Third Man* is not so much a city in ruins as a city at night on its way to becoming, very much like the Los Angeles of Raymond Chandler a decade earlier, "a dark place of quasi-Weimarian grandeur" (Davis 36), something Mike Davis traces to the literary tradition, the classic template for which was laid down by Charles Dickens, Eugène Sue, Edgar Allan Poe and Charles Baudelaire. Protagonist Holly Martin (Joseph Cotton) finds himself confronted, upon his arrival in Vienna, with not only an occupied city in ruins, but also a mystery. The plot revolves around "the familiar trope of the 'evil genius' masterminding the metropolitan underworld" while "the modern fear of the irruption of the irrational within everyday normality […] is linked to a specifically post-imperialist paranoia about the 'return' of the alien" (Donald 1993, 174). This corresponds to what Said's reading of Dickens's London suggests: "[…] subjects can be taken to places like Australia, but they cannot be allowed a 'return' to metropolitan space, which as all Dickens's fiction testifies, is meticulously charted, spoken for, inhabited by a hierarchy of metropolitan personages" (Said xvi). In the case of *The Third Man*, Harry Lime must not leave the Russian zone. However, this relation to a centre of power does not obtain in the same way as it does for imperial metropolises like London and Paris with colonies strewn around the globe. It is not only the Russian zone which is rendered as a colonial space, but the whole occupied city: the international zone is itself the maze, compared to a Babel of languages, and violence erupts as easily between the Brit and the American as among the "natives."

The colonial urban space in *The Third Man* is also more profoundly ambivalent because it is haunted, as is so typical for the city's representation, by its own – imagined – history. Throughout the movie, there is a subtext, the presence of post-war Vienna's imagined other: its own past. This is evident even in the narrator's voiceover at the beginning of the movie. "I never knew the old Vienna before the war, with its Strauss music, its glamour and easy charm," the narrator claims. Yet this old Vienna is in plain sight, literally being staged in the Theater in der Josephstadt, where ladies frolic and curtsy in powdered wigs and corsets [Figure 1.28 and 1.29]. This is not the only scene in the film in which Viennese high culture

Figure 1.28: *The Third Man* (Images ©1949 London Film Productions/ British Lion Film Corporation).

Figure 1.29: *The Third Man* (Images ©1949 London Film Productions/ British Lion Film Corporation).

erupts forcefully into the not-quite-colonized space of post-war Vienna. At the literary society talk, at which Holly Martin, who has written some Westerns, is invited to expound upon his views regarding literature, the competing image of Vienna as a place of backward-oriented high culture, a place that remembers a very European, very Western modernity (Joyce, stream-of-consciousness), contains the exoticism that an American reading tries to impose on it. *The Third Man*'s Vienna manages to avoid being turned into an exotic other – a post-war colonial space – by conjuring up not only its own imminently Western past but also its own homemade "others," specifically the newly Communist east, peopled by vaguely swarthy, generically Eastern types, such as the female protagonist, who poses as an Austrian but is later unmasked as Czech on account of her forged documents.

This powerful nostalgic presence of a Vienna of the past that still maintains its status even when occupied is ultimately the basis on which the post-war re-imaging of Vienna was built by the preachers of a high culture and a Western European modernity that exorcized any (Central European) demons from its quaint, museum-like imaginary. In Vienna, it was not the return of the exotic other that makes the city threatening and alluring, but the return of a tame, quaint, exclusionary, self-important capital of music that did not allow for the existence of the other within its not-so-modern, not-so-noir urban space. It has only been recently that the Viennese, hostile to the depiction of their city when the film was produced, could afford to recuperate the popularity of the film and commodify a filmic imaginary in "Third Man" guided tours, advertised in prominent locations in the city [Figure 1.30].

Fortunately, as we have seen in this section, labour migration and the opening up of the country to the EU and beyond has finally allowed others – both working class and foreign – to become present in the Viennese urban imaginary in ways unimaginable a century ago, when

Figure 1.30: Third Man tour poster (Photo: S. Ingram).

they could only register at a threatening, if alluring, level but did not have access to means of self-representation that could either penetrate the class barriers and travel beyond them, or champions to represent them. That they now do, and have added to the Wiener Chic mix, has been the thrust of this part of the book. The thrust of the next one is to show how this opening up has been equally pivotal for the fashion system.

Notes

1   A longer account of this event is available in Ingram 2012 ("Schlingensief's Container").

2   Landa also draws attention to the protagonist's profession and how it allows Allahyari to distance him from the usual descriptions of foreigners, who are commonly infantilized on account of their lack of mastery of German grammar.

3   "Ich habe diese Zeit als Jüdin bewußt miterlebt."

4   These were her father's parents. She describes their background as a "real German" one ("Der Hintergrund meiner Familie vom Vater her ist ein echt deutscher" (21) but also somewhat murky ("hat nebelhafte Hintergründe, wie andere jüdische Familien auch" (22). Her father's father was from Russian-Poland and came to Breslau after WWI as a deserter, while her father's mother was "120% German" (22), who had attended "eine höhere Töchterschule" in east Germany and whose father had won a medal for fighting in the German-French war of 1870-1. Her mother's parents, on the other hand, worked in a Polish liqueur factory in "Lemberg," where Okladek's mother was born. They emigrated to Vienna in 1906 (20–21), and her mother's mother died there in 1913 (20).

5   "Ich hätte mich wohl dem Synagogendiener vorstellen und ihm sagen können: 'Ich bin ein Flüchtling!' Aber nein, das habe ich nicht gesagt. Vielmehr redete ich mir ein, jetzt selbstständig sein zu müssen."

6   "Nach ungefähr fünf Stunden Marsch, immer den Bach entlang, standen wir vor einer Hirtenhüte, vor der ein Mann Schafe hütete [...] Er hatte sofort gemerkt, daß wir Flüchtlinge waren, und wies uns darauf hin, daß man in dem Dorf schon öfters Flüchtlinge aufgenommen habe."

7   The information on this prize is available at: http://de.wikipedia.org/wiki/Karl-Renner-Preis, accessed 10 June 2013.

8   "Das nostalgische, in die Geschichte zurück projizierte Wien-Image ist, wie verschiedene Studien zeigen, eine Erfindung des frühen 19. Jahrhunderts, und wurde in späterer Folge in unterschiedlichen sozialen und ökonomischen Kontexten immer wieder neu aufgegriffen und interpretiert. Die Vorstellung eines ursprünglichen Wiens voll von verwinkelten Gassen, alten Häusern, gotischen Stadtvierteln und mittelalterichen Sakralbauten entstand im Vormärz. [...] Mit dem "Alt-Wien" Topos wurde eine verallgemeinerbare Regressionsphantasie der Stadt geschaffen, die immer dann zur Anwendung kommen konnte, wenn soziale und kulturelle Krisen zusammen mit markanten urbanen Modernisierungsschuben von eingesessenen Bevölkerungengruppen als Bedrohungsszenarien empfunden wurden."

9   Cf. Reisenleitner 2004. The following material is drawn from that source.

PART II

Staging Fashion in Vienna

"When in Vienna one asks oneself again and again why fashion doesn't make the headlines here and haute couture doesn't play a major role, then one is thinking, unconsciously comparatively, about Parisian haute couture, and forgetting the very different preconditions."

(Bönsch 17)[1]

In Gerda Buxbaum's monumental *Mode aus Wien, 1815–1938*, the only major monograph so far on fashion in Vienna, which is conspicuously named to avoid claiming that there is such a thing as Viennese fashion but rather only "Fashion from Vienna" that came to an end with the march into Vienna of Hitler's troops, one of the key developmental chapters is entitled "Die Laufstege der Wiener Mode" (The Catwalks of Vienna Fashion). After having chronologically outlined in the previous chapter the various forces that affected fashion from Vienna between the Congress of Vienna in 1815 and the Nazi *Anschluß* of 1938, Buxbaum goes on to enumerate the catalysts that played an "important, irreplaceable role in advancing fashion" during the period in question (Buxbaum 1986, 107). In addition to larger societal processes such as improvements in education, the founding of clubs and societies, advantageous customs agreements as well as faster and more cost-efficient access to raw materials, Buxbaum concentrates primarily on printed materials, beginning with the first magazine to appear in Vienna with the word "Mode" in its title: the *Mode-, Fabriken- und Gewerbezeitung* (*Fashion, Factory and Trade Magazine*), which Schönfeld published in Vienna and Prague between 1787 and 1789. In the following chapters, her focus then turns to the fashion salons in Vienna, the representations of fashion in the fine arts, and the Viennese women who acted as "figureheads of fashion," primarily women in the so-called "second society," that is, non-aristocrats such as actresses, who on the basis of their prominence and popularity had access to aristocratic circles. *Mode aus Wien* is thus structured on the basis of the access that the Viennese had to fashion, where they learned about it and how they came into contact with it.

While we are rather averse to the causal implications inherent in strict chronologizing, our study too takes cultural practices as its focus and in this part seeks to survey the contemporary cultural institutions that have brought fashion to visibility in Vienna.[2] We begin with the observation that whenever fashion is staged in Vienna, the chics identified in the previous part as key components of the city's urban imaginary seem to come into play in one form or another. In the first instance, fashion is primarily staged in the city's

Figure 2.1: Fashion show @ the MQ (Photo: M. Reisenleitner).

baroque tradition of conspicuous display. In comparing nineteenth-century Vienna, Paris and London, Donald Olsen confirms that "Vienna placed greater stress on public life than Paris, immensely more than London" (Olsen 239-240), which he attributes to the fact that

[t]he triumph of Habsburg absolutism not only deprived the old Viennese *Bürgertum* of its independence but took from the old feudal aristocracy its political functions. It could justify its wealth and privileges not on the basis of services it performed for society – as the English aristocracy could – but on the basis of the splendour and conspicuousness with which it lived. To maintain a position based on symbolic rather than functional grounds, it was necessary to invest every aspect of behaviour with high ceremonial content. The consequences were awesome: the permanent 'self-presentation' demanded a formalized manner of moving, speaking, and dressing (Olsen 240).

Even though the regime was no longer an absolute monarchy during the Ringstrasse era, the aristocracy nonetheless still conducted itself as it had during the Baroque. As Olsen notes, it "felt equally constrained to live in a punctilious, splendid and public fashion. Since no two members of that aristocracy were precisely equal, it was as important to establish and maintain one's position in the social hierarchy as it had been in the Versailles of the duc de

Figure 2.2: Champagne reception at *Meinl am Graben* during Fashion Night 2012 (Photo: M. Reisenleitner).

Saint-Simon" (ibid.). That is, unlike the nouveau elites in the new world such as the Rockefellers, who wanted to hide among themselves and who left representation to their monumental buildings, the Viennese elites, whether pre-modern aristocrats or contemporary social icons, have always needed to be seen to reinforce their assumed superiority [Figure 2.2]. This relationality has led to fashion being made at least partially available for the masses, unlike the fashion events and trade shows in the leading global fashion cities, where access is more strictly controlled.

As we see in this part, the Viennese fashion system is a relatively porous and conflictual field, marked by tensions between the competing demands of centripetality, a liberal agenda, and social concern. How these various priorities have been balanced has played out differently in different kinds of institutions; the more permanent, most pertinently those of learning and display, such as museums, institutes, shops and print material, tend more towards social concerns while the more temporary, such as fashion events, advertising brochures and web presences, tend more towards commerce. However, given the small size of the system, the tight weave of its networks, and the fact that institutions like museums and shops have found the programming of events useful in developing and maintaining their clientele, determining degrees of permanence becomes increasingly difficult. There is, however, no doubt that these institutions have had a crucial influence on taste cultures, and have been understood, and have understood themselves, as formative for what counts as stylish, timely and, increasingly, globally competitive in terms of fashion and design.

The following chapters probe what appear to be the most relevant of these institutions and explore their specific genesis and contribution to Wiener Chic.

Notes

1   "Wenn man sich in Wien immer wieder fragt, warum hier die Mode keine Schlagzeilen macht und die Haute Couture keine große Rolle spielt, dann denkt man, unbewußt vergleichend, an die Pariser Haute Couture und vergißt dabei die durchaus verschiedenen Voraussetzungen."

2   While we are hardly political or social scientists of the mould identified by De Frantz in her work on the new institutional paradigm in those disciplines, of the various perspectives she outlines, such as rational choice and normative, we would ascribe to the historical understanding of institutions as she outlines it, namely, "Historical approaches define institutions as long-established conventions guiding individuals' behavior along paths that are consolidated over time. Once set up, collective processes become path-dependent because they are either difficult to change or unquestioned, even despite emerging inefficiencies in a changing context" (De Frantz 2008, 467). One would need to make a proviso, however, on the question of what constitutes "long established"; clearly some of the newer collective processes and practices are of markedly shorter duration than some of the older ones.

Chapter 5

Museum Chic

In this chapter, we focus on institutions that have a history of displaying fashion and include fashion-related activities in their programming. While there are also small collections housed in institutions such as the Österreichisches Theater Museum (Austrian Theater Museum), in terms of imprinting fashion on the city's imaginary it is to three major museums that one must look: the Wien Museum, the Museum für Angewandte Kunst (applied arts, better know by its acronym, MAK) and the Museumsquartier (MQ).

Wien Museum: A museum for the Viennese

In many ways, the Wien Museum is an unlikely location for one of the most comprehensive fashion collections in Europe. Founded in 1887 as the "Historisches Museum der Stadt Wien" (Historical Museum of the City of Vienna), it was originally located in the Rathaus (City Hall), the neo-Gothic prestige building on the Ringstrasse between the University and the Parliament that was meant to emphasize the independence of city government from Habsburg rule by recuperating communal urban self-governance during the Middle Ages. It included, and put on display, the holdings of the city's armoury (the Zeughaus), where not only the weapons that armed the citizens of Vienna were stored but also the spoils of the two failed Ottoman sieges of 1529 and 1683. Displays emphasized the city's historical role as a bulwark against the threats thought to be emanating from the East and characterized Vienna as a feisty place whose spirit of independence was temporarily subdued during the early modern absolutist period of the Habsburg's reign, only to be resurrected by the Liberals wresting away the Ringstrasse urban modernization project from the imperial rulers. While this somewhat triumphalist origin of a large part of the permanent collection might not seem to be an auspicious starting point for engaging with the multifaceted and globally connected strands of the city's history and collective memory, the lineage of the collection contributed to establishing a tradition that focused on material culture, rather than the elite forms of artistic practice that one finds in museums like the Albertina and the Kunsthistorisches Museum (Museum of Art History).[1]

While City Hall provided a clear line of connection between the Vienna city council and the self-presentation of the city, a more prominent location was envisaged at an early stage of the museum's history, and the favoured location was the Karlsplatz – an awkwardly dimensioned traffic hub that connects several major traffic arteries while being visually dominated by the baroque church that recalls imperial power from the

Figure 2.3: "Reflecting Fashion" exhibition at the MUMOK. (Photo: S. Ingram).

Age of Absolutism [Figure 2.4] in sharp contrast with the bourgeois signature buildings of the Künstlerhaus and the Musikverein across the street [Figure 2.5]. The design of a representative museum building figured prominently in several attempts to re-imagine this space and to align it with the modernization Vienna was undergoing during the *fin-de-siècle*. Otto Wagner's monumental re-conceptualization of the square was never realized, and he had to content himself with designing the city railway station opposite the cathedral [Figure 2.6].

Plans for a dedicated museum space were only realized in 1959, when a competition was held on the occasion of the eightieth birthday of ex-mayor Körner. In line with the somewhat authoritarian strand characteristic of a city council dominated by Social Democrats, the jury selected the fourth-ranked design by Oswald Haerdtl, which was understatedly modern and conformed perfectly with the party's avowed ambition to present a visual image of the city that would return it to world city status [Figure 2.7]. The city's intentions in this regard are shown by the title of a 1956 piece published by the Austrian "Städtebund" (federation of cities) together with the Wiener Kulturamt: "Wien wird wieder Weltstadt" (Vienna is again becoming a world city), as well as the 300+ page "Prachtband" (*Wiedergeburt einer Weltstadt* – Rebirth of a World City), which was published in 1965 (Payer 1).

In the new building on the Karlsplatz, a permanent exhibition was set up that follows a chronological sequence of the city's history from Roman fortress to modern city, with a predictable emphasis on the Ottoman sieges and the Ringstrasse eras. Special exhibitions

Figure 2.4: Wien Museum and the Karlskirche (Photo: S. Ingram).

Figure 2.5: Künstlerhaus and the Gesellschaft der Musikfreunde (Photo: M. Reisenleitner).

Figure 2.6: Otto Wagner's city railway station at the Karlplatz (Photo: M. Reisenleitner).

Figure 2.7: Wien Museum at night (Photo: S. Ingram).

during the first decades of the new exhibition space emphasized urban history, prominent Viennese artists (Otto Wagner) and architectural history, especially of the *fin-de-siècle* ("Das Stadtbild Wiens im 19. Jahrhundert von der Festung zur Großstadt," 1960 – Vienna's Cityscape in the 19th Century from Fortress to Metropolis), but they already included social history topics that would have been considered daring within the walls of Austrian university history departments of the day, which were dominated by political and diplomatic history ("Exhibition childhood" in 1960). Also remarkable is the strong focus on urban imaginaries (*Stadtbilder*).

An important development in this period was the founding, in 1946, of the Modeschule Hetzendorf and the assembling, by its first director Alfred Kunz (1894-1961), of a fashion collection that has in the meantime grown to well over 20,000 objects.[2] The Modeschule's predecessor institution was the *Wiener Frauenakademie* (Viennese Women's Academy), a public art school founded in 1897 under the impetus of painter Olga Prager for females who wanted to study art but were not allowed entry into the existing art academies. The Nazis had "downgraded" the academy to a fashion school, and the school building it occupied in the 3rd district had been destroyed by bombs in 1944. After the war, Kunz – who had successfully established himself as a costume and set designer in film (among other things he did the costumes for Willi Forst's 1942 *Wiener Blut* as well as a series of short documentaries on *Wiener Mode*) and who had been the artistic director of the *Wiener Haus der Mode* (Viennese House of Fashion) in the Palais Lobkowitz from 1938 to 1945 – led the efforts to re-establish the Modeschule in the baroque palace in Hetzendorf that Maria Theresia had bought from Countess Eleonore Thun-Hohenstein and her husband Duke Anton Florian von and zu Liechtenstein in 1742 and had expanded for the sake of her elderly widowed mother's health [Figure 2.8].

Elis Blauensteiner, who was responsible for *Modeentwurf und Modegrafik* (Fashion Design and Graphic Design) at the school from 1946 to 1986, has described the "spirit" that developed in the early days on account of Schloß Hetzendorf's location and the general conditions:

It [Schloß Hetzendorf] had also been damaged in the war – and it was far to walk to! The Philadelphiabrücke – a boardwalk. The streetcar unreliable. Something was born in those days that I would like to call 'the spirit of Hetzendorf.' Teamwork instead of hierarchy! Together we stamped across the snow, together we froze in unheated rooms, together and in a chain we cleared out the various bombed sites, together we organized the books in the fashion collection and discussed possible fashion activities. We made our first designs out of paper and coloured molino. We invited the press, the city councillor responsible for culture, the guild, school authorities and textile firms – and lo and behold: they all came! And we got front-page coverage in the Viennese dailies and the material that we longed for was donated. Soon the students were exhibiting 'their' own designs on the runway in the garden. In groups! We thus also introduced something new. (Fashion at that time was only celebrated individually and exclusively!) (Blauensteiner 8–9).[3]

Figure 2.8: Schloß Hetzendorf (Photo: S. Ingram).

In addition to offering five-year courses of study in the practical areas of fashion design and dressmaking, knitwear and hosiery, tailor-made leather goods, tailor-made millinery and textile design, the Modeschule also houses a library with over 12,000 volumes, including fashion journals dating back to 1786 and over 3000 copperplates from the second half of the nineteenth century, and it organizes events like the "Hetzendorfer Gespräche" (Hetzendorfer Talks), a series of lectures that was published as *Fashion in Context* (Buxbaum 2009).

The fashion collection itself, which now claims over 22,500 items of clothing and accessories, is based on the holdings of the *Verein für Kultur und Mode* (Association for Culture and Fashion), Alfred Kunz's private collection, and subsequent donations and acquisitions. While its emphasis is on nineteenth- and twentieth-century women's fashion, it also includes items of men's, children's and sports clothing as well as accessories and items that have fallen out of fashion.[4] The thrust of the collection is decidedly local.[5] While some international designers are represented (Giorgio Armani, Yves Saint Laurent, Helmut Lang, Vivienne Westwood and Dries van Noten), they are dwarfed by items associated with notable Viennese personalities, such as one of Maria Theresia's cashmere shawls, a pair of ballerina Fanny Elssler's shoes, one of playwright Johann Nestroy's dressing gowns, a parasol from the opening of the Suez Canal, boots belonging to Helene Vetsera, the mother of Crown Prince Rudolph's lover, Mary (the suicidal pair of the Mayerling tragedy), dresses belonging to Franz Joseph's mistress, actress Katharina Schratt, gloves belonging to Franz Joseph and Empress Elisabeth, the Hungarian court uniform that Emperor Karl I wore to his coronation as King of Hungary in 1916, Kolo Moser's reform clothing, and smocks belonging to the Secessionist artists Gustav Klimt, Josef Engelhart and Anton Hanak. Clothiers from the Biedermeier period are represented (Thomas Petko, Josef Georg Beer and Gottfried Röhberg for women; Josef Gunkel for men) as well as the most important fashion studios of the *fin-de-siècle*: Bohlinger & Huber, Emanuel Braun & Co., Christoph Drecoll, the sisters Flöge, Heinrich Grünbaum, Heinrich Grünzweig, L. & H. Laufer, Jungmann & Neffe, G. & E.Spitzer, Ignaz Bittmann, Stone & Blyth, the fashion division of the Wiener Werkstätte, the luxury department store Ludwig Zwieback & Bruder, Popp & Kretschmar (for leather goods), Riedel & Beutel (for undergarments) and Ignaz Bittmann (for children's clothing). From the twentieth century, one finds exemplars by the designers W.F. Adlmüller, Vera Billiani, Franz Faschingbauer, Berta Farnhammer, Herta Gross, Gertrud Höchsmann, and an important collection of Adele List's hat creations.

This collection, while initially not connected to the Wien Museum, became its property in 1954 and resulted in an exhibition that was held at Schloß Hetzendorf, on "Die Wiener Mode im Wandel der Zeiten" (Viennese Fashion through the Ages, 15 June 1960 to 22 October 1960).[6] It was followed by two exhibitions, also at Schloß Hetzendorf, that were organized in conjunction with larger period exhibitions at the Wien Museum on the Karlsplatz: "Wiener Mode des Empire und Biedermeier" (Vienna Fashion of the Napoleonic and Biedermeier Periods, 8 June 1969 to 21 September 1969) and "Mode in Wien 1850–1900" (Fashion in Vienna 1850–1900, 22 May 1973 to 23 September 1973).

The fashion collection clearly formed an important part of the museum's holdings, but the role of fashion in the programming strategy remains somewhat ambivalent and was certainly not central during the following decades. Rather, exhibitions on fashion topics were relegated to the outskirts of the city, especially after the Hermesvilla was acquired as an additional exhibition space in 1971 [Figure 2.9].

The historicist villa, built in 1881 by Franz Joseph for his wife Empress Elisabeth in the Lainzer Tiergarten at the western outskirts of Vienna, not only represents the aristocratic taste culture that gave rise to couture; there could also not be a more pronounced architectural contrast than between this Ringstrasse-era building based on dynastic tastes and built at a time when the Liberals had already taken control of Vienna's more centrally located signature architecture (e.g. the Künstlerhaus and the Musikverein) and the international style of Haerdtl's museum on the Karlsplatz. The role of the Hermesvilla was showcased in the exhibition "200 Jahre Mode in Wien" (200 Years of Fashion in Vienna, 10 April 1976 to 31 October 1976). Consequently, fashion exhibitions based on the fashion collection and loans were staged regularly but never in the central location on the Karlsplatz. Rather, they were held both at the Hermesvilla and at Hetzendorf.[7]

It was not until the new millennium that fashion moved to the centre, under the directorship of Wolfgang Kos, a former radio journalist and prominent 68er, who assumed the directorship

Figure 2.9: Hermesvilla (Photo: M. Reisenleitner).

of the Historisches Museum der Stadt Wien in 2003. Shortly thereafter, the museum was rebranded as the Wien Museum. An exhibition on "Wiener Couture: Gertrud Höchsmann 1902–1990" was put on together with the Academy for Applied Arts (7 November 2002 to 25 January 2003), and followed by "Hutsalon Susi & Milchfrau Rosa: Wiener Verkaufskultur fotografiert von Petra Rainer" (Hat Salon Susi & Milkmaid Rosa: Viennese Commodity Culture Photographed by Petra Rainer, 21 August 2003 to 28 September 2003) and the first presentation of gifts to the Fashion Collection ("Erstmalige Präsentation der Schenkungen an die Modesammlung des Wien Museum," 7 July 2004 to 12 December 2004). Fashion began to be wrested away from associations of elitism and class distinction and recognized as a relevant part of the culture of everyday life that characterized the Wien Museum's mandate and contributed to the complexities of the cultural mix informing Vienna's urban identity.

The Wien Museum played a significant role in relocating, centralizing and popularizing fashion discourse in Vienna as part of its mission to create an urban identity for the Viennese that provided them with a historical narrative along the lines of our chics. Adopting a very liberal notion of culture that is somewhat sensitive to class issues, minorities and forgotten and non-hegemonic histories has resulted in presenting a very diverse picture of the city's urban fabric. Exhibition programming has affirmed and on occasion also transcended and queried the city's alignment with national (or even regional) narratives and identity constructions. The institution has a reputation for (occasionally) not shying away from controversial topics such as the restitution of art expropriated by the Nazis or the history of squatting in the city – the topic of an exhibition in the spring and summer of 2012. Titled "Besetzt! Der Kampf um Freiräume seit den 70ern" (Occupied! The Struggle for Free Spaces since the 1970s), the exhibition "examines the political visions and successes of the various generations of squatters and their quest for a different city."[8] Its centrepiece was the 100-day-long squat in an abandoned slaughterhouse during the summer of 1976 and the demands for an autonomously governed cultural centre. The Arena occupation is credited with "arous[ing] Vienna from its slumber," creating a new appreciation and understanding of popular and youth culture that draws on Viennese locality (such as local dialect) and a socially subversive, partly even radical social vision that found its afterlife in the career of Ostbahn Kurti (cf. Chapter 3).[9]

What the museum achieves in the context of Vienna's urban imaginary stands in stark opposition to the campaigns by the city's tourist board that aim at a Vienna "brand" (which, as discussed in the Introduction, has shifted from "Wien ist anders/Vienna is different" to "Wien, jetzt oder nie/Vienna – now or never"). While attempts to brand, that is condense the imaginary of a city to a visual meme or tag line, are usually directed at tourists, most of the museum's exhibits seem to strive to unpack the multiple threads of the city's texture and do justice to the complexities of its history for its citizens. What is remarkable in this context is that this development has moved the role of fashion – understood as part of a wider discursive realm of urban culture – to the centre and given it visibility by taking it out of the rarefied strata of elite taste, culture and distinction and making it part of the city's multi-layered collective cultural and historical identity, which is presented as being a diverse, complex, and often resistant part of Vienna's opening up to consumption and lifestyle, particularly in the wake of 1968. For example, next door to the "Occupied" exhibition was a relatively small-scale (one room) fashion exhibition featuring model-turned-designer Katarina Noever, who is credited with internationalizing Vienna's fashion and design scene in the late sixties and seventies:

A fashion collection as a document of Vienna's avant-garde lifestyle since the 1960s. Katarina Noever was a top model at the time and wore creations from the 'Étoile' boutique, which was a breath of fresh air in fusty Vienna. In 1971 she and Peter Noever founded the now legendary Section N [Figure 2.10].[10] This store, designed by Hans Hollein, was 'a kind of urban salon' (Laurids Ortner): the Viennese public was introduced to international design in an unconventional way. On offer next to lamps by Achille Castiglioni and furniture by Marcel Breuer were felt slippers from Styria and ethno-fashion from Asia. (Folder text)[11]

In 1971 Katarina Noever mixed up Vienna which was a bit colourless at the time. Together with her husband and former MAK director Peter Noever she opened the 'Section N' (with the appendix 'Warenhandel für Umweltgestaltung GmbH' as required by the authorities) – today it would be a classic concept store. Through her job as well

Figure 2.10: Section N (Photo: Eduard Hueber).

Figure 2.11: "Occupied" exhibition at the Wien Museum (Photo: S. Ingram).

as through her passion for fashion, Noever has acquired many dresses. From suits by Armani to dresses by Missoni and items by Issey Miyake (Czerny).[12]

Much less advertised than "Occupied," whose presence was announced loudly and clearly on the facade of the museum [Figure 2.11], "Mehr als Mode – Die Sammlung Katarina Noever" (More Than Fashion – The Katarina Noever Collection) was extended due to great public interest.

While no official attempt was made in the museum to connect the stroppy world of the often working-class, left-leaning, mildly anarchist culture rebels in the slaughterhouse to the glossy inner-city-meets-global fashion world of Noever (or to connect either to the Klimt exhibit on the main floor that was the Wien Museum's contribution to Klimt year 2012, Figure 2.12), the parallels between the two exhibitions upstairs are striking and point to the role of both the Wien Museum and fashion in the city's urban fabric. Both exhibitions emphasize Vienna's cultural "awakening" in a core period of youth upheaval and mobilize histories that matter more to the Viennese than an international audience, who would

Figure 2.12: "Klimt" exhibition at the Wien Museum (Photo: S. Ingram).

presumably not venture beyond the Klimt exhibition on the main floor across from the gift shop. Both the Occupy and Katarina Noever exhibitions also rely on a comprehensive understanding of culture, its history, and its importance for Vienna's identity. While the museum's overall focus on fashion and design might be partly the result of serendipity – early donations and the close institutional links to the fashion school, which is also operated by the city –, an inclusive concept of culture, understood as always already inextricably intertwined with the fabric of Viennese everyday life and the museum's dedication to probing the specific cultural and historical mix of Vienna's local specificities, has resulted in a quite unique approach that has consistently created localized knowledge.[13] The museum is a public memory project that speaks to the Viennese more than to tourists.

The centrality of the Wien Museum's activities for Viennese identity can also be seen in the very public debates being waged about the future location of the central exhibition space. The building on the Karlsplatz is in dire need of renovation and expansion, and the city would like to relocate it to the corporate space of the prestige urban renewal project around the Hauptbahnhof (central train station), a mega-redevelopment along the outer ring road of the city which rivals the nineteenth century's urban renewal project in both scale and ambition in trying to create a "cultural district" (tentatively titled "Quartier Belvedere" because of the vicinity of the baroque palace that has become an icon of Austria's national history, cf. Reisenleitner 2008) – on property owned by one of Austria's largest financial institutions, the Erste Bank. The attention that the museum's relocation plans have garnered, and Director Kos's resistance to be affiliated with public-private partnerships that commodify urban culture into prestige projects directed mainly at tourists and aligned with strategies of "city branding," would seem to indicate that the Wien Museum will not be moved to the Hauptbahnhof, at least not without some resistance.[14]

The Austrian Museum of Applied Arts Vienna (MAK): Reaching out to the world of art and design

At the same time as Katarina Noever's work was being showcased in the Wien Museum, her ex-husband Peter Noever was making headlines after resigning from his post as director of the MAK in 2011. The circumstances surrounding his resignation are still under investigation at the time of writing; what interests us here is the controversial understanding of style and taste culture that Peter Noever promoted successfully as Austria's longest-serving museum director, an understanding that deliberately challenged the historical role of the institution he led while at the same time partaking of, and mobilizing, its international orientation and tendency to take its cues from, and contribute to, new developments abroad. From the time he was appointed MAK director in 1986, Noever relentlessly presented himself in interviews, publications and events as a visionary who had turned around, almost singlehandedly, a "fusty" institution whose historical legacy was to be seen more as a burden than an asset [Figure 2.13]. Noever's public statements and self-promotion in connection with his role in positioning the MAK have been permeated by the same rhetoric of change already rehearsed in the founding of Section N, the influential design- and lifestyle-oriented boutique he and Katarina opened in 1971. Former model Katarina was celebrated in the summer of 2012 as the closest thing to Mary Quant Vienna could produce in the sixties, emphasizing her connection to Helmut Lang and her having introduced designer names such as Armani and Miyake to Vienna (Czerny; Figure 2.14). While she was cast as a sustainable fashion designer avant-la-lettre (making her into a role model for the generation of Viennese fashion designers

Figure 2.13: Portrait of Peter Noever (Photo: Noever, courtesy of Creative Commons).

who rose to local prominence in the first decade of the twenty-first century), Peter has had a rougher ride. Not unlike the corporate fixers who reshaped companies at will in the 1980s, his program for the MAK was idiosyncratic and deliberately controversial in aligning applied arts with avant-garde artistic practices rather than commercially viable design concepts. A look at the history of the museum reveals why this could be presented as a radical move in the landscape of Viennese taste culture and how it ended up reinvigorating the museum's historical connections to the world of fashion.

The urban engineering of Vienna during the Ringstrasse period stemmed from a host of (sometimes diverging) motivations, interests and intentions (cf. Chapter 2), and aesthetic

Figure 2.14: Katarina Noever (Photo: Roland Pleterski/
AnzenbergerGallery Vienna).

considerations were certainly a crucial part of the mix; "geschmückt durch Kunst" (decorated with art) is one of the mottos inscribed on the leaflet of the "Allerhöchst genehmigter Plan der Stadterweiterung" (highest approved plan for city expansion) of 1860 (Schorske 32–33). Another part was the need for urban renewal in Vienna after the profound social changes that 1848 and its aftermath brought about, which accelerated, albeit unevenly, the speed of industrialization, urbanization and social reform in the Habsburg lands and raised questions of competitiveness with other nations, most prominently England and France.

In the second half of the nineteenth century, a novel form for demonstrating the competitiveness of a nation was institutionalized: the world exhibitions. These large-scale demonstrations of the manufacturing prowess of the leading nations necessitated an aestheticized and popularized representation of industrial and technological progress. The marriage of craftsmanship, industrial production and patterns of consumption manifested itself in several categories of consumer products but was particularly noticeable in "Kunstgewerbe" (decorative or applied arts), which was taken to be indicative of both the economic power and the taste culture of a nation (represented through its capital city). Following the enormous success of the first exhibition – the so-called Great Exhibition of the Works of Industry of all Nations of 1851, a "Museum of Manufactures" was established in London the following year: "Its founding principle was to make works of art available to all, to educate working people and to inspire British designers and manufacturers."[15] It is here that the founding father of the MAK, Rudolf Eitelberger, found his inspiration. Eitelberger was the first Professor of Art History and Theory ("für Theorie und Geschichte der bildenden Kunst") at the University of Vienna, a university department that was founded in 1852 with his appointment as chair (Egger 271) after he had regained favour with the government following a short dalliance with revolutionary liberalism (Pokorny-Nagel 59). A man with considerable political influence, Eitelberger worried about the deterioration of taste in the Habsburg lands with the onset of industrialization and lobbied the government to create a remedy along the lines of the British model to improve the taste culture and create a meeting place for industry, commerce and aesthetics.

> Presumably he put the argument about the profitability of Austrian products in the foreground to make it easier to achieve his own ideas of founding a museum. In competitive ability he saw the conditions for peaceful political and economic competition and attached great hopes to the world exhibitions, which beginning in 1851 began to take place with great rapidity as 'trade fairs of the decorative arts' that created a hitherto unknown situation of mutual influence and exchange (Pokorny-Nagel 61).[16]

The perceived need to "catch up" with the industrializing empires of Western Europe, and the imaginaries they created, by emphasizing Kunstgewerbe as a leading indicator of taste culture led to the "Maiausstellung" (May Exhibition), organized in 1860 by the Österreichischer Kunstverein (Austrian Art Association). The event resulted in an intense public debate about the need for a "*Kunstgewerbemuseum*," that is, an institution dedicated to the display of applied and decorative arts. Eitelberger's visit to the South Kensington Museum in connection with the London World Exhibition of 1862 further cemented his determination (Pokorny-Nagel 64); he convincingly argued that the South Kensington Museum had successfully contributed to the "progress" *Kunstgewerbe* had made in Britain, subscribing to the pedagogical understanding of the function of museums that would make a *Kunstgewerbemuseum* crucial for the success of the Vienna World Exhibition that was to take place in 1873:

> Connecting these rational considerations with the patriotic idea of improving Austria's world exhibition proved successful. On 7 March 1863 Emperor Franz Joseph issued a written order for the foundation of such an institution and at first assigned the new 'taste-building' museum the Ballhaus as a location (Boeckl 19).[17]

Eitelberger was appointed director when the k.k. Österreichisches Museum für Kunst und Industrie (the Imperial Austrian Museum for Art and Industry) opened in 1864. Together with his fellow academic and second-in-command Jacob von Falke (Pokorny-Nagel 70), he implemented an academic program that was built on historicist academic tenets and thus fit well into the Ringstrasse concept. Taste (*guter Geschmack*) was to be acquired by studying the best the past had to offer, and the museum's collections reflected this. Organized according to materials (a system derived from the South Kensington model), the collections were meant to be inspirations and educational tools for designers who started out by copying them faithfully. This method was also the guiding principle for the Kunstgewerbeschule/ School of Applied Arts (Franz 90), which has complemented the museum since 1867 and which shared its administration until 1900, and for the annual exhibitions of industrial products which have been held since 1874. Addressing a public with its taste-building mission,[18] this institution dedicated to art and industry remained firmly rooted in a historicist understanding of the model character of the past, out of which a "national" style was to develop.

The orientation towards past models, which proved to have enormous longevity for Vienna's imaginary, as well as for the institution's international inspiration and aspirations, is reflected in the style of the new building in which the museum was to be housed. Heinrich von Ferstel, the young architect of the painstakingly historicist neo-Gothic Votivkirche (the first major building commissioned for the Ringstrasse redevelopment) and the exhibition space on the Ballhausplatz, who had established his reputation as a designer for *Kunstgewerbe* exhibits, won the commission for the new museum building in 1867 (Pokorny-Nagel 63, 69). The original plan was to integrate the museum as a separate wing into a monumental complex called the Kaiserforum, planned for housing the Habsburg collections between the Imperial Stables and the Hofburg, where the Museums of Art History and Natural History are now located. This plan was rejected when it became clear that such a complex would not give the Ringstrasse – the central element in Vienna's urban renewal – enough visual prominence. The eventual location of the museum in a rather remote part of the Ringstrasse development (the site of what was then a military parade ground, Franz 96) provoked public controversy and distanced the museum from the *Bildung* context of the two "big" museums. Its location reflects the odd in-between position of the institution in Vienna's representational museum culture: it was not part of the core building complex, but it was still steeped in the bourgeois educational ideology of the period.[19]

Ferstel's building, which opened on 4 November 1871, continued the historicist legacy by evoking Renaissance façades and architectural structures of Renaissance palaces in ways that were functional for a museum (Figure 2.15, Pokorny-Nagel 78). His basic tenet, already manifest in the Votivkirche, was "exactitude in the reproduction of historical motifs" (*Exaktheit in der Reproduktion historischer Motive*, Boeckl 21), but here he shifted from the Gothic to a firm belief in the "exemplary nature of the Renaissance" ("*Vorbildlichkeit der Renaissance*," Franz 101). Agreeing with Eitelberger on the timelessness of an aesthetics derived from the Mediterranean, he felt its character apposite for what could become a "national" taste culture in the Empire's capital:

The Viennese Renaissance was based for the most part on the Italian Renaissance, and here and there in albeit very limited ways and never without a foreign feel on the art of Greek antiquity. In this borrowing from Italy and Greece, our artists are following a healthy instinct, and we can only wish that they will not go off their heads in this direction. For all of our artistic progress rests upon the spiritually cleansing atmosphere that reaches us and increasingly emanates from Tuscany and Greece [...] A Renaissance is untenable without important sculpture and painting, without artistic, technically accomplished ornamentation. What matters about Renaissance structures is not that they were built in the

Figure 2.15: MAK (Photo: S. Ingram).

shapes of the Renaissance; rather, the sculptors and painters had to be completely steeped in the principles and spirit of the Renaissance (Eitelberger 185, 188, cited in Franz 102).[20]

The tight integration of the School of Applied Arts and the museum and its firm grounding in historicist thinking, legitimated by the prevailing academic tenets of the second half of the nineteenth century, prevented the cross-fertilization with industry envisaged by its founders. A style culture oriented towards the past was not necessarily conducive to reflecting, on the level of style and taste, the modernizing thrust of the last decades of the nineteenth century (culminating in the Secession movement of 1897) and was at best ambivalent towards the commercialization of design culture that was part of its mission.

It was only under the influence of Secession artists that these values came under increasing scrutiny. The institution's inability to address contemporary demands by turning to the past was raised by a new generation of artists, most prominently by Otto Wagner (Pokorny-Nagel 88). This led, in 1900, to an administrative separation of the School of Applied Arts and the museum, a move that opened the School of Applied Arts to modern influences by recruiting teachers from the Secession movement such as Josef Hoffmann, Koloman Moser and Alfred Roller (Scholda 233), which set the institution on a trajectory of innovation that has characterized its reputation and teaching style ever since. The School became an institution of higher education in 1941, was given university status in 1970, and renamed the "University of Applied Arts" in 1998.

Fashion appeared on the scene courtesy of the Wiener Werkstätte (Viennese Workshops), a *Produktivgenossenschaft* (cooperative) of visual artists led by Josef Hoffmann and Koloman Moser that evolved from the Secession's interest in reforming the applied arts along the lines of several foreign models, including Ruskin and Morris's arts and crafts movement, "Ashbee's British Guild of Handicrafts, which Hoffmann visited in 1902 [...] the United Workshops for Arts and Crafts, founded in 1897, to which Peter Behrens and Hermann Obrist belonged, and the Dresden Crafts Workshop, founded in 1898" (Cunningham 194). The group adhered to the principle of lifestyle as *Gesamtkunstwerk*, which bears striking similarities to Bradley Quinn's fashion space – the idea that all design aspects of a space should harmonize. In the case of the Wiener Werkstätte, it became clear to them that fashion would have to be part of their considerations when they began working on the Palais Stoclet in Brussels in 1905 and Mme. Stoclet's Parisian wardrobe proved more of a challenge to incorporate into their plans than they expected (Fahr-Becker 187). In 1905 the group established a textile workshop:

> Hoffmann and Moser had already worked successfully with the textile firm of Backhausen & Söhne for carpets and upholstery, but set up the in-house operation to focus on more lavish hand-printed and painted silk designs. With such luxury cloth, manufactured in literally thousands of patterns constantly replenished by the Werkstätte's leading artists – Hoffmann, Dzeschka, et al – Vienna first made its mark on the international fashion scene (Fahr-Becker 101).[21]

Next to be founded was a fashion workshop, by Eduard Josef Wimmer-Wisgrill, who had been a private student of Moser's and studied with Hoffmann and Roller at the Kunstgewerbeschule from 1901 to 1907. Upon completion of his studies he founded the fashion workshop and led it until 1922. While Hoffmann taught a master class in architecture whose students produced a fashion magazine in 1914 (Buxbaum 1986, 265), it is Wimmer-Wisgrill who is considered "the Viennese answer to Paul Poiret, and a review of his designs as well as those of his colleagues shows a constant dialogue with Paris fashion and Poiret's designs in particular" (Fahr-Becker 101).

With the coming of World War I, that dialogue became more of a call to arms, namely, "*los von Paris*," away from Paris. For the fashion industry, this meant increasing emancipation. The fashions of the Wiener Werkstätte became trendsetting especially in Switzerland, where fashion shows in Bern and Zurich helped to seal their success. By 1916 they had their own production space and a sales branch in the Palais Esterházy at Kärnterstrasse 41 (Buxbaum 1986, 219). Further shops followed both in Vienna and abroad (Karlsbad in 1909, Marienbad and Zürich in 1916–17, New York in 1922, and Berlin in 1929), but the post-war years were not kind to the Werkstätte. A group that catered to the rarefied tastes of the 1 per cent of their day was not destined to do well in the lean, inflation-ravaged, post-war years: "standards of quality declined, and an unmistakable element of kitsch marked too many of its productions" (Varnedoe 103).

In 1922 Wimmer-Wisgrill left for the US, where he worked as a fashion and theatre illustrator in New York and taught fashion at the Art Institute of Chicago. Upon his return in 1925, he assumed leadership of a "Meisterklasse in Mode" at the Kunstgewerbeschule, which has enjoyed increasing renown with each of its directors. In contrast to the fashion school at Hetzendorf, which concentrates more on projects and practical matters, the Modeklasse is connected to other disciplines at the Kunstgewerbemuseum and enjoys a productive exchange with graphic design and the arts (Percher 2009). After Wimmer-Wisgrill's 30-year tenure, leading designers Gertrud Höchsmann (1959–72) and Fred Adlmüller (1973–79) assumed the position, while the likes of Karl Lagerfeld, Helmut Lang, Veronique Branquinho, Jean Charles de Castelbajac, Viktor&Rolf, Raf Simons and Vivienne Westwood have all taught there. Its alumni have brought the institution a measure of renown as well, from Gustav Klimt and Emilie Flöge [Figure 2.16] to Anna Aichinger, and it has also developed a small fashion collection, which Elizabeth Frottier is currently in charge of.

While the school, and later university, embraced the innovations the Vienna modern ushered in, the museum remained dedicated to its increasingly antiquarian mission, with historicism baked into its DNA and exhibition style. Indicative of its character is the fact that what is now considered the pinnacle of Vienna's modern turn in *Kunstgewerbe*, the Wiener Werkstätte, only became a part of the museum's collection in 1955, more than 20 years after the movement's demise (Noever 1995, 12). When Peter Noever became its director in 1986, the appointment was made in the midst of a public debate about the role of state-financed museums, a global turn towards blockbuster exhibitions, and a revival of interest in *fin-de-siècle* Vienna that had manifested itself in the blockbuster 1985 "Traum und Wirklichkeit" (Dream and Reality) exhibition at the Künstlerhaus.

The rather neglected, cozily antiquarian MAK did not escape attention. It was seen as directionless, dilapidated and in need of renewal, and Noever, a well-known designer who associated with the likes of Arthur C. Clarke and Marshall McLuhan, was seen as just the man for the job.

> Already at the beginning of this [the 20th] century it was not quite free of anachronisms; now, a century later, it had blatantly outlived itself. The Museum of Applied Arts' lack of profile was basically nothing other than the visible result of the institution's spiritual climate, which could be characterized as a kind of vacuum in terms of content and ideology (Waechter-Böhm 77).[22]

So writes one of Noever's admirers in one of the flood of publications that accompanied Noever's tenure at the MAK and hammered home his concept of giving museal *Geschmacksbildung* (taste formation) a new direction.

Figure 2.16: Portrait of Emilie Flöge in the Wien Museum (Photo: S. Ingram).

That new direction was to bring it "back to the present" (Waechter-Böhm 88) and reorient it programmatically towards contemporary art (Noever 1995, 13). Unlike the V&A, which opened itself up to commercial culture under similar pressures (which ultimately led to a proud tradition of incorporating fashion exhibitions and collections), the MAK insisted on the importance of social relevance over popularity and over visitor numbers as its principal criterion of quality and success, which implied for Noever and his circle the necessity of radically divorcing the museum from its historical orientation and opening it up to critical impulses from abroad. In an interview, Noever states this very succinctly:

The institution was practically suffocating on its own past. That's why it was my first priority to stop this losing oneself in history, this unreflected, undistanced fixation on a tradition. It would be totally absurd to try today to carry out the original foundational purpose 'according to the letter,' so to speak [...] In such an institution in particular, it should be about daring into new territory (Waechter-Böhm 79).[23]

While "Traum und Wirklichkeit" managed to musealize a Vienna modern that had questioned the MAK's historicist foundation during the fin-de-siècle, the institution itself turned away from its historical legacy and found a new mission in critical contemporary art and architecture as the turn of the millennium approached. At the time of its reorientation, Vienna lacked a museum dedicated to the display of such art.[24] Noever saw contemporary art as inspiring taste and denied mass production any relevance for the mission of the museum:

In the age of mass production, objects of applied art are primarily interesting as cultural and historical objects, but can hardly be taken as models for contemporary aesthetic production [...] Neither applied arts nor design are in themselves adequate role models or stimuli for contemporary debate. Art is a much more powerful ignition force (Noever 1995, 13).

Noever's rhetoric played well in an atmosphere in which the common sense was that there was too much attention to history and that Vienna was always somewhat "behind" in questions of contemporary artistic and taste culture. He picked the right enemies against which to position the museum as something Vienna sorely lacked, while also not disguising his contempt for the popular and the culture industries:

At the same time the culture industry makes use of art and forces artists into the role of entertainer-cheerleaders of an expanding culture-society. The contempt for art that the makers of a growth-oriented leisure-time and tourist society feel is thereby made clear. Culture is responsible for everything, also in part for art [...] The discussion of such a development has established itself in this country, as in so much else, with considerable time delay (Noever 1988, 121).[25]

This institution, the Austrian Museum for Applied Art, certainly has the chance, after all it has achieved, to become a place of confrontation, a place of resistance, an arena for conflicts, but also to remain a place of the mysterious, a place of feelings and dreams (Noever 1988, 125).[26]

It seems ironic that Noever's relentlessly avant-garde ideology and rhetoric, which quickly manifested themselves in architectural changes to the museum, were somewhat anachronistic for the mid-1980s, precisely the time when Vienna's globalizing taste culture was opening up to the global popular, to street style and international designer brand names. However, this program did not prevent Noever from adopting strategies of commodification that had proven successful elsewhere, pursuing sponsoring initiatives, wooing contemporary artists (and social circles close to contemporary artists, cf. Noever 1988, 123) to his institution, and organizing society events that helped sponsor his plans. Assisted by the "first 'Museums Billion,' one billion Schillings earmarked for the restoration of Austria's national museums" (Noever 1995, 15), the renovations he spearheaded included not only important and welcome extensions of exhibition spaces but also a swank restaurant that soon became a go-to place for stylish crowds that demonstrated their elite tastes by proximity to contemporary art – and not by its appreciation of mass-produced design icons, as in London's Design Museum, which was founded in 1989 by Terence Conran and whose Blueprint Café was designed to attract a similar crowd.

Another example of the international orientation of the museum that prioritizes contemporary art over Vienna's historicist tradition is the MAK Center for Art and Architecture in Los Angeles whose founding in 1995 Noever spearheaded (cf. Noever 2002). Propagating "the spirit of the life's work of Rudolph M. Schindler (1887–1953), the Vienna architect and student of Otto Wagner who emigrated to the USA in 1914" (Noever 2002, 204), the Center consists of three separate modernist dwellings Schindler designed in the interwar period: the Pearl M. Mackey Apartments, the Fitzpatrick-Leland House and the Schindler House [Figure 2.17].[27] It continues the spirit of the MAK's reorientation and "aims for a radical contemporary orientation. Its program concentrates on new spatial and architectural trends and developments emanating from the interface of art and architecture" (ibid.). The spread attempted here is interesting. Clearly, Vienna modernism, of which Otto Wagner was a figurehead and advocate, was not (quite) an apposite model for what the MAK was trying to accomplish because it had already been musealized and domesticated as the dream world of *fin-de-siècle* coffeehouse culture and was no longer the avant-garde, utopian type of project Noever encouraged; however, Noever still seems to have felt the need to establish a connection to the Vienna modern.

Since being acquired by the Austrian government, the MAK Center for Art and Architecture in Los Angeles has sponsored artists in residence, public outreach activities, as well as the museum, which occupies the house the architect designed for himself and runs a residency program out of the apartments.[28] It almost seems as if the historical lineage that connects the artistic, social and cultural visions of Vienna's *fin-de-siècle* modernism to contemporary art – its social criticism, international outlook, and spirit of renewal and innovation – needed to be transplanted to America's west coast in order to be made meaningful for Noever's concept.

In taking up the directorial reins that Peter Noever was forced to relinquish, Christoph Thun-Hohenstein, formerly the Director of the Austrian Cultural Forum in New York and Managing Director at departure, the creative agency of the City of Vienna responsible for providing the fashion scene with important funding, now has the mandate of steering the

Figure 2.17: Schindler House (Rudolf Schindler), 1922 (Photo: S. Ingram).

institution in a new direction.[29] However, as of late 2012, the public statements of the former career diplomat reveal little of substance about the new direction – the most noticeable change is in the rhetoric. At his first program presentation, Thun-Hohenstein displayed none of Noever's radical and confrontational overtones when he explained that "Applied art needs to be filled with new life. Utilizing its potential as a motor of positive change in our society – socially, ecologically and culturally – is the main mission of an active museum of applied arts."[30] It is a program that is hard to object to, a diplomatic marriage of Noever's program of social change, the tradition of the museum and a timely, if somewhat generic, bow to environmental sustainability:

Although I greatly respect this tradition, my mission is clearly to steer the museum into the 21st century. We have about four sections: applied art – though I am not very clear what it is – design, architecture, contemporary art, and intercreativity, that is interdisciplinary ideas and projects involving those fields. To me it is important that the MAK does not become solely a design museum or a museum for the decorative arts. All these things belong together. […] But the focus in general will be on positive change, or, to be more precise, on the contributions architecture (as well as design, applied art, and contemporary art) can make to positive ecological, social, and cultural change.[31]

Compromise seems to be the main message, communicated diplomatically: not a rupture with Noever's legacy, but mobilizing the institution's roots and rediscovering the historicist legacy of its permanent collection. "Christoph Thun-Hohenstein, Director of the MAK since September, has achieved an artistic feat: he acknowledges the way his predecessor positioned the museum – and yet does everything differently" is how the Austrian newspaper *Der Standard* summarizes Thun-Hohenstein's diplomatic tap dance.[32]

In the winter of 2012–13, one of the exhibitions featured at the MAK was "Wien 1900: Wiener Kunstgewerbe 1890–1938" (Vienna 1900: Viennese Decorative/Applied Arts 1890–1938), and Thun-Hohenstein's opening remarks capture the conciliatory, tame but still clearly elite spirit of the program:

> What moved us to again take an interest in Vienna 1900? Simply the circumstance that we have a world-class collection and Vienna around 1900 is a central part of this collection. It is my conviction that every art museum should be a contemporary museum that engages with the past from the perspective of the present and does not just have an art-historical point of view but rather also has a cultural-historical one and also tries to go beyond it to see was it relevant for today[33] [Figure 2.18].

While viewers are treated to this firm commitment to both the historical legacy *and* contemporary critique, as well as to some truisms about art and the museum that are so

Figure 2.18: Thun-Hohenstein at the opening of the Wien 1900 exhibition (vimeo.com/54454923).

vague that neither the firmly antiquarian Eitelsberger nor radically avant-garde Noever could possibly object, the camera of the vimeo clip from which this quote is taken presents *fin-de-siècle* furniture and period paintings. The only slightly disruptive moment comes when the camera pans from Claudia Schmied, the Austrian Education Minister (from the Social Democratic Party), in whose portfolio the MAK is situated and who formally opened the exhibition, to a political poster exhorting early twentieth-century voters to "renovate" and vote for the Social Democrats of their time ("Sanierung – wählt sozialdemokratisch" [00:32]).

The presence of the MAK in social media (with two dedicated vimeo channels) and its continuing organization of major society events for (aspiring) celebrities in Vienna also shows that the traditions Noever created to attract a particular crowd with the habitus of a socially aware taste elite are being continued.[34] Clearly, the MAK is not going to transform itself into a design museum that embraces mass production in the way the institution on the Thames did 20 years ago; Vienna is not seen as a fulcrum of design in Thun-Hohenstein's imaginary. "Should Vienna become a place of design like Milan? No!" he declared firmly at the opening of the "Design 4 You" exhibition held from 6 June to 7 October 2012, curated by Hartmut Esslinger and Thomas Geisler, and focusing on "over 80 examples of designers' output to examine new tendencies and strategic approaches of the twenty-first century that point out forward-looking social, ecological and cultural innovations."[35] The catalogue is not reticent about its intended audience:

> It is aimed neither exclusively at the small group of wealthy design customers, nor generally at the other 90 per cent to whom design is not and partly cannot be of conscious concern. Rather, it is conceived to address the steadily growing number of people who, in their decisions as consumers and otherwise, are in the happy situation of being able to choose between different options. Excellent design must be so convincing that it motivates as many people as possible to make the right choice. Here, 'right' means: in the interest of society's positive further development, especially with regard to environmental issues (Thun-Hohenstein et al. 3).

Something of a vision emerges here: design as an ecologically aware "fun" culture for those who can afford it (not the "other" 90 per cent!), an educational program of the right form of consumerism with seduction as its strategy:

> Politically correct persuasion is important. But broad swaths of the populace will only begin to assume responsibility based on literacy and agency when the 'fun factor' is properly included. Design represents the ideal artistic tool with which to communicate the fun to be had and the joy to be found in assuming responsibility for sustainable change. During my tenure at departure, the slogan 'irresistibly responsible' was coined for this idea – and since then, probably no better expression has been found with which to sum up what this is all about (Thun-Hohenstein et al. 5).

Much could be said about the glib marriage of a neo-liberal rhetoric of consumer choice, the palpable condescension to the less educated, a vision of social engineering straight out of the modernists' playbook, and its articulation to issues of environmental protection and sustainability that drives so much of current "creative" design and technology. However, for the role of the museum in Vienna's taste culture, suffice it here to point out that the vernacular does not seem to be on the taste horizon of a descendant of the Habsburg empire's high nobility, whose education and career trajectory are firmly tied to Austria's social elites, who also consider themselves taste elites. Under Thun-Hohenstein, the MAK seems set to continue its tradition and mission of *Geschmacksbildung* with an elitist understanding of what constitutes taste and how to communicate it.[36]

The Museumsquartier (MQ): Going global by creating a fashion-oriented place to meet

The MQ is both the latest addition to the Viennese museum scene to become involved in fashion and the one housed in the oldest building. The motto under which it opened to the public in June 2001 – "Baroque meets Cyber Space"– is telling (Rakuschan). Located in the Habsburg's former stables, which were designed and built by Fischer von Erlach father and son in the first quarter of the eighteenth century in a space then across from one of the city's outer gates (the Burgtor), the building has the longest baroque façade in Vienna, occupying the entire length of the street behind the Museums of Art History and Natural History between the Mariahilferstraße and the Volkstheater [Figure 2.19].

The site went through an iteration beginning in the interwar period as a place for trade fairs (Peter Noever held international exhibitions for office organization there, for example)[37] before being turned into its current form: a future-oriented museum cluster flagship development, which could boast upon opening that it was "one of the ten largest cultural complexes in the world" (De Frantz 2005, 53). As the name suggests, museum clusters are "geographic concentrations of interconnected museums which work closely with local suppliers, tourist attractions and public sector entities. [...] Notable examples of good practice exist in the technology industry in Silicon Valley, the Hollywood movie industry, the clothes industry in Hong Kong and the Covent Garden theatre district" (Tien 69–70). In the case of the MQ, which has also achieved international recognition for its "good practice" in clustering (Tien 69), the cluster brings together, in the same shared space, three main museums: 1) the Leopold Museum, which contains Rudolph and Elisabeth Leopold's 5,000+ piece collection of modern Austrian art, including the world's largest Schiele collection; 2) the Museum of Modern Art Foundation Ludwig Vienna (MUMOK – Moderner Kunst Stiftung Ludwig Wien), which contains 7,000+ modern and contemporary works by the likes of Andy Warhol, Pablo Picasso, Joseph Beuys, Gerhard Richter, Jasper Johns and Roy Lichtenstein; and 3) the Kunsthalle Wien, which is an exhibition space for international contemporary art that originally opened in 1992 on the Karlsplatz, moved into the section of the stables that incorporated the former Winter Riding Hall in the MQ

Figure 2.19: Aerial shot of the MQ and the Natural History and Art History museums (Photo: Peter Korrak).

in 2001 and is attached to the MUMOK [Figure 2.20]. Both the MUMOK and the Leopold Museum [Figure 2.21] are strikingly contemporary designs by the Austrian architectural firm Ortner & Ortner.

The complex also includes a centre for contemporary dance (Tanzquartier Wien), a centre for architecture (Architekturzentrum Wien), and facilities that promote artistic activity for adults (quartier21) and for children (Zoom Kindermuseum, wienXtra-kinderinfo, Dschungel Wien), as well as a number of gastronomic options. Fashion is among the emphases of the activities that quartier21 promotes, together with digital culture and design (*Museumsquartier Wien* 2, Figure 2.22). A former CEO of the MQ, Dieter Bogner, considers the concept a success because of "the presence of many festival agencies, editorial offices of art magazines, and cultural agencies that today consider

Figure 2.20: Courtyard of the MQ (Photo: M. Reisenleitner).

Figure 2.21: Enzis in front of the Leopold Museum (Photo: M. Reisenleitner).

Wiener Chic

Figure 2.22: quartier21 (Photo: S. Ingram).

Figure 2.23: Enzis in use (Photo: M. Reisenleitner).

140

quartier21 the ideal address for communication, a central workplace and professional meeting ground in one" and because symbolically it "has managed to secure a prominent position for young 'applied arts' in the middle of Austria's most central cultural complex" (27). Bogner considers it surprising that the MAK has not cultivated this area, for which it "at least nominally can be considered the responsible party," and unfortunate that "the eight million euros in public tax money earmarked annually for this area of art still go to the MAK, even though it has largely become inactive in the fields of design and fashion" (28). Perhaps under Thun-Hohenstein's stewardship, the MAK will make more visible use of these opportunities.

The space inside the MQ is scattered with colourful geometric blocks called Enzis after Daniela Enzi, who was the MQ's general manager until May 2012, when she left the cultural complex to lead a revitalization project of the area around the Konzerthaus, the ice palace and the Hotel Intercontinental ("Museumsquartier: Enzis ohne Enzi"). In good weather, the Enzis have proven to be popular places to hang out [Figure 2.23] and have given the MQ an edge over comparable sites like the Museum Island in Berlin in terms of the creation of effectively used public space (Badelt). This is in keeping with observations "from culture-led schemes world-wide [...]: despite the architectural and media attention to the design experiments which house otherwise traditional performing and visual arts spaces and programmes, public preference is still strongly directed at the prosaic bridges, ferris wheels and waterfront boardwalks and the reuse of industrial structures" (Evans 974). The prosaic filling of the MQ's courtyards with casual, non-commodified public places to spend time was a strategically savvy decision; having only a paying crowd in restaurants and cafés would have made the MQ an entirely different type of institution, and one that would have had a much more difficult time distinguishing itself in Vienna's vast cultural scene.

Other characteristics of that conflictual, politically charged, and internecine scene helped to turn the planning process for the MQ into a controversial, drawn-out affair, as alluded to in Chapter 1 on Baroque Chic. A "citizen initiative and its political speakers prioritized the protection of the 'baroque treasures' against new architecture. Some extreme voices even argued for an authentic reconstruction of the original baroque plans that had never actually been realized" (De Frantz 2005, 57), and the building of a reading tower that would have intruded into the city's skyline and interfered with the city's application for its historic cityscape to qualify for UNESCO world heritage status ended up being axed. (That status was granted in 2003.) Because the general demands for historic protection predominantly concerned preservation, "the historic protection zone was stretched out beyond the baroque buildings to include also the late nineteenth-century parts of the complex as a consistent 'historically grown ensemble'" (ibid.). That zone now anchors a wedge that radiates from the MQ into the 6th and 7th districts, an area that has in the meantime evolved into an up-and-coming place for fashion and is very much in keeping with the MQ's function as a flagship cultural institution.[38] The Museumsquartier debate has been described as a "'turning-point' in Austria's political culture where the old ideological struggle 'between left and right' was replaced by a new opposition 'between small and large' associated with the question of whether 'globalization and capitalism bring homogeneity, uniformity and alienation'" (De Frantz 2005, 61).

Unlike, and therefore conceived as a supplement to, the Wien Museum and the MAK, the MQ is driven by a more national, and internationalizing, political agenda, something in line with the fact that the complex is owned by the Republic of Austria (75% federal and 25% provincial, since Vienna enjoys provincial status). The complex has therefore been "associated rather with transformative ambitions that aimed to mobilize a climate of creative innovation internally and diversify its tourism attractiveness externally" (De Frantz 2005, 61). As De Frantz details:

> Under pressure from increased competition with neighbouring cities such as Prague and Budapest, the need for 'self-representation' as a 'European metropolis' turned cultural investment into an 'interest of the republic.' To make 'Austria aware' that losing the competition for investments meant losing innovation and falling into 'anti-progressive passivity,' the flagship project would add the touch of a 'contemporary metropolis' to Vienna's image of a 'capital city and imperial residence of the past.' [...] In contrast to the second-tier city Bilbao and the new capital Berlin, which both used culture for regenerating their otherwise negative images of either deindustrialization or former partition, Vienna could rely on a well-established worldwide reputation as an old European capital full of valuable historic heritage and high culture. Yet the media spectacles initiated recently in those cities were interpreted in Vienna as pressures to join the competitive 'search for an urgently needed new identity at the dawn of the new millennium.' In these times of globalization, spectacular flagship architecture stood for a 'new vision of development,' positioning the city 'at the node of international brain and transport flows instead of at the margins' just as the 'crown' had represented the medieval symbol of urban autonomy (De Frantz 2005, 60).

Fashion was assigned a key role in establishing Vienna's new global identity as chic, and the area in and around the MQ became the site for institutions that would drive this process forward.

The first key moment in this process was the founding in 2000 of "Unit F büro für mode" (Unit F office for fashion) by Ulrike Tschabitzer-Handler and Andreas Oberkanins.[39] The Federal Ministry for Education, the Arts and Culture (BM:UKK, Bundesministerium für Unterricht, Kunst und Kultur) and the department in the city government responsible for culture (Wien Kultur Magistratsabteilung 7) teamed up to provide an annual budget to be used to support fashion designers with the potential of establishing themselves internationally.[40] Unit F acted quickly to establish the AFA Austrian Fashion Awards, and in its first year hosted a "small but exquisite" presentation of the new prizes in the basement of its office in the Gumpendorferstrasse in the 6th district. The event grew into a gala at the Wienmuseum on the Karlsplatz, and from 2002 to 2005 it became part of Austrian Fashion

Week, which was the first fashion week to be held in the city. Based in the MQ's Kunsthalle Wien, it featured shows in various spots around the city.[41]

In 2006 this fashion week morphed into a "festival for fashion & photography," which from 29 May to 6 June 2012 saw its sixth iteration.[42] The English-language names as well as an emphasis on the visuality of the events and strong presence in social media are in keeping with the MQ's and Unit F's global orientation. Unit F supported a wide range of activities from exhibitions to publishing endeavours, such as the issues of *Wien Live* that accompany the festivals for fashion and photography, and symposia. Among the major projects Unit F was involved in was the "CFA – Contemporary Fashion Archive," an online fashion platform that ran from 2002 to 2007 and helped five European fashion institutions – Central Saint Martins College of Art and Design (London), Dutch Fashion Foundation (Amsterdam), Flanders Fashion Institute (Antwerp), Hochschule für Gestaltung, Technik und Wirtschaft (Pforzheim) and Unit F büro für mode – to "establish a unique information network," the results of which are still available online.[43] Also online are the results of "The Vienna Fashion Observatory," an exhibition that ran for 66 days in 2009, accumulating "359 individual observations on fashion and the city [...] by the 25 different bloggers, photographers, fashion-designers and artists that participated in the project. The exhibition in the Freiraum at the Museumsquartier in Vienna had 3811 visitors, while the blog was visited by 41642 visitors from all over the world" (ibid.). Among those who participated in the Observatory were Yvan Rodic of *Facehunter* fame[44] and MILCH's Chloed Priscilla Baumgartner [Figures 2.24, 2.25 and 2.26].[45]

Figure 2.24: Lisi, The Vienna Fashion Observatory (Photo: Cloed Priscilla Baumgartner).

Figure 2.25, 2.26: Jules, The Vienna Fashion Observatory (Photo: Cloed Priscilla Baumgartner).

In the fall of 2003, Unit F was joined on the fashion funding scene by departure, a "creative agency" established by the City of Vienna to encourage economic activity in branches of the creative industries such as fashion, music, audio-vision, multimedia, design, publishing, the art market and architecture that are located in or have their main headquarters in Vienna. In addition to helping new designers get established,[46] it offers a further funding node for publishing and networking and structural enhancements to creative scenes, such as events

Figure 2.27: MQ fashion show (Photo: M. Reisenleitner).

that happen in conjunction with the Vienna Fair (Austria's largest fair for contemporary art with a focus on Central, Eastern and Southern Europe), the "sound:frame" festival (a festival "for audio-visual expressions"), Vienna Art Week and Vienna Design Week.[47] One sees the convergences and relationalities involved in Unit F and departure funding in the fact that a "departure fashion night" takes place during the Unit F-organized "festival for fashion and photography," at which selected projects that have received departure funding are presented.[48]

Also a part of the mix is the Akademie der bildenden Künste Wien (Academy of Fine Arts Vienna), which has a substantial department of "Fashion and Styles." They offer degree programs that qualify students to teach in secondary schools and to pursue careers in "creative and educative professions beyond the school context"[49] and organize events such as the "Textiles: Open Letter | A Haptic Space: Praxis and Discourse" conference.[50]

The MQ responded to this activity by upping the fashion ante and taking back the lead in setting the tone for Vienna's fashion scene [Figure 2.27]. In 2009 it established its own "Vienna Fashion Week,"[51] which since then has been held each September. Sponsored by Vöslauer, an Austrian mineral water company which belongs to the Ottakringer corporation (Ottakringer is the last remaining brewery in Vienna), it is organized by creative headz, a group that provides, according to its self-promotion, "ideas, concepts and art direction for fashion events, coordination and production of

Figure 2.28: Summer of Fashion catwalk (Photo: S. Ingram).

fashion and lifestyle events, choreography and directing for entertainment shows, and show production and casting for fashion shows," and is located at Gumpendorferstrasse 36 (Unit F is a few doors down at Gumpendorferstrasse 56 – both are within easy walking distance of the MQ).[52]

In 2012, Vienna Fashion Week was the culmination of the MQ's "Summer of Fashion," which ran from 14 June to 16 September and added a bright-red temporary Summer of Fashion catwalk to the complex's attractions [Figure 2.28]. The catwalk was designed with the MQ's priority of participatory visibility in mind:

> The catwalk seems to grow out of the ground throughout different areas of the Museumsquartier transforming these into real action zones. The Summer of Fashion will be open and visible to everyone and at all times, whether there is an event going on or not. The structure varies in height, making the person walking on it automatically visible for others, whether it be, a model or simply a passer-by. This enables a change in roles; everyone can now be the Model. The idea plays with the confusion between the observer and the observed and provokes self-reflection. The theme of the mix-up between actor and spectator can also be read in the formations of the catwalk structure. Everyone is the model and the spectator at once.[53]

Summer of Fashion provided an entire summer of fashion-oriented events, including a number of widely advertised (and very accessible) fashion shows, public talks and exhibitions, including "Reflecting Fashion: Kunst und Mode seit der Moderne" (Reflecting Fashion: Art and Fashion since the Modern), which was on display at the Museum of Modern Art Foundation Ludwig Vienna (MUMOK – Museum moderner Kunst Stiftung Ludwig Wien) from 15 June to 23 September 2012.[54] "Reflecting Fashion" was something of a departure for the MUMOK. While its use of the English language in titling events is in keeping with the image the MQ encourages for the complex as a global player (the exhibition which ran before Reflecting Fashion was "Pop and the Sixties"), the MUMOK specializes in modern and contemporary art and was devoting an exhibition to fashion for the first time, in keeping with the MQ's ambitions to create an inclusive, non-elite space for the creative industries in the city.

Of the museums in the complex, the Kunsthalle Wien is the one with the most experience in fashion. In conjunction with one of the first exhibitions it put on after moving to the new space in the MQ (on "Flash Afrique – Fotografie aus Westafrika"), a symposium was organized on "Die andere Moderne: Über/Leben zwischen Digital Culture, Fashion und Trash Art" (The Other Modernity: Living On between Digital Culture, Fashion and Trash Art).[55] Even before its move to the MQ, the Kunsthalle Wien had put on an exhibition in which the artistic work of Viennese-born designer Helmut Lang was featured along with that of Louise Bourgeois and Jenny Holzer (from 9 October 1998 to 10 January 1999). It also hosted the Austrian Fashion Awards in 2004 and 2005, the Modepalast from 2003 to 2010 and the opening of the "7 festival for fashion & photography" in 2007. A lecture on "Mode und Film" was part of the 2007 festival, while an exhibition on the fashion photography of Viennese label Schella Kann showed at the Kunsthalle's Karlsplatz project space in January 2008. In the fall and winter season of 2011–12, the Kunsthalle Wien adopted fashion as its main theme, organizing a series of talks on "Fotografie und Mode im Wandel" (Photography and Fashion in Transformation, 17 November 2011), "Fashion Transmitters: Von Vogue zu the Sartorialist. Wohin geht der Trend?" (Fashion Transmitters: From Vogue to the Sartorialist. Where are the Trends Leading?, 24 November 2011), and "Image Makers: Aus der Zeitschrift ins Museum. Ist Modefotografie Kunst?" (Image Makers: From the Magazine into the Museum. Is Fashion Photography Art?, 1 December 2011). On 19 January 2012, a Burgtheater actress did a reading of prose texts about fashion by Nobel Prize winner Elfriede Jelinek in the Karlsplatz project space (according to the website, the texts included "Mode" (2000), "Claudia" (2001), "in Fetzen" (2003), and "Rudi Gernreich" (2000)). The Kunsthalle Wien's interest in Jelinek's work corresponds to the overall MQ view of fashion as a privileged intermediary between art and the everyday. Therefore it announced her as follows:

Elfriede Jelinek is one of the most important authors in the German-speaking realm, and at the same time one of the most controversial. In her wide-ranging literary oeuvre, she connects art indivisibly with sociopolitical positioning. Her approach to fashion is also self-reflexive and critical: 'There are only a few things I understand as much about as clothes. I know little about myself, and am not very interested in myself, but it seems to me that my passion for fashion can stand in for that in myself […]. I take an interest in clothing so that I don't have to deal with myself, because myself I would immediately lose interest in the minute I had myself in hand.' Characteristic of her critical works are heelless textual surfaces, through which she weaves different genres and linguistic levels.[56]

The success of the two fashion-related exhibitions held at the Kunsthalle Wien as part of its winter of fashion – "Vanity," on fashion photography from F.C. Gundlach's collection (21 October 2011 to 12 February 2012) and the ironically titled "No fashion, please!: Fotografie zwischen Gender und Lifestyle" (Photography between Gender and Lifestyle, 10 November 2011–29 January 2012) – seems to have encouraged the MQ to be bolder in its fashion-related programming and follow up with a summer extravaganza. After being extended, the former closed on 1 April 2012 on a wonderfully Viennese note with a well-attended "Finissage," so-called "interventions in the Vanity exhibition," which parodied the original image by F.C. Gundlach that had been chosen for the exhibition's catalogue and was given the good baroque title "Vanitas" [Figures 2.29 and 2.30].[57] If the MQ had been

Figure 2.29: Vanity (Photo: F.C. Gundlach).

Figure 2.30: Vanitas poster (© Hausleitner/Knebl).

wondering how its programming was resonating with local fashion-lovers, this event would have convinced it of the wisdom of taking its flagship strategy literally and using fashion to infuse the city's powerful baroque heritage with contemporary global street style-hipness.

One of the first accounts of the MQ when it opened in 2001 shows that this hybrid of baroque-global performativity was a deliberate part of the design process and evident to its first visitors:

When one enters through the main entrance (to be more specific, the median resalit or avant-corps) of the Fischer von Erlach tract, one finds oneself in a large square flagged with light stones and looks, in the words of architect Laurids Ortner, at the area as though it were built on a stage. The theatricality of the imperial Ringstrasse indeed continues inside the MuQua compound, if with minimalist, neo-modern restraint. The monumental staircases, which lead to the entrances of the museums and have been the subject of critique, also contributes to the theatricality. Seen sociologically they make sense. 'Self-presentation, self-staging will become of central importance for people who have to live their lives like artworks,' said Ulrich Beck once in an interview in the mid-1990s, when asked about the role of the individual in the twenty-first century. And Laurids Ortner confirms, 'One goes down there like on a tiered stage. Everyone can see everyone else' (*Falter* 25/01). Much that was once the privilege of art has now become part of everyday social practice (Rakuschan).[58]

That fashion is now an integral part of that everyday social practice is shown by its having been able to respond to the demands the MQ placed on it, mediating successfully between art and the social.

Despite its contested origin and the initial resistance against establishing it in a baroque building complex, the MQ seems to have been quite effective in negotiating the pressures exerted by the legacy of the materiality of the architectural structures and articulating it to an inclusive public space, a space that manages to uphold the baroque legacy of providing spectacle (e.g. the spectacle of fashion shows) while at the same time democratizing those shows and dissociating them from elite tastes. While the MAK's reinvention in the 1980s vocally separated its new mission from the style and taste pressures of any historical legacy while perpetuating an elitist approach to taste culture, the MQ's activities show a more relaxed approach to the past, mobilizing its legacies with a Benjaminian sense for presenting creativity and style to the Viennese as well as the world and creating a sense of local belonging (75% of "users" are local compared with 15% from abroad, of whom 55% are German).

The baroque legacy that permeates Vienna's built environment is highly ambivalent as a meme. While the baroque social structure was profoundly hierarchical, anti-egalitarian, and based on divine legitimation of its social structure, the absolutist system that gave rise to its cultural manifestations was also the foundation of defining its subjects as part of a homogeneous audience that had been levelled, whose members had become equals in the act of observing the staging of the spectacle of power on which the baroque was based (and one that could be mobilized dialectically in order to further a democratic and egalitarian agenda, as became clear with the French Revolution). While the organizers of the second Vienna Fashion Night along the *Luxusmeile* chose to use the baroque residence of the Habsburgs as a backdrop to a fashion show that was by invitation only for the new aristocracy of celebrity culture,[59] the MQ's show on the next day was open to everyone, and the catwalk was positioned in a way that it made use of the baroque axes of the building to make visible to a large number of people what Vienna fashion design had produced, mobilizing the mass appeal of its historical legacy.

Notes

1   It is worth drawing attention to the fact that unlike other European cultural centres, Vienna's museums have more recently tended to concentrate on avant-garde and everyday forms of art rather than traditionally elite ones.

2   That is the figure given on the collection's website: http://www.wienmuseum.at/de/standorte/ansicht/modesammlung.html, accessed 11 June 2013.

3 "Es war ebenfalls kriegsbeschädigt – und der Anmarsch war weit! Die Philadelphiabrücke – ein Holzsteg. Die Straßenbahn ungewiß. In diesen Tagen wurde etwas geboren, was ich den 'Geist von Hetzendorf' nennen möchte. Teamwork statt Hierarchie! Gemeinsam stapften wir durch den Schnee, gemeinsam froren wir in den ungeheizten Räumen, gemeinsam und in Kette schafften wir den Schutt in die diversen Bombentrichter, gemeinsam ordneten wir die Hefte in der Modesammlung und diskutierten mögliche Modeaktivitäten. Unsere ersten Modelle machten wir aus Papier und eingefärbtem Molino. Wir luden Presse, Kulturstadtrat, Innung, Schulbehörde und Textilfirmen ein – und siehe: Sie kamen alle! Und wir bekamen Titelseiten in den Wiener Tageszeitungen und das ersehnte Material gespendet. Bald konnten die Schülerinnen 'ihre' eigenen Modelle auf dem Bretterlaufsteg im Garten vorführen. In Gruppen! Damit brachten wir auch etwas Neues auf die Beine. (Mode wurde damals nur einzeln und exclusiv zelebriert!)."

4 This information is available on the collection's website: http://www.wienmuseum.at/de/standorte/ansicht/modesammlung.html, accessed 11 June 2013.

5 The following information in this paragraph is from Karner 2007.

6 An online archive of the Wien Museum exhibitions is available at http://www.wienmuseum.at/nc/de/ausstellungsverzeichnis.html, accessed 11 June 2013.

7 Those at the Hermesvilla included: "Die Frau im Korsett: Wiener Frauenalltag zwischen Klischee und Wirklichkeit" (The Corseted Woman: Viennese Women's Everyday Life between Cliché and Reality, 14 April 1984 to 8 April 1985); "Elisabeth von Österreich: Einsamkeit, Macht und Freiheit" (Elisabeth of Austria: Loneliness, Power and Freedom, 22 March 1986 to 22 March 1987); "Drüber und Drunter: Wiener Damenmode von 1900 bis 1914" (Over and Under: Viennese Women's Fashion from 1900 to 1914, 11 April 1987 to 28 February 1988); "Emilie Flöge und Gustav Klimt: Doppelporträt in Ideallandschaft" (Emilie Flöge and Gustav Klimt: Double Portrait in an Idealized Landscape, 30 April 1988 to 19 February 1989); "Rudolf: Ein Leben im Schatten von Mayerling" (Rudolf: A Life in the Shadow of Mayerling, 18 March 1989 to 4 March 1990); "Kaiserin Elisabeth: Keine Thränen wird man weinen..." (Empress Elisabeth: One Won't Cry Any Tears..., 2 April 1998 to 16 February 1999); and "Mode von Kopf bis Fuß 1750–2001" (Fashion from Head to Toe 1750–2001, 17 May 2001 to 17 February 2002). Eventually a somewhat short-lived "permanent" exhibition was set up at the Hermesvilla called "Chic: Damenmode des 20. Jahrhunderts" (Chic: Women's Fashion in the 20th Century, 12 April 2005 to 7 January 2009). Meanwhile, exhibitions on fashion were also taking place at Schloss Hetzendorf: "Krinolinenzeit: Damenmode 1849–1867" (Time of Crinolines: Women's Fashion 1849–1867, 6 May 1992 to 11 April 1993); "Von der Tournüre zum Cul de Paris: Wiener Damenmode von 1868 bis 1888; im Schauraum der Modesammlung" (From the Bustle to the Parisian Posterior: Viennese Women's Fashion from 1868 to 1888, 6 May 1993 to 10 April 1994); "Fin de Siècle – Wiener Damenmode von 1889 bis 1914" (Fin de Siècle: Viennese Women's Fashion from 1889 to 1914, 5 May 1994 to 9 April 1995); "Vom Empire zur Belle Epoque – Wiener Damenmode von 1805 bis 1910" (From Empire to Belle Epoque – Viennese Women's Fashion from 1805 to 1910, 4 May 1995 to 6 April 1997); "Benjamin, ich hab' nichts anzuzieh'n – Wiener Damenmode von 1920–1930" (Benjamin, I Don't Have Anything to Wear – Viennese Women's Fashion from 1920 to 1930, 22 May 1997 to 26 December 1999);

"Glamour: Wiener Damenmode der 30er Jahre" (Glamour: Viennese Women's Fashion of the 1930s, 25 May 2000 to 30 December 2001).

8   http://www.wienmuseum.at/en/exhibitions/detail/ausstellung/besetztkampf-um-freiraeume-seit-den-70ern.html, accessed 29 June 2013.

9   http://www.wienmuseum.at/de/ansicht/ausstellung/besetztkampf-um-freiraeume-seit-den-70ern.html, accessed 29 June 2013.

10   Designed by star architect Hans Hollein, the store introduced international brand names to Vienna and became the social focus of a taste elite and closed in 1987. "Das Programm der Section N reichte von Marcel Breuers 'Wassily' bis zum Leiter-Sessel 'Ottakringer', vom Loos-Glas bis zum irischen Tweedhut aus Connemara. Katarina Noever: 'Wir haben uns auf eine Gruppe von Menschen ähnlicher Gesinnung und Geschmacks spezialisiert, nicht aber auf Produktgruppen. Die Section N war ein Einrichtungshaus und Informations-Zentrum für ein neugieriges, qualitätshungriges Publikum, Anlaufstelle für ausländische Kulturpublizisten und -touristen, Auftraggeberin und Vermittlerin von Künstlern, Architekten und Designern.'"

11   "Eine Modesammlung als Dokument der Wiener Lifestyle-Avantgarde seit den 1960er-Jahren. Katarina Noever war damals Top-Model und trug die Kreationen der Boutique 'Étoile', die im muffigen Wien für frischen Wind sorgte. 1971 gründete sie mit Peter Noever die heute legendäre Section N. Dieses von Hans Hollein gestaltete Geschäft war 'eine Art urbaner Salon' (Laurids Ortner): Auf unkonventionelle Weise wurde dem Wiener Publikum internationales Design nahegebracht. Neben Lampen von Achille Castiglioni und Möbeln von Marcel Breuer waren auch steirische Filzpatschen und Ethno-Mode aus Asien im Angebot."

12   http://www.wienmuseum.at/de/ansicht/austellung/mehr-als-mode-die-sammlung-katarina-noever.html, accessed 29 June 2013.

13   One also sees this approach in catalogues of high academic quality that are usually either not translated into English and/or out of print or both.

14   Cf.http://derstandard.at/1336697980227/Richtungsstreit-um-Zukunft-des-Wien-Museums, accessed 11 June 2013, and http://www.simmoag.at/en/services/newsletter/news/artikel/presentation-of-new-quartier-belvedere-564.html, accessed 11 June 2013.

15   "The Museum moved to its present site in 1857 and was renamed the South Kensington Museum. Its collections expanded rapidly as it set out to acquire the best examples of metalwork, furniture, textiles and all other forms of decorative art from all periods. It also acquired fine art – paintings, drawings, prints and sculpture – in order to tell a more complete history of art and design" (http://www.vam.ac.uk/content/articles/a/a-brief-history-of-the-museum/, accessed 11 June 2013). In 1899 the museum moved to its present site and was renamed Victoria and Albert Museum.

16   "Vermutlich steht für ihn das Argument, aus österreichischen Produkten wirtschaftlichen Profit schlagen zu können, im Vordergrund, um seine eigenen Ideen der Museumsgründung leichter durchsetzen zu können. In der Konkurrenzfähigkeit sieht er die Bedingungen für den friedlichen politischen und wirtschaftlichen Wettstreit und knüpft große Hoffnungen an die sich ab 1851 an verschiedenen Orten in rascher Folge wiederholenden Weltausstellungen als 'Jahrmärkte des Kunstgewerbes', die eine bis dahin unbekannte Situation gegenseitiger Beeinflussung und Austauschbarkeit schaffen."

17 "Die Verbindung dieser sachlichen Überlegungen mit dem patriotischen Gedanken, Österreichs Weltausstellung zu stärken, war erfolgreich: Am 7. März 1863 ordnete Kaiser Franz Joseph per Handbillet die Gründung einer solchen Institution an und wies dem neuen Geschmacksbildungsmuseum zunächst das Ballhaus als Standort zu."

18 "Der Glaube, Kunst und Kunstgewerbe im speziellen durch Lehre und Wissenschaft qualitativ verbessern zu können, war in Wien durch Rudolf von Eitelberger zur Doktrin erklärt worden" (Pokorny-Nagel 81). *Geschmacksbildung* meant an appreciation of historical models. The collections consequently strove to include exemplary objects from each era, with copies and photographs complementing originals and copying faithfully from those models was the core way of instruction in the attached Kunstgewerbeschule, originally housed in the museum's attic (Scholda 220).

19 History repeated itself in a public debate that started in the late 1980s when the Museumsquartier (cf. next section) was constructed. Plans to incorporate the MAK into the complex were ultimately dropped.

20 "Die Wiener Renaissance lehnt sich grosstheils an die italienische Renaissance an, hie und da, allerdings sehr vereinzelt und nie ohne fremdartigen Beigeschmack, an altgriechische Kunst. In diesem Anlehnen an Italien und Griechenland folgen unsere Künstler einem gesunden Instincte und wir können nur wünschen, dass sie sich in dieser Richtung nicht irre machen lassen. Denn all' unser künstlerischer Fortschritt beruht darauf, dass die geistig reinigende Atmosphäre, die aus der Toscana und Hellas zu uns herüberstreicht, immer mehr sich verbreite [...] Eine Renaissance ist ohne bedeutende Sculptur und Malerei, ohne eine künstlerisch und technisch vollendete Ornamentik ganz haltlos. Bei den Renaissance-Bauten kommt es nicht darauf an, dass in·den Formen der Renaissance überhaupt gebaut wird, sondern es müssen auch der Bildhauer und der Maler von den Principien und dem Geist der Renaissance ganz durchdrungen sein."

21 Backhausen converted the basement of its shop in Vienna's first district (at Schwarzspanierstrasse 10) into a textile museum so that it could display its comprehensive archive of 3500 original sketches of textile designs, which it claims is the largest in the world (http://www.backhausen.com/index.php?m=museum&s=geschichte, accessed 11 June 2013).

22 "Es dürfte schon zu Beginn dieses Jahrhunderts nicht ganz frei von Anachronismen gewesen sein, jetzt, ein gutes Jahrhundert später, hatte es sich längst eklatant überlebt. Im Grunde war der Mangel an Profil des Museums für angewandte Kunst nichts anderes als die sichtbare Folgeerscheinung des geistigen Klimas im Haus, das sich auch als eine Art inhaltliches und ideologisches Vakuum charakterisieren ließe."

23 "Das Haus ist an seiner eigenen Vergangenheit fast erstickt. Daher ging es mir zunächst einmal darum, dieses Sich-Verlieren in der Geschichte, diese unreflektierte, distanzlose Fixierung auf eine Tradition zu unterbinden. Es wäre doch völlig absurd, wollte man heute versuchen, den ursprünglichen Gründungsauftrag sozusagen 'buchstabengetreu' weiterzuführen [...] Gerade in einem solchen Haus kommt es darauf an, sich auf Neuland hinauszuwagen."

24 In the meantime several institutions have developed to fill this void, including the KunstHausWien, which was designed by Friedensreich Hundertwasser and opened in 1991, the Museum Moderner Kunst Stiftung Ludwig Wien in the Museumsquartier, which was

gifted with a major collection of contemporary art in 1981 and opened in its new location in 2001, and the 21er Haus, which used to be the 20er Haus but reopened in 2011 with a new mandate to display contemporary Austrian art.

25   "Gleichzeitig bedient sich der Kulturbetrieb der Kunst und drängt die Künstler in die Rolle von Animateuren einer expandierenden Kulturgesellschaft. Die Verachtung der Kunst durch die Macher einer wachstumsorientierten Freizeit- und Tourismusgesellschaft wird damit deutlich. Kultur ist für alles zuständig, am Rande auch für die Kunst [...] Die Diskussion über solche Phänomene einer Entwicklung hat in diesem Land, wie vieles andere, mit erheblicher Zeitverzögerung eingesetzt."

26   "Dieses Haus, das Österreichische Museum für angewandte Kunst, hat nach dem bisher Erreichten durchaus eine Chance, ein Ort der Auseinandersetzung, ein Ort des Widerstandes, eine Austragungsstätte für Konflikte zu werden, aber auch ein Ort des Geheimnisvollen, ein Ort der Gefühle und Träume [...] zu bleiben."

27   Schindler is an intriguing link to Los Angeles and has an interesting position in the city's own tradition. Influenced more by Frank Lloyd Wright than Wagner (he apprenticed with Lloyd Wright after having emigrated in 1914 in response to a job offer and being left stranded due to the war), Schindler contributed a particular strand of modernism to the urban texture of Los Angeles, one characterized by a strong vision of social reform that was subsequently all but forgotten in the imaginary Los Angeles acquired as the city of theme parks and postmodernism *avant la lettre* (cf. Reisenleitner 2002).

28   Details are available on the Center's website: www.makcenter.org, accessed 11 June 2013.

29   http://www.nytimes.com/2007/08/30/arts/music/30thun.html, accessed 18 December 2012.

30   http://www.e-flux.com/announcements/new-director-christoph-thun-hohenstein-to-re-position-mak-vienna/, accessed 11 June 2013.

31   http://archpaper.com/news/articles.asp?id=5635, accessed 11 June 2013.

32   "Christoph Thun-Hohenstein, seit September Direktor des MAK, ist ein Kunststück gelungen: Er bekennt sich zur Positionierung des Museums unter seinem Vorgänger – und macht doch alles anders." http://derstandard.at/1319183690114/Die-Plaene-des-neuen-Direktors-Christoph-Thun-Hohenstein, accessed 11 June 2013.

33   "Was hat uns bewogen, hier uns um Wien 1900 wieder zu kümmern? Einfach der Umstand, dass wir eine Weltklassesammlung haben und Wien um 1900 ein zentraler Bereich dieser Sammlung ist und nach meiner Überzeugung jedes Kunstmuseum ein zeitgenössisches Museum sein muss, das sich immer wieder aus der Gegenwart heraus mit der Vergangenheit beschäftigt und nicht nur den kunsthistorischen Blick tätigt, sondern auch den kulturhistorischen und darüber hinaus auch herauszuarbeiten versucht, was davon auch heute noch relevant ist." https://vimeo.com/54454923, accessed 11 June 2013.

34   vimeo.com/36409253 [3:20], accessed 11 June 2013.

35   "Soll Wien Mailand werden als Designstadt? Nein!" (https://vimeo.com/44249750; http://www.mak.at/en/more_mak/videochannel/made_4_you_design_for_change_5, both accessed 11 June 2013).

36   It might seem contradictory that this elitism is being sponsored by a minister from the Social Democratic Party. However, in the Austrian context, there is a strong strand of

Bildungsbürgertum pervading the party, with Bruno Kreisky being the outstanding example. This also defines a strong dividing line between the Social Democratic movement at the federal level, and the Social Democrats who operate at the city level.

37   "In 1970, together with Helmut R. Scholz and H. Laszlo, Peter Noever founded the IFABO (Internationale Fach-Ausstellung für Büro-Organisation) an international exhibition for office organization that was held annually till 2002. First held in February of the same year at the Messepalast in Vienna, it will now also be extended to Prague ('Austrobüro')" (http://peternoever.mak.at/e/html/03/c_03_2.html, accessed 11 June 2013).

38   Since 2008, 7tm has provided a platform for retailers in the area. According to its press materials, "7tm promotes the most unique viennese fashion & design scene to tourists and locals. 58 selected stores present themselves within the framework of numerous co-operations" (http://www.7tm.at/home/en/press). Among the qualities it stands for are individuality, a special taste, slowness, and local supply, and it is against standardization (http://www.7tm.at/home/en/about, accessed 11 June 2013).

39   The following information is from the mission statement and links available on their website (http://www.unit-f.at/jart/prj3/unitf/main.jart?rel=de&content-id=1234436335111&reserve-mode=active, accessed 11 June 2013). In December 2012, Unit F – büro für mode announced it was ceasing operations after 12 years of supporting the Austrian fashion scene. In that time it sponsored 181 projects by 71 labels, awarded 11 different prizes, and made participation in many trade fairs, publications and pop-up stores possible. It is set to be replaced in 2014 by a similar model ("Modeförderung: Unit F stellt Tätigkeit ein derstandard.at." from http://derstandard.at/1353208546484/Modefoerderung-Unit-F-stellt-Taetigkeit-ein, accessed 11 June 2013).

40   In 2012 BM:UKK's share was EUR 180,000, while Wien Kultur put up EUR 136,000.

41   See the Unit F büro für mode website: http://www.unit-f.at/jart/prj3/unitf/main.jart?rel=de&reserve-mode=active&content-id=1239028817460&ref_projekte_id=1239028817004, accessed 11 June 2013.

42   The program for it is online at: http://www.12festival.at/de/programm, accessed 11 June 2013.

43   See http://www.contemporaryfashion.net/index.php/none/none/0/uk/about.html and http://www.unit-f.at/jart/prj3/unitf/main.jart?rel=de&reserve-mode=active&content-id=1239028817460&ref_projekte_id=1239698344148/, both accessed 11 June 2013. The net itself claims to have run for five years, while Unit F seems only to have funded it from 2002 to 2005.

44   http://theviennafashionobservatory.com/?cat=75, accessed 11 June 2013.

45   http://theviennafashionobservatory.com/?cat=59, accessed 11 June 2013.

46   A list of those who have been supported is available at http://www.departure.at/de/gefoerderte_projekte, accessed 11 June 2013. Since 2004, 56 projects have been funded (of 161 applications).

47   "Neben den Förderaktivitäten setzt departure auch diverse Strukturverbesserungsmaß-nahmen für die jeweiligen Kreativszenen. Initiativen wie zum Beispiel das parallel zur VIENNAFAIR stattfindende Projekt curated by_vienna oder diverse Veranstaltungen im Rahmen des sound:frame-Festivals, des festivals for fashion & photography, der VIENNA

ART WEEK und der VIENNA DESIGN WEEK sowie einer Kooperation mit dem MAK über neue Design-Strategien sollen Wien als Kreativstandort zusätzlich stärken" (http://www.departure.at/de/presse/departure_allgemein/departure__wirtschaftsfoerderer_im_urbanen_gefuege, accessed 11 June 2013).

48   "In der departure fashion night, die im Rahmen des festival for fashion & photography stattfindet, werden ausgewählte Projekte aus dem Bereich Mode präsentiert, die seitens departure Förderungen erhielten. Unit F büro für mode, als Veranstalter des festival for fashion & photography, übernimmt mit seiner auf österreichisches Modedesign gerichteten Kernkompetenz die Organisation und Veranstaltung der seit 2005 jährlich stattfindenden departure fashion night."

49   http://www.akbild.ac.at/portal_en/studies/institutes/education-in-the-arts, accessed 11 June 2013.

50   http://www.akbild.ac.at/Portal/studium/institute/kunst-und-kulturwissenschaften/vortrage-veranstaltungen, accessed 11 June 2013.

51   www.mqviennafashionweek.com, accessed 15 June 2012.

52   http://www.creative-headz.com/about.html, accessed 11 June 2013.

53   http://www.mqw.at/en/program/detail/?event_id=7120&page=7&filter_keyword_ids=125, accessed 11 June 2013.

54   http://www.mqw.at/en/program/detail/?event_id=6944, accessed 11 June 2013.

55   The symposium took place on 18 October 2001 in the MQ (http://old.kunsthallewien.at/cgi-bin/event/event.pl?id=91;lang=de;event_cat=12, accessed 29 June 2013).

56   "Elfriede Jelinek zählt zu den bedeutendsten und gleichzeitig umstrittensten AutorInnen des deutschsprachigen Raums. In ihrem vielfältigen literarischen Schaffen verbindet sie Kunst untrennbar mit gesellschaftspolitischer Stellungnahme. Selbstreflexiv und kritisch ist auch ihr Zugang zur Mode: 'Von wenigen Dingen verstehe ich so viel wie von Kleidern. Ich weiß wenig von mir, interessiere mich auch nicht sehr für mich, aber mir kommt vor, daß meine Leidenschaft für Mode mir mich selbst ersetzen kann […]. Ich beschäftige mich mit Kleidung, damit ich mich nicht mit mir beschäftigen muß, denn mich würde ich sofort fallen lassen, kaum daß ich mich einmal in der Hand hätte.' Charakteristisch für ihre pointierten Werke sind absatzlose Textflächen, in denen sie unterschiedliche Textgattungen und sprachliche Ebenen verwebt." (http://old.kunsthallewien.at/cgi-bin/event/event.pl?id=4581&lang=de)

57   The poster reprinted here can also be found on the event's Facebook page: http://www.facebook.com/events/243456592418058/, accessed 11 June 2013.

58   "Kommt man durch den Haupteingang bzw. den Mittelrisalit des Fischer von Erlach-Trakts, gelangt man auf einen großen mit hellen Steinplatten ausgelegten Platz und sieht, nach den Worten des Architekten Laurids Ortner, das Gelände wie auf einer Bühne aufgebaut. In der Tat setzt sich die Theatralik der imperialen Ringstraße auch innerhalb des MuQua-Geländes weiter fort, wenn auch mit minimalistisch-neomoderner Zurückhaltung. Zur Theatralik tragen auch die kritisierten Monumentalstiegen bei, die zu den Eingängen der Museen führen. Soziologisch gesehen, machen sie aber Sinn. 'Selbstdarstellung, Selbstinszenierung wird eine zentrale Bedeutung erlangen, die Menschen werden ihr Leben

wie ein Kunstwerk gestalten müssen', sagte Ulrich Beck einmal Mitte der 90-er Jahre in einem Interview, als er über die Rolle des Individuums im 21. Jahrhundert befragt wurde. Und Laurids Ortner bestätigt: 'Man geht da runter wie auf einer Showtreppe. Alle sehen alle.' (*Falter* 25/01) Vieles was einmal Privileg der Kunst war, ist in die gesellschaftliche Alltagspraxis eingegangen."

59 It took place in the Michaelerplatz-Passage on 14 June 2012.

Chapter 6

Designer Chic

Uncompromising understatement meets material potentiality

"You were seen as having a very serious approach to fashion. Has art relaxed you? I am always serious and I am always relaxed. Nothing has changed."
(http://www.nowness.com/day/2011/7/23/1559/helmut-lang-make-it-hard)

The Viennese fashion designer to have achieved the greatest renown internationally thus far is Helmut Lang. One of the "new generation of designers that shaped 90s fashion," Lang is often mentioned together with "Martin Margiela and Walter van Beirendonck, later followed by Raf Simons, Viktor & Rolf, Bless and Balenciaga."[1] In contrast to these other designers, Lang has insisted on maintaining a relationship to the fashion world resolutely on his own terms, something we will show in this section to be indicative of, and in keeping with, the larger Viennese fashion system.

Born in one of the newer districts on the northern outskirts of the city the year after the Soviets officially left Vienna (1956), Lang was raised by his maternal grandparents in a small village in the Styrian Alps for ten years before returning to Vienna when his father remarried.[2] According to the account of his youth he gave John Seabrook in an interview, Lang's childhood was very black and white or, more precisely, white and black, with ten idyllic years followed by eight tortuous ones:

'In the mountains there was a very elegant way about basic necessities,' Lang told me, 'a great beauty in a certain way that is completely refined but not about money. Then money comes in and it gets over the top. People who grow up in the city don't have that sense of taste, they don't experience it as connected to a real life, to nature, as I did. I was really very lucky to have that experience, though I was perhaps unlucky that my parents' divorce and my mother's death made me have it.'

The mountain idyll ended abruptly when Helmut was ten. His father remarried, and Helmut went back to Vienna. The next eight years were 'the most unhappy period of my life,' Lang has said. His stepmother forced him to wear suits and hats that had belonged to her father, a Viennese businessman. He had to wear them to school as well as around the house. Of course the suits didn't fit. 'It was completely painful to have to wear these clothes,' he said. 'The other kids at school were dressing like hippies, but I was not allowed to wear jeans. My chance to find my style as a teen-ager, which is a very formative time, was taken away from me. I'm not completely sure, but maybe this is why I became a fashion designer. Because I was denied my own identity.'

On the day Lang turned eighteen, in 1974, he told his parents he was leaving. He never saw either of them again (Seabrook).

Rather, Lang taught himself how the kind of clothes he wanted to wear were made and, in 1979, opened his own boutique in Vienna, called Bou-Bou Lang. It lasted five years and propelled him on to Paris, where in 1986 he showed a collection in conjunction with the monumental exhibition that had brought to Vienna a renewed appreciation of Jugendstil/art nouveau and popularized it elsewhere, namely "Vienne 1880-1939: L'apocalypse joyeuse" (Vienna 1900/Traum und Wirklichkeit) at the Centre Georges Pompidou. The success of this venture led to his founding his own label and showing his first ready-to-wear collection later that year.

The 1990s were a propitious time for a designer of Lang's proclivities. As Seabrook sums up:

The recession of 1992, which followed the grunge movement, set the stage for Helmut's minimalist style. The eighties had been about showing money; the nineties were about hiding the money. Lang's secretive aspect perfectly suited the zeitgeist. Anna Wintour said recently, 'Helmut came along and at first it was "Wait a moment, what's this? This is not in the spirit of the mid-eighties," which was all about opulence. But then everything crashed and fashion reflected that, and Helmut was there to take advantage.'

During the 1990s Lang remained based in Europe, teaching for a while in the prestigious Modeklasse at Vienna's University of Applied Arts and showing innovative women's and men's lines in Paris that were based on newly designed fabrics like thermal leather, paper, holographs and new kinds of nylon. Paris appreciated his innovation, which included restructuring the usual fashion show format as a "séance de travail," as did the art world, which he entered in 1997 by presenting work at two exhibitions: "I Smell You On My Clothes" at the Florence Biennale and "art/fashion" at the Guggenheim SOHO in New York.

A decade after he had introduced the Helmut Lang Men's collection in Paris, and two decades after the opening of his boutique in Vienna, Lang showed a men's collection in New York and began working with the American conceptual artist Jenny Holzer on a series of boutiques. He relocated the company from Vienna to New York the next year, in 1998, and advertised his first collection there in a variety of new ways. It was the first ever Internet-based fashion show and the first time a fashion house had advertised on the top of New York cabs (the campaign featured the controversial photography of Robert Mapplethorpe and Bruce Weber). Less than two years later, in April 2000, he became the first non-American designer to become part of the Council of Fashion Designers of America (CFDA), a group which had named him Best International Designer of the Year in 1996. His not appearing to accept their award that year for Menswear Designer of the Year was not taken kindly by the industry: "'We all have to do things we don't want to do sometimes,' said André Leon Talley, the editor-at-large of *Vogue*. Anna Wintour described Helmut's decision as 'a mistake.' [...] 'If I had known he wasn't coming, I would have called him. It was discourteous not to turn up'" (Seabrook).

In the second half of 1999, the Prada Group set about "consolidat[ing] its position as a leading luxury conglomerate by acquiring – in addition to a share of Helmut Lang – Jil Sander, the company run by its namesake, a German-born designer who shares Lang's minimalist approach; Church's, the English shoemaker; and fifty-one per cent of Fendi, together with LVMH Moët Hennessy Louis Vuitton" (Seabrook). There was much speculation about Lang's decision to sell 51 per cent of his company, and even more when Jil Sander resigned from her company in January 2000, less than six months after having sold 75 per cent of it to Prada. Lang lasted somewhat longer, selling the rest of his company to the Prada Group in October 2004. In spring of the next year he left the company, by the end of 2005 the boutiques in New York, Tokyo, Hong Kong, Singapore, Seoul, Paris, Milan, Munich and Vienna had closed (the one in London's Westbourne Grove remains – Figure 2.31), and in 2006 Prada sold the company to the American-Japanese Link Theory Holdings.

Figure 2.31: Helmut Lang boutique in Westbourne Grove, London (Photo: S. Ingram).

Since then Lang has remained in Long Island and devoted himself to art. While his work has been included in a number of group exhibitions, it is two of his solo shows that have garnered the most attention for the austerity and depth of their vision. The ambiguously titled "Alles Gleich Schwer" (Everything Equally Heavy/Difficult) was part of the "Hannover Goes Fashion" project held in the summer of 2008, during which all ten of the city's large museums and exhibition houses coordinated exhibitions on the theme of fashion. Lang's response when asked about the title by curator Neville Wakefield makes clear what a relief it must be for him to no longer be part of the corporately controlled fashion world:

As one of the sentences in Jenny Holzer's 'Truisms' states, 'Everyone's Work Is Equally Important.' I believe that the idea of a creative equality for every kind of word is one of the fundamental principles of human coexistence. There is a similar kind of importance to mastering a process independently of the goal one is attempting to achieve. But independent of this, I would like the title to be considered on another level, specifically, so that it does not suggest that things have the same difficulty or weight on account of the committment of activity. According to my understanding, 'Alles Gleich Schwer' should bring about a new consideration of ideas and feelings that are fundamental to human existence. An appreciation of which significance and which meaning every individual measures things by in a time of changing values (Lang et al. 39).[3]

Among the works on display was "Séance de travail 1993-1999," on which Lang had collaborated with Jenny Holzer and Louise Bourgeois and which had already been displayed in the Kunsthalle Wien in 1998. Also featuring "Next Ever After" (2007) and "Three" (2008) – "elements which came from his fashion offices on Greene Street in the New York district of Soho and which were already displayed there in their originally unadapted form as *objets trouvés*" (Lang et al. 105), namely, a mirror-lined sphere and tar-covered mahogany eagles – the exhibition drew attention to the passage of time and the question of material memory, making use of both organic materials like wood and the more reflective, screen-like substances Lang also is comfortable working with. These effects were strengthened by the "Arbor" maypoles, the "Life Form" pieces, and the "Surrogate Skins," all of which, Lang agreed with Wakefield, addressed the "ritual celebration of potential" (Lang et al. 35).

Lang's more recent "Make It Hard" exhibition pushed the question of material potentiality to a highly personal extreme. From 22 July to 8 August 2011, column-like artworks with textured bark were on display in East Hampton "across the road from the house formerly owned by Jackson Pollock and Lee Krasner" (Syson). The fire that struck his fashion archive in February 2011 – fortunately after he had generously donated "a large volume of his work to select fashion, design and contemporary art collections worldwide" ("Helmut Lang: Make it Hard") – provided him with the exhibition's impetus. Sorting through charred remains spawned the idea to shred and repurpose "6000 garments from his eponymous label into a series of terrestrially textured, stalactite columns that stretch from floor to ceiling" (ibid.). According to writer and creative director Neville Wakefield, who presented the exhibition,

"Lang's sartorial oeuvre now takes the form of 'strangely beautiful excretions,' which erase the past and bear witness to 'the transience of our creative endeavours'" (Syson). Wakefield may be correct in his assessment of this being a case of expelled waste matter, the remains expunged after being subject to Lang's digestive juices. However, the tree-like shapes and colours of the columns point in another direction: that of regeneration, which could also be seen as the credo that links Lang's work in the fashion and art worlds. For ideas to live on, they require some kind of substance at some point. As a child, one suspects that Lang recognized in the shoes that his cobbler-grandfather made both something that connected their materiality to their surroundings and something that reminded him of his grandfather's values, and he channelled that into the chic "uniform for the new casual world" (Seabrook) he created for the post-Yuppies, which champions the independent, proletarian heritage of jeans. What his more recent art makes clear about the fashion that he used to design is that he sees an organic connection between them and ascribes a virility to, and revels in being able to, transform, regenerate and repurpose materials in strikingly upwardly mobile forms that at the same time gesture to an independence of purpose and style.[4]

What can Helmut Lang's oeuvre tell us about fashion in Vienna? Is there anything we would want to characterize as Viennese about his cultural production? If one calls up the website of Viennese-born Anna Aichinger, who studied fashion design with the luminaries at Vienna's University of Applied Arts, graduated in 2003 with the best diploma of the year and began presenting her own label in Paris in 2006, its firm black lettering will tempt one to attribute the city with an aesthetics of stark, almost severe, cultivation and craftsmanship, one that, upon examination, can be seen to have grown out of a dialectical history of showy baroque extravagance tempered by periods of privation, austerity and the ideological rejection of opulent elite lifestyles.[5] Looking back in history, one finds in influential periods the manifestations of this ethos of chic. At the first occasion that Viennese fashion had to prove itself on an international stage, the 1815 Congress of Vienna at which the post-Napoleonic order was negotiated:

[t]he Viennese gentlemen chose their clothes with an assured sense of what suited them best from among the many possibilities available. They never stepped outside the mainstream of the international development of men's fashion, which was dominated by the English, but they adopted the western European fashions in a way that was practical and suited their temper as well as their customs. It required great skill to create a simple line, such as that of trousers that fit 'like marble' (Cone 102).

Over a century later, celebrating the twenty-fifth anniversary of the Wiener Werkstätte in 1928, Josef Hoffmann declared its main achievement to have been giving

'practical and appropriate forms to all objects and then to make these unique and valuable through pleasing proportions and harmonious shapes. [...] We do not dictate to an artist,' Hoffmann continued, 'but seek only to encourage him [sic] to follow his

[sic] own intuition and develop his [sic] creative power. [...] The idea of accepting a style without building on it and making it one's own leads to stagnation and decline. We are reacting to this unwholesome artistic atmosphere, which has recently been current in Europe. We believe in looking back to a healthy tradition – for instance, the Empire style – drawing inspiration from it, and creating new forms. Mere copying, no matter how well done, is always worthless and can never replace an original' (Cone 161).

Similarly, one finds that Aichinger's designs "have more to do with shape, cut and attitude than decoration, attempting to emphasise the personality and elegance of women" (http://www.notjustalabel.com/editorial/anna_aichinger). She can thus be firmly located in a longer Viennese tradition that rejects ostentatious non-functional ornament and national costume and bears some family resemblance to Armani's similarly cosmopolitan rejection of Italian glamour in favour of a more timeless and placeless style of his own. However, one would also want to note that the Viennese ethics that Janik and Toulmin draw attention to in their work on Wittgenstein – "the man who rejected all his traditional privileges as a fellow of Trinity College, Cambridge, who was never seen around the town except wearing an open-necked shirt and one or two zipper-fastened parkas, and who insisted passionately – as a point of ethics rather than aesthetics – that the only movies worth seeing were Westerns" (Janik and Toulmin 20-21) – are also a key part of Lang's and Aichinger's style and independent sensibilities. In describing the idea behind her 2008 summer collection "Alphagirls," Aichinger evokes a figure one could easily position as Lang's sister:

I'd rather see the Alphagirl as a woman who reaches out into the world and goes her own way without paying attention to what others might think. Who tries new ways of combining all things she wants to be in life. It's about escaping the stereotypes we still have in mind today of what a career woman is, what a good wife is, what a good mother is. Alphagirls try to define all of this according to their own needs and desires. And lead their own life. Not following someone else's ideas (Sark 2011, "Anna Aichinger").

The sentiment motivating Aichinger's 2010 collection "All we want baby...is everything" is similar [Figure 2.32]. When asked whether she really believed today's women can have it all, she replied:

Of course we can. The only problem is that people never take their time to really get into themselves and find out what they really want. They get so many stereotypes of so-called happiness stuffed into their head, all day long from all sides, that they hardly find the time to listen to their inner voice that tells them what they really need in life to be happy. So once you discovered what truly makes you happy, most of the time it's not that hard to live it (ibid.).

Just as one has the sense that Aichinger understands and sympathizes with Helmut Lang's having left the fashion world and turned to art, one can believe the same of Christiane Gruber,

Figure 2.32: Anna Aichinger website.

who graduated from the University of Applied Arts the year before Aichinger, founded her own label "Awareness and Consciousness" in 2005, and presented collections in Paris until 2009 (since the birth of her daughter in 2010, she has been developing a new concept).[6] Her collections bear names like "Never Get Lost," "Never Get Cold," "Ease," "Fuse," "Falling Down," "Let Loose," and "Running," and feature simple, flowing organic designs that clearly express the label's philosophy, of which it is, as its name suggests, very aware and conscious [Figure 2.33].

Another evocatively named Viennese label that shares in an aesthetics of "un-ostentatious elegance" and an ethos one is tempted to dub "sustainable satisfaction" is Maria Steiner's "Ruins of Modernity," which was founded in 2010 (Sark 2012, "Ruins of Modernity") [Figure 2.34].

Figure 2.33: Awareness & Consciousness website.

Figure 2.34: Ruins of Modernity website.

As Steiner relates, the name of the label was taken from her first collection, as it seemed to her to sum up the larger idea she was trying to achieve with her designing:

I found it to be so much more, it's about society in a time between black and white, after modernity. When modernity dawned on the world and rationality and science set their light in people's minds, black and white started to fade to a million different shades of grey. The encrusted, rigid towers of set morals, values and truths crumbled piece by piece. Reason fought its way into the highness of church and throne and slowly tore apart the breathtaking corset that held people in their place. What is good and true, what is wrong and bad? The view of the world ever widened to different opinions, reality and perception became individual. Free from the tight corset of answers, we nearly tumble under the overwhelming complexity of questions and questionable layers of reality and truth. What do you believe and why should you think it's true? We stand in midst of the ruins of modernity, fallen and broken buildings of values and truth, in midst of the ashes of our past – free to build something new (ibid.).

In Steiner's case, what she feels free to build are collections that reflect her own sense of broken elegance.

Steiner, Gruber and Aichinger are but three of a large number of fashion designers who have called Vienna home, but they are also three among the many with an international presence that contributes to the meme of an elegant, understated Viennese style in the spirit of Helmut Lang's minimalism.[7] All three feature on the successful NJAL "notjustalabel" website, which claims to be "the world's leading designer platform for showcasing and nurturing today's pioneers in contemporary fashion."[8] Aichinger and Gruber regularly present their collections in Paris, while Steiner showed her first collection at the Museumsquartier (MQ) Vienna Fashion Week as soon as she completed her studies.

The sustainability principle: We're all in this together

Central to the unostentatious elegance of Lang's, Aichinger's, Gruber's and Steiner's work is the value they place on quality materials. That it is not only sustainable satisfaction that matters in Vienna but also the satisfaction of sustainability, of creating something that not only looks timeless but will endure well beyond the throw-away life cycle of increasingly faster fashion, is something we have already encountered in the cooperative "7tm" initiative of retailers in the growing fashion district that has emerged around the Museumsquartier, which stands for individuality, a special taste, slowness, local supply, and is against standardization. This ethos is perhaps most evident in the work of Cloed Priscilla Baumgartner, who in 2000 began producing small collections for her eco-friendly MILCH label and has since been involved in a number of initiatives that have contributed substantially to the building up of Vienna's fashion community and its sustainable sense of self.

The recycling ethos has been a prominent feature of the label since its first artistic productions, such as aprons she designed out of old floppy disks that were used for sound performances in real-time audio streaming sessions [Figure 2.35].[9] Whereas many labels have philosophies, MILCH has a manifesto that makes a point of its "upcycling" clothing, that is, making new clothes not just out of recycled materials but out of donated clothes:

> Both the environmental and societal aspects are taken into account in the whole production chain. Not only are natural fabrics from up-cycled clothing used, but all MILCH garments are hand sewn under fair working conditions [... They] buy the raw material (trousers and skirts) from the Volkshilfe Box in Vienna, [...] wash the clothes at Green&Clean Waschsalons, [... and t]he Upcycling and Sewing is done at Merit and Dalla (Vienna).[10]

One cannot help but wonder whether Lang's recycling his garments into art was inspired by this type of fashion practice.[11] It is in any case part of a mix that works against ostentatiousness and conspicuous consumption as well as against the kind of fast fashion that is characteristic of the contemporary global fashion capitals. On the contrary, Baumgartner won a "slow fashion" award in 2012.[12]

It is thus possible to find in Vienna established designers who not only support each other but "also help out younger designers, photographers, and even bloggers who are just starting out."[13] Baumgartner is proud of the key role she has played in these networking efforts, which include managing a mailing list where designers can exchange information (it currently has over 350 subscribers), inviting young designers to sell their clothes in her

Figure 2.35: Apron (Photo: Cloed Priscilla Baumgartner).

showroom in the Yppenplatz just off the Ottakringer Strasse in the 16th district (the same part of town which experienced the 1911 uprising that Maderthaner and Musner discuss), showcasing their work to her clients, and encouraging already established designers to switch to organic, recycled and fair trade fabrics [Figure 2.36].[14]

The most prominent and influential of the community-building fashion initiatives Baumgartner has been involved in has to be the Modepalast, which she and Jasmine Ladenhaufen founded in 2003 and which in the meantime has grown into Austria's largest fashion sales fair.[15] Explicitly making a point of raising awareness for high-quality, sustainable fashion, the Modepalast offers local and regional designers direct access to their customers.[16] The success of the annual direct-buy fashion trade show can be seen in its growth ("from 200 to 3000 square meters of exhibition space for more than 160 established and young designers from Austria, Berlin, and Eastern Europe"), its expansion in 2010 from its original quarters in the MQ to a larger space in the Austrian Museum of Applied Arts (MAK), and its branching out for its tenth anniversary to a second event in Linz. According to Baumgartner, "[m]ost designers make about 10% of their annual income at Modepalast; it allows many to start their own shops, and many make their first successful sales there" (Sark 2011, "MILCH").

Sustainability may have become as much of a buzzword in Vienna's fashion community as elsewhere. However, it has also created a quite unique ethos of eschewing both fast fashion and the glitz of the global brand names, which have taken to locating their boutiques in

Figure 2.36: MILCH storefront (Photo: K. Sark).

the narrow confines of the *Luxusmeile* in Vienna's central district. Not exactly street style, these young designers seem to be moving in tandem with Lang's decisive renunciation of a global fashion system that has increasingly become dominated by a handful of corporate players. Instead, the creative design scene that has been emerging in the new millennium in Vienna draws on local arts-and-crafts traditions and the collective ethos of the *Vorstadt,* the still proletarian outskirts – no longer exactly unruly but definitely very specific in both its aesthetics and its aspirations.

Notes

1   http://www.contemporaryfashion.net/index.php/none/none/0/uk/about.html, accessed 12 June 2013.
2   Lang is a notoriously private person. The information is this section is based on Seabrook, which offers the most detailed account of Lang's early years available.
3   We have modified the translation (35) so that it more accurately reflects the original. The original text reads: "Wie eine der Sentenzen in den 'Trusims' von Jenny Holzer

ausführt: 'Die Arbeit Eines Jeden Zählt Gleich Viel.' Ich glaube, dass die Vorstellung einer kreativen Gleichwertigkeit jeglicher Arbeit zu den fundamentalen Prinzipien des menschlichen Zusammenlebens gehört. Es entsteht auch eine ähnliche Wichtigkeit in der Bewältigung eines Arbeitsprozesses unabhängig vom Ziel, das man zu ereichen versucht. Aber unabhängig davon möchte ich, dass man den Titel auch noch in anderer Weise andenkt, und zwar, dass er nicht vorschlägt, dass die Dinge das gleiche Gewicht oder Schwierigkeit haben durch das Engagement der Aktivität. 'Alles Gleich Schwer' soll nach meinem Verständnis eine Neubestimmung von Vorstellungen und Gefühlen einbringen, die fundamental für die menschliche Existenz sind. Eine Absägung, welchen Stellenwert und welche Bedeutung ihnen jeder Einzelne von uns in einer Zeit des Werteumbruchs beimisst.'

4   The exhibition with which Lang followed up "Make It Hard" was "Sculptures": 20 black "totem pole-like stacks of found objects" made of industrial rubber (Michael).

5   Aichinger's website is located at: www.annaaichinger.com. The quotes in the following paragraph are from an editorial on her on the "Not Just A Label" website: http://www.notjustalabel.com/editorial/anna_aichinger (both accessed 12 June 2013). We are grateful to Katrina Sark for her suggestion to situate the Viennese designers in a larger context.

6   http://www.notjustalabel.com/awareness_and_consciousness.   See   also   http://www.awarenessandconsciousness.com/ABOUT2, accessed 12 June 2013.

7   We would not want to be misunderstood as suggesting that it is due to Helmut Lang's influence that these collections contain echoes of his; rather, we would want to see them all as part of the larger system, one, moreover, that tends to produce a quite unique, more understated look than one tends to find in the fashion capitals.

8   http://www.notjustalabel.com/about, accessed 12 June 2013.

9   http://milch.mur.at/aprons.html, accessed 12 June 2013.

10   http://milch.mur.at/collection/, accessed 12 June 2013.

11   We are, of course, not claiming that recycling is unique to Vienna. Rather, the eco-fashion that is a component of the city's fashion scene and that it shares with other places takes on a particular form and resonance in Vienna given the city's history of social-democratic sensibility.

12   http://milch.mur.at/info/, accessed 12 June 2013.

13   The information in this paragraph is from http://suitesculturelles.wordpress.com/2011/07/31/milch-eco-fashion-from-vienna/, accessed 12 June 2013.

14   A list of Baumgartner's iniatives can be found at: http://milch.mur.at/projects/, accessed 12 June 2013.

15   Baumgartner sold the Modepalast at the end of 2012 in order to do a Master's in Innovation Management (personal communication with K. Sark, 10 December 2012).

16   The President of the Vienna Chamber of Commerce and Industry, Brigitte Jank, makes this point in her congratulatory column in the 2011 *Modepalast Magazin* (http://www.modepalast.com/2011/material/MODEPALAST_MAGAZIN2011.pdf).

Conclusion

Vienna Now, Not Never

W hat we have tried to shed light on in this study are the mechanisms that constitute Vienna's urban imaginary as chic, a task not made any easier by the fact that their primary characteristic is that of being on display, being, as we put it in our introduction, *toujours paru*. How does one illuminate something whose main feature is precisely being so visible that it is taken not so much for granted but for something else, namely, a handful of clichés? Focusing on the city's fashion system was our way of bringing the city's display tendencies to the fore and showing how they have been reacting to the onset of the globalization that has been gathering momentum since 1989. What became apparent in our investigations is that Vienna's urban imaginary is so intimately linked to its historical legacy that its fashion system's inherently modern, change-oriented dynamic is constantly forced to define itself in relation to its past. In other words, unlike the *déjà disparu*, which is based on clichés of things that have never been, the historical materiality of Vienna's built environment continues to make itself felt and has been a force that has had to be negotiated at every turn. As we have seen, this has manifested itself in many different ways – ranging from the glorification and close imitation of past models, such as characterized the historicist origins of the MAK, to radical renunciation, as in the case of the Secession and Peter Noever's avant-garde program.

One finds eruptions of the past, and the specific mix of a baroque-modernist past, in truly the darnedest of places in Vienna's cultural imaginary: in the structuring thematics of *Before Sunrise* and the Schmetterlings' *Proletenpassion*, in the spectacular concert at the Arena in *Blutrausch,* in the evocative image of Sisi on the Schönbrunn balcony in *I Love Vienna,* on the stage of the Josefstadt in *The Third Man,* in the denial of a reading tower for the MQ; even the emotionally charged materiality of Helmut Lang's art is resonant and laden with the residue of Vienna's historical legacy. More often than not, we find the past articulated to the present of specific projects, such as the sustainable fashion designs of the millennial generation and the MQ's redefinition of baroque spaces for accessible fashion shows, some of which even feature the Baroque (such as "The History of Fashion" one in August 2012 [Figure 3.3]).

All of these eruptions of past clichés work to prevent any kind of simple preservationalism. On the contrary, they spawn discourses that make it necessary to frame what is specific about Vienna style at a particular juncture, what makes it timely, as a form of rupture or "awakening" – whether it was the seceding of artists from their academic masters at the *fin-de-siècle*, the 68ers tame revolution against a benign but authoritarian welfare state, the playing catch-up to the global creative industry players that happened in the 80s, or the turn to creative city aspirations in the 00s. "Wien bleibt Wien," Vienna remains Vienna, no matter

Figure 3.1: Clowning around in the Böhmischer Prater
(Photo: M. Reisenleitner).

Figure 3.2: Fiaker sunset (Photo: M. Reisenleitner).

Figure 3.3: The History of Fashion: Barock (©Mato Johannik Weinper at Idee Konzept Mario Soldo).

Figure 3.4: Vienna Tourist Board advertising poster
(www.wien.info).

Figure 3.5: WIEN JETZT ODER NIE poster in Berlin (Photo: S. Ingram).

Figure 3.6: Apple-banana sign in the Blindengasse (Photo: S. Ingram).

what – the burden of the historical foil against which any kind of specificity, attraction and hipness needs to be set has remained an ineluctable other for the city's creative efforts.

That is why the new Vienna Tourism campaign slogan mentioned in the introduction almost, but not quite, succeeds. If we cast a final look in concluding at the "Vienna Now or Never" campaign, we see that as much as it attempts to mobilize the city's imperial heritage and play up its other historical attributes, the present of *SOKO Donau* with all of its conflictual, global-flow elements also makes itself felt. The saying – "At this moment the Danube is reflecting a smile. Too bad it's not yours" – is typical of the campaign both in concept and in attitude [Figure 3.4]. The poster images are constructed with empty squares in the middle into which a range of sayings can be inserted that all suggest in a competitively capitalist way that those viewing the poster are worse off than those who do not have the good fortune of living in Vienna and being able to enjoy its taste culture on a regular basis. A billboard in Berlin, for example, states: "At this moment an original Sacher Torte is waiting for you in Vienna. What are you waiting for?" [Figure 3.5]. The tourist board campaign thus addresses foreigners exclusively and cuts itself off from the Viennese it supposedly represents. Its Vienna is not ready to acknowledge the otherness at Vienna's core, the foreign presences that saturate Vienna's past, and the uniqueness of a mix that, as we hope to have shown, help to make Vienna's present distinctively and inspiringly *chic* [Figure 3.6].

References

Abbas, M.A. *Hong Kong: Culture and the Politics of Disappearance*. Minneapolis, MN: University of Minnesota Press, 1997.

Appadurai, Arjun. *Modernity at Large: Cultural Dimensions of Globalization*. Minneapolis, MN: University of Minnesota Press, 1996.

Auden, W.H. "As I Walked Out One Evening." *Another Time*. London: Faber and Faber, 1940.

Badelt, Udo. "Mehr Leben für die Kunst." *Der Tagesspiegel Online* 20 October 2009. <http://www.tagesspiegel.de/berlin/museumsinsel-mehr-leben-fuer-die-kunst/1618692.html> accessed 31 May 2013.

Bancroft, Alison. "Book Review: *Fashion: A Philosophy* by Lars Svendsen." *Fashion Theory: The Journal of Dress, Body and Culture* 12.3 (2008): 393–96.

Barthes, Roland. *Empire of Signs*. Trans. Richard Howard. New York: Farrar, Straus and Giroux, 1982 (*L'Empire des signes* 1970).

———. *The Fashion System*. Trans. Matthew Ward and Richard Howard. New York: Hill and Wang, 1983 (*Système de la mode* 1967).

Baudelaire, Charles. "Le Cygne (The Swan)." *Selected Poems from Les Fleurs du Mal: A Bilingual Edition*. English renderings and notes by Norman R. Shapiro; foreword by Willis Barnstone; engravings by David Schorr. Chicago, IL: University of Chicago Press, 1998.

———. "The Painter of Modern Life." *The Painter of Modern Life and Other Essays*. Translated and edited by Jonathan Mayne. 2nd Edition. London: Phaidon Press, 1995. 1–34.

Bauer, Werner T. *Zuwanderung nach Österreich*. Wien: Österreichische Gesellschaft für Politikberatung und Politikentwicklung, January 2008. <http://www.forschungsnetzwerk.at/downloadpub/zuwanderung_nach_oesterreich_studie2008_oegpp.pdf>.

Beller, Steven. *Rethinking Vienna 1900*. New York: Berghahn Books, 2001.

Benjamin, Walter. *The Arcades Project*. Ed. Rolf Tiedemann. Cambridge, MA: Belknap Press, 1999.

Berenson, Edward, and Eva Giloi, eds. *Constructing Charisma: Celebrity, Fame, and Power in Nineteenth-Century Europe*. New York: Berghahn Books, 2010.

Berger, John. *Ways of Seeing*. London: BBC/Penguin, 1972.

Bettelheim, Bruno. "The Birthplace of Psychoanalysis." *The Wilson Quarterly* 14.2 (Spring 1990): 68–77.

Bhabha, Homi K. *The Location of Culture*. London; New York: Routledge, 1994.

Blauensteiner, Elis. "Die Modeschule aus meiner Sicht." *Festschrift Modeschule der Stadt Wien im Schloss Hetzendorf, 1946–1996*. Ed. Günter Baumgartner. Vienna: Modeschule der Stadt Wien, 1996. 8–9.

Boeckl, Matthias. "'…ein echtes Werk aus dem Geist und Stil der Renaissance': Die Bauten des Museums 1863–1909: Heinrich Ferstels Haus am Stubenring, seine Vorgeschichte und spätere

Erweiterung." *Tradition und Experiment: Das Österreichische Museum für Angewandte Kunst, Wien.* Ed. Peter Noever. Salzburg; Wien: Residenz, 1988. 14–35.

Bönsch, Annemarie. *Wiener Couture: Gertrud Höchsmann 1902–1990* [*Katalog zur gleichnamigen Ausstellung*]. Wien: Böhlau, 2002.

Boorstin, Daniel. *The Image: A Guide to Pseudo-Events in America.* New York: Harper, 1964.

Brenner, Neil, and Roger Keil, eds. *The Global Cities Reader.* London; New York: Routledge, 2006.

Breward, Christopher, and Caroline Evans. *Fashion and Modernity.* Oxford: Berg, 2005.

———, and David Gilbert, eds. *Fashion's World Cities.* Oxford, New York: Berg, 2006.

Brickner, Irene. "Die konfliktreiche Rückkehr der Ute Bock." 13 April 2012. <http://derstandard. at/1334132568637/Umgang-mit-Anrainern-Die-konfliktreiche-Rueckkehr-der-Ute-Bock> accessed 31 May 2013.

Brooker, Peter, and Andrew Thacker, eds. *Geographies of Modernism: Literatures, Cultures, Spaces.* London; New York: Routledge, 2005.

Bunzl, Matti. *Symptoms of Modernity: Jews and Queers in Late-Twentieth-Century Vienna.* Berkeley, CA: University of California Press, 2004.

Burri, Michael. "Vienna: City of the Imagination." *World Film Locations: Vienna.* Ed. Robert Dassanowsky. Bristol: Intellect, 2012. 6–7.

Buxbaum, Gerda. *Mode aus Wien,* 1815–1938. Salzburg: Residenz Verlag, 1986.

———, ed. *Fashion in Context.* Vienna; New York: Springer, 2009.

Chakrabarty, Dipesh. *Provincializing Europe: Postcolonial Thought and Historical Difference.* With a new preface by the author. Princeton, NJ: Princeton University Press, 2007 (2000).

Chambers, Iain. *Popular Culture: The Metropolitan Experience.* London; New York: Routledge, 1986.

Cheah, Pheng. "Non-Dialectical Materialism." *New Materialisms: Ontology, Agency, and Politics.* Eds. Samantha Frost, and Diana H. Coole. Durham, NC; London: Duke University Press, 2010. 70–91.

Comerford, Philip. "The Olympic Security Fence Is a Modern Day Form of Enclosure." *Open Democracy* 27 July 2012.

Cone, Polly, ed. *The Imperial Style: Fashions of the Hapsburg Era: Based on the Exhibition, Fashions of the Hapsburg Era, Austria-Hungary, at the Metropolitan Museum of Art, December 1979–August 1980.* New York: Rizzoli, 1980.

Craik, Jennifer. *The Face of Fashion: Cultural Studies in Fashion.* London; New York: Routledge, 1994.

Csendes, Peter, and Ferdinand Opll, eds. *Wien: Geschichte einer Stadt.* Wien: Böhlau, 2001.

Cunningham, Patricia A. *Reforming Women's Fashion, 1850–1920: Politics, Health, and Art.* Kent, OH: Kent State University Press, 2003.

Czerny, Katharina. "Interview with Katarina Noever at the Wien Museum in the Course of the Opening of the Exhibition 'MORE THAN FASHION' – the Collection Katarina Noever." 6 March 2012. <http://www.zip-magazine.com/2012/03/interview-with-katarina-noever-at-the-wien-museum-in-the-course-of-the-opening-of-the-exhibition-more-than-fashion-the-collection-katarina-noever/> accessed 31 May 2013.

Dassanowsky, Robert. "Introduction: World Film Locations: Vienna." *World Film Locations: Vienna.* Bristol: Intellect, 2012. 5.

Davis, Mike. "Bunker Hill: Hollywood's Dark Shadow." *Cinema and the City: Film and Urban Societies in a Global Context.* Eds. Mark Shiel, and Tony Fitzmaurice. Oxford: Blackwell, 2001. 33–45.

Dawkins, Richard. *The Selfish Gene.* 30th anniversary edn Oxford; New York: Oxford University Press, 2006 (1976).

De Frantz, Monika. "Contemporary Political Theories of the European City." *European Journal of Social Theory* 11.4 (November 2008): 465–85.

———. "From Cultural Regeneration to Discursive Governance: Constructing the Flagship of the 'Museumsquartier Vienna' as a Plural Symbol of Change." *International Journal of Urban and Regional Research* 29.1 (2005): 50–66.

Donald, James. "How English Is It? Popular Literature and National Culture." *Space and Place: Theories of Identity and Location.* Eds. Erica Carter, James Donald, and Judith Squires. London: Lawrence & Wishart, 1993. 165–86.

———. *Imagining the Modern City.* Minneapolis, MN: University of Minnesota Press, 1999.

Driver, Felix, and David Gilbert, eds. *Imperial Cities: Landscape, Display and Identity.* Manchester: Manchester University Press, 2003.

Ebert, Roger. "Eight Miles High." *Chicago Sun Times* 21 August 2008.

Ebner, Claudia C. *Kleidung verändert: Mode im Kreislauf der Kultur.* Bielefeld: Transcript, 2007.

Ebner, Paulus, and Karl Vocelka. *Die zahme Revolution: '68 und was davon blieb.* Wien: Ueberreuter, 1998.

Egger, Hanna. "Die Anfänge des k.k. Österreichischen Museums für Kunst und Industrie und der Wiener Schule der Kunstgeschichte." *Kunst und Industrie: Die Anfänge des Museums für Angewandte Kunst in Wien.* Ed. Peter Noever. Ostfildern DA: Cantz, 2000. 271–83.

Ehmer, Josef. "Handwerk und Gewerbe." *Das Zeitalter Kaiser Franz Josephs I. Beiträge.* Wien: Amt der Niederösterreichischen Landesregierung, 1984. 138–44.

Eitelberger, Rudolf von. *Mittheilungen des k.k. Österreichischen Museums für Kunst und Industrie* II.29 (1867).

Evans, Graeme. "Measure for Measure: Evaluating the Evidence of Culture's Contribution to Regeneration." *Urban Studies* 42.5/6 (May 2005): 959–83.

Fahr-Becker, Gabriele. *Wiener Werkstaette: 1903–1932.* Ed. Angelika Taschen. Köln; London: Taschen, 2008.

Fassmann, Helmut, and Ursula Reeger. "'Old' Immigration Countries in Europe: The Concept and Empirical Examples." *European Migrations: Trends, Structures, and Policy Implications.* Ed. Marek Okólski. Amsterdam: IMISCOE Research, Amsterdam University Press, 2012. 65–90.

Felsenthal, Julia. "Listening to Dylan Thomas Read Auden: An Antidote to Heartbreak." <http://www.slate.com/blogs/procrastinatebetter/2010/12/22/listening_to_dylan_thomas_read_auden_an_antidote_to_heartbreak.html> accessed 7 June 2013.

Fischer, Wladimir. "'I haaß Vocelka – du haaßt Vocelka.' Der Diskurs über die 'Gastarbeiter' in den 1960er bis 1980er Jahren und der unhistorische Vergleich mit der Wiener Arbeitmigration um 1900." *Wien und seine WienerInnen: Ein historischer Streifzug durch Wien über die Jahrhunderte. Festschrift für Karl Vocelka zum 60. Geburtstag.* Eds. Martin Scheutz, and Vlasta Valeš. Wien; Köln; Weimar: Böhlau, 2008. 327–54.

Franz, Erich, and Bernd Growe. *Georges Seurat, Dessins*. Paris: Hermann, 1984.

Franz, Rainald. "Vom Kaiserforum zum Exerzierplatz: Die Errichtung und Architektur des k.k. Österreichischen Museums für Kunst und Industrie am Stubenring." *Kunst und Industrie: Die Anfänge des Museums für Angewandte Kunst in Wien*. Ed. Peter Noever. Ostfildern DA: Cantz, 2000. 90–102.

Gallop, Jane. "The American Other." *The Purloined Poe*. Eds. John P. Muller and William J. Richardson. Baltimore, MD: Johns Hopkins University Press, 1988. 268–82.

Gans, Herbert J. "Kubrick's Marxist Finale – An Eye-Opening Review of *Eyes Wide Shut*, Stanley Kubrick's Last Movie." *Social Policy* 30.1 (1999): 60–2.

Girtler, Roland, and Friederike Okladek. *Eine Wiener Jüdin im Chor der Deutschen Wehrmacht*. Wien: Pichler Verlag, 1994.

Göktürk, Deniz, David Gramling, and Anton Kaes, eds. *Germany in Transit: Nation and Migration, 1955–2005*. Berkeley, CA: University of California Press, 2007.

Haar, Ania. "50 Jahre Gastarbeiter in Österreich." *Die Presse com*. 15 November 2011. <http://diepresse.com/home/panorama/integration/708980/50-Jahre-Gastarbeiter-in-Oesterreich>

Haffenden, John. *W.H. Auden, the Critical Heritage*. London; Boston: Routledge & Kegan Paul, 1983.

Hahn, Sylvia. "Inclusion and Exclusion of Migrants in the Multicultural Realm of the Habsburg 'State of Many Peoples.'" *Social History/Histoire Sociale* 33.66 (2000): 307–24.

Hampel-Fuchs, Maria. *Wien ist anders. Das dritte Modell des Föderalismus in Österreich*. Wien: Lois Weinberger-Institut für christlich-soziale Politik in Wien, 2008.

Hare, David. *The Blue Room*, freely adapted from Arthur Schnitzler's *La ronde*. New York: Grove Press, 1998.

Haslinger, Tina. *Guided* Vienna. City Guide for Fashion & Design*. Wien: Guided Vienna, 2013. <www.guided-vienna.com> accessed 31 May 2013.

"Helmut Lang: Make It Hard." *NOWNESS*. 23 July 2011. <http://www.nowness.com/day/2011/7/23/1559/helmut-lang-make-it-hard> accessed 31 May 2013.

Hemetek, Ursula, and Initiative Minderheiten. *Am Anfang war der Kolaric: Plakate gegen Rassismus und Fremdenfeindlichkeit*. Wien: Südwind, 2000.

Henderson, Amy. "Media and the Rise of Celebrity Culture." *OAH Magazine of History* 6.4 (April, 1992): 49–54.

Herbert, Robert L. *Seurat: Drawings and Paintings*. New Haven, CT: Yale University Press, 2001.

Herzog, Hillary Hope. *"Vienna is Different": Jewish Writers in Austria from the Fin de Siècle to the Present*. New York: Berghahn Books, 2011.

Herzog, Todd. "Wonder Wheel: The Cinematic Prater." *World Film Locations: Vienna*. Ed. Robert Dassanovsky. Bristol: Intellect, 2012. 88–9.

Holzheu, Barbara. "'... und der Emigrant kommt anders zurück.'" *Gedenkdienst* 01/04. <http://www.gedenkdienst.at/index.php?id=407> accessed 31 May 2013.

Horak, Roman et al. *Metropole Wien: Texturen der Moderne*. Wien: WUV, 2000.

Huyssen, Andreas, ed. *Other Cities, Other Worlds: Urban Imaginaries in a Globalizing Age*. Durham, NC: Duke University Press, 2008.

Ingram, Susan. "Meet Me in Vienna (Alt-Wien), Meet Me at the Fair." *Placing History: Themed Environments, Urban Consumption and the Public Entertainment Sphere = Orte Und Ihre Geschichte(n)*. Eds. Markus Reisenleitner, and Susan Ingram. Vienna: Turia & Kant, 2003. 83–103.

———. "Schlingensief's Container: Translating Europe in the Age of Media Spectacle." *Historical Textures of Translation: Traditions, Traumas, Transgressions.* Eds. Markus Reisenleitner, and Susan Ingram. Vienna: Mille Tre, 2012. 165–74.

———. "Schnitzler as a Space of Central European Cultural Identity: David Hare's *The Blue Room* and Stanley Kubrick's *Eyes Wide Shut.*" *spaces of identity* 3.1 (2001): 7–32.

———, and Katrina Sark. *Berliner Chic: A Locational History of Berlin.* Bristol: Intellect, 2011.

———, and Markus Reisenleitner. "I Love Vienna." *World Film Locations: Vienna.* Ed. Robert Dassanovsky. Bristol: Intellect Books, 2012. 94–5.

Jahn, George. "Dream and Reality Looks at Vienna in Transition." *Lawrence Journal* 20 Oct. 1985, World: 6D.

Jameson, Fredric. *A Singular Modernity: Essay on the Ontology of the Present.* London; New York: Verso, 2002.

Janik, Allan. *Wittgenstein's Vienna Revisited.* New Brunswick, NJ: Transaction Publishers, 2001.

Janik, Allan, and Stephen Toulmin. *Wittgenstein's Vienna.* New York: Simon and Schuster, 1973.

Jay, Martin. *Downcast Eyes: The Denigration of Vision in Twentieth-Century French Thought.* Berkeley: University of California Press, 1993.

———. "Scopic Regimes of Modernity." *Vision and Visuality.* Ed. Hal Foster. Seattle: Bay Press, 1988. 2–23.

Jones, J. Sydney. *Vienna 1900.* <http://www.jsydneyjones.com/vienna1900.html> accessed 31 May 2013.

Kadivar, Cyrus. "Dialogue of Murder." *Payvand Iran News* 1 November 2003.

Kalliney, Peter J. "Reading Maps, Writing Cities." *Modernism/modernity* 13.4 (2006): 747–54.

Karner, Regina. *Wien Museum Modesammlung.* <http://www.wienmuseum.at/de/sammlungen/geschichte-und-stadtleben/modesammlung.html> accessed 28 June 2013.

———, and Historisches Museum (Wien). *Chic: Damenmode des 20. Jahrhunderts: Permanente Modeausstellung in der Hermesvilla; Katalog.* Wien: Museen der Stadt Wien, 2003.

Kauffmann, Kai. *Es ist nur ein Wien! Stadtbeschreibungen von Wien 1700 bis 1873: Geschichte eines literarischen Genres der Wiener Publizistik.* Wien: Böhlau Verlag, 1994.

Keeling, Kara. *The Witch's Flight: The Cinematic, the Black Femme, and the Image of Common Sense Perverse Modernities.* Durham, NC: Duke University Press, 2007.

King, Anthony D. *Global Cities: Post-Imperialism and the Internationalization of London.* London; New York: Routledge, 1990.

Kos, Wolfgang, ed. *Alt-Wien, die Stadt, die niemals war.* Wien: Czernin, 2004.

Kreider, Tim. "Review of *Eyes Wide Shut.*" *Film Quarterly* 53.3 (2000): 41–8.

Kropf, Robert, ed. *Be Inside, Vienna.* Wiener Neustadt: insiderei.com, 2012.

Landa, Jutta. "Lovable Foreigners: Gestures of Cross-Cultural Embracing in Austrian Film." *After Postmodernism: Austrian Literature and Film in Transition.* Ed. Willy Riemer. Riverside, CA: Ariadne Press, 2000. 94–105.

Lang, Helmut, Veit Görner, Matthew Gaskins, and Kestner-Gesellschaft. *Alles gleich schwer Helmut Lang* [anlässlich der Ausstellung Helmut Lang, Alles gleich schwer, Kestnergesellschaft, Hannover, 31 August – 2 November 2008]. Köln: König, 2009.

Lehmann, Ulrich. *Tigersprung: Fashion in Modernity.* Cambridge, MA: MIT Press, 2000.

Lehne, Inge, and Lonnie Johnson. *Vienna, the Past in the Present: A Historical Survey.* Wien; Riverside, CA: Österreichischer Bundesverlag; Ariadne Press, 1995.

Lipovetsky, Gilles. *The Empire of Fashion: Dressing Modern Democracy.* Trans. Catherine Porter. Princeton, NJ: Princeton University Press, 1994 (eBook).

Loacker, Armin, ed. *Wien, die Inflation und das Elend: Essays und Materialien zum Stummfilm Die freudlose Gasse.* Wien: Filmarchiv Austria, 2008.

Lutter, Christina. "Spacing History, Historicizing Culture: Urban History, Cultural Studies, and Vienna." *Modern Intellectual History* 9.02 (2012): 463–75.

McEwen, Britta. *Sexual Knowledge: Feeling, Fact, and Social Reform in Vienna, 1900–1934.* New York: Berghahn Books, 2012.

———. "Symptoms of Modernity: Jews and Queers in Late-Twentieth-Century Vienna (review)." *Journal of the History of Sexuality* 15.1 (2006): 132–135.

McQuiston, Kate. *"We'll Meet Again": Musical Design in the Films of Stanley Kubrick.* Oxford: Oxford University Press, forthcoming.

Maderthaner, Wolfgang, and Lutz Musner. *Die Anarchie der Vorstadt: Das andere Wien um 1900.* Frankfurt am Main; New York: Campus, 1999.

———. *Unruly Masses: The Other Side of Fin-de-Siècle Vienna.* Trans. David Fernbach and Michael Huffmaster. New York: Berghahn Books, 2008.

Martin, Fran. "Review of Hamid Naficy. An Accented Cinema: Exilic and Diasporic Filmmaking." *Screening the Past* 25 July 2002 < http://tlweb.latrobe.edu.au/humanities/screeningthepast/current/cc1102.html>.

Massey, Doreen. "Travelling Thoughts." *Without Guarantees: In Honour of Stuart Hall.* Eds. Lawrence Grossberg, Angela McRobbie, and Paul Gilroy. London: Verso, 2000. 224–32.

Michael, Apphia. "Helmut Lang: Sculptures Exhibition, New York." *Wallpaper** 4 May 2012. <http://www.wallpaper.com/art/helmut-lang-sculptures-exhibition-new-york/5776> accessed 31 May 2013.

Millikan, Ruth Garrett. *Varieties of Meaning: The 2002 Jean Nicod Lectures.* Cambridge, MA: MIT Press, 2004.

Mitten, Richard. "Jews and Other Victims: The 'Jewish Questions' and Discourses of Victimhood in Post-War Austria." *Austria in the European Union.* Eds. Michael Gehler, Anton Pelinka, and Günter Bischof. New Brunswick, NJ: Transaction Publishers, 2002. 223–70.

Mohanty, Chandra. "Under Western Eyes: Feminist Scholarship and Colonial Discourses." *Feminist Review* 30 (1988): 61–88.

Morley, David. *Home Territories: Media, Mobility and Identity.* London; New York: Routledge, 2000.

Moser, Joseph W. "Vienna Imperial at Home and Abroad: The City as Film Myth in the 1930s and 1940s." *World Film Locations: Vienna.* Ed. Robert Dassanovsky. Bristol: Intellect, 2012. 8–9.

Museumsquartier Wien – Eine Bilanz. Eine Verlagsbeilage der Wiener Zeitung. September 2009. http://www.mqw.at/mediafiles/21/MQ-WienerZeitung-DE.pdf.

Musner, Lutz. *Der Geschmack von Wien: Kultur und Habitus einer Stadt.* Frankfurt am Main: Campus, 2009.

Naficy, Hamid. *An Accented Cinema: Exilic and Diasporic Filmmaking.* Princeton, NJ: Princeton University Press, 2001.

Ndalianis, Angela. *Neo-Baroque Aesthetics and Contemporary Entertainment*. Cambridge, MA; London: MIT Press, 2004.

Noever, Peter. "Die Realität des Ortes als Herausforderung." *Tradition und Experiment: Das Österreichische Museum für Angewandte Kunst, Wien*. Ed. Peter Noever. Salzburg; Wien: Residenz, 1988. 120–25.

———. *MAK Austrian Museum of Applied Arts Vienna*. 2nd edn. München: Prestel, 1995.

———, ed. *Vienna by MAK*. Munich: Prestel, 2002.

Nussbaumer, Martina. *Musikstadt Wien: Die Konstruktion eines Images*. Freiburg im Breisgau: Rombach, 2007.

Olsen, Donald J. *The City as a Work of Art: London, Paris, Vienna*. New Haven, CT: Yale University Press, 1986.

Park, Robert E. *The City* (with R.D. McKenzie and Ernest Burgess). Chicago, Il: University of Chicago Press, 1984 (1925).

Parsons, Nicholas. *Vienna: A Cultural History*. Oxford; New York: Oxford University Press, 2009.

Paterson, Tony. "Uschi: Groupie, Addict, and Heroine of the Left." *The Independent Web* 2 February 2007 <http://www.independent.co.uk/news/world/europe/uschi-groupie-addict-and-heroine-of-the-left-434740.html> accessed 31 May 2013.

Paulicelli, Eugenia, and Hazel Clark, eds. *The Fabric of Cultures: Fashion, Identity, and Globalization*. New York; London: Routledge, 2009.

Payer, Peter. "'Gehen Sie an die Arbeit': Zur Geschichte der 'Gastarbeiter' in Wien 1964–1989." *Wiener Geschichtsblätter* 1 (2004): 1–19.

Percher, Petra. "Gerda Buxbaum: "Wien war nie Modemetropole." *Die Presse.com* 25 April 2009. <http://diepresse.com/home/leben/mode/473899/Gerda-Buxbaum_Wien-war-nie-Modemetropole> accessed 31 May 2013.

Perloff, Marjorie. "Seductive Vienna." *Modernism/modernity* 10.2 (2003): 221–38.

———. *The Vienna Paradox: A Memoir*. New York: New Directions Books, 2004.

Poe, Edgar Allan. "The Man in the Crowd" and "The Purloined Letter." *The Fall of the House of Usher and Other Writings: Poems, Tales, Essays and Reviews*. Edited with an introduction and notes by David Galloway. London: Penguin, 2003.

Pokorny-Nagel, Kathryn. "Zur Gründungsgeschichte des k.k. Österreichischen Museums für Kunst und Industrie." *Kunst und Industrie: Die Anfänge des Museums für Angewandte Kunst in Wien*. Ed. Peter Noever. Ostfildern DA: Cantz, 2000. 52–89.

Potvin, John, ed. *The Places and Spaces of Fashion 1800–2007*. New York and Oxford: Routledge, 2009.

Quinn, Bradley. *The Fashion of Architecture*. London: Berg, 2003.

Rakuschan, F.E. "MuQua: Hammer oder Spiegel?" *Telepolis* 11 July 2001.

Raphael, Frederic. *Eyes Wide Open: A Memoir of Stanley Kubrick and Eyes Wide Shut*. London: Orion, 1999.

Rathkolb, Oliver. *The Paradoxical Republic: Austria, 1945–2005*. Trans. Otmar Binder, Eleanor Breuning, Ian Fraser, and David Sinclair-Jones. New York and Oxford: Berghahn Books, 2010.

Reisenleitner, Markus. "A Question of Residence: Early Modern Court Society and the Urban Texture of Contemporary Vienna." Paper delivered at Florida International University, 16 November 2009.

———. "Beach-Haus vs. Traum(a) Factory: The L.A. Experience through Central European Eyes." *Reverberations: Representations of Modernity, Tradition and Cultural Value in-between Central Europe and North America*. Eds. Susan Ingram, Markus Reisenleitner, and Cornelia Szabo-Knotik. Frankfurt am Main; New York: P. Lang, 2002. 241–58.

———. "Das Belvedere – ein Palast mit Ausblick: Europäische Geschichte und Gedächtnis im urbanen Raum." *Wien und seine WienerInnen: Ein historischer Streifzug durch Wien über die Jahrhunderte. Festschrift für Karl Vocelka zum 60. Geburtstag*. Eds. Martin Scheutz and Vlasta Valeš. Wien; Köln; Weimar: Böhlau, 2008. 355–72.

———. "The American Traveling Detective and the Exotic City: *Pépé Le Moko, Macao* and *The Third Man*." *Ports of Call: Central European and North American Culture/s in Motion*. Eds. Susan Ingram, Markus Reisenleitner, and Cornelia Szabo-Knotik. Berlin; New York: P. Lang, 2004. 259–67.

Rider, Jacques le. *Modernité viennoise et crises de l'identité*. Paris: PUF, 1990, 2nd edn 2000.

Riemer, Willy. "Films for Entertainment and Reflection: An Interview with Houchang Allahyari." *After Postmodernism: Austrian Literature and Film in Transition*. Ed. Willy Riemer. Riverside, CA: Ariadne Press, 2000. 89–93.

Robertson, Roland. *Globalization: Social Theory and Global Culture*. London: Sage, 1992.

Rose, Alison. *Jewish Women in Fin de Siècle Vienna*. Austin, TX.: University of Texas Press, 2008.

Rotenberg, Robert. *Landscape and Power in Vienna*. Baltimore, MD: Johns Hopkins University Press, 1995.

Said, Edward. *Culture and Imperialism*. New York: Knopf, 1994.

Sark, Katrina. "Anna Aichinger." *Suites Culturelles*. 2 August 2011. <http://suitesculturelles. wordpress.com/2011/08/02/anna-aichinger/> accessed 1 June 2013.

———. "Baustelle Berlin: Post-Reunification Voids." *World Film Locations: Berlin*. Ed. Susan Ingram. Bristol: Intellect, 2012. 88–9.

———. "MILCH. Eco Fashion from Vienna." *Suites Culturelles*. 31 July 2011. <http://suitesculturelles. wordpress.com/2011/07/31/milch-eco-fashion-from-vienna/> accessed 1 June 2013.

———. "Ruins of Modernity." *Suites Culturelles*. 15 August 2012. <http://suitesculturelles. wordpress.com/2012/08/15/ruins-of-modernity/> accessed 1 June 2013.

Sassen, Saskia. *Cities in a World Economy*. 4th edn Thousand Oaks, CA: SAGE/Pine Forge, 2011 (1994).

Schnitzler, Arthur. *Dream Story*. Translated by J.M.Q. Davies. Harmondsworth: Penguin Classics, 1999.

———. *Reigen*. Stuttgart: Reclam Verlag, 2008.

———. *Traumnovelle und andere Erzählungen*. Frankfurt am M: Fischer Verlag, 2008.

Scholda, Ulrike. "'Die ausführende Hand der Theoretiker': Die Verbindung von Kunstgewerbeschule und k.k. Österreichischem Museum für Kunst und Industrie unter ihrem Direktor Josef von Storck." *Kunst und Industrie: Die Anfänge des Museums für Angewandte Kunst in Wien*. Ed. Peter Noever. Ostfildern DA: Cantz, 2000. 219–234.

Schorske, Carl E. *Fin-de-siècle Vienna: Politics and Culture*. New York: Knopf: distributed by Random House, 1979.

Schwarz, Egon. "Some Cultural Aspects of Alban Berg's Vienna." *The German Quarterly* 61.1 (1988): 50–66.

Seabrook, John. "The Invisible Designer: Helmut Lang." *The New Yorker* 18 Sept. 2000 <http://www.booknoise.net/johnseabrook/stories/design/lang/index.html> accessed 1 June 2013.

Seibel, Alexandra. *Vienna, Girls, and Jewish Authorship: Topographies of a Cinematic City, 1920–1940*. Thesis (Ph.D.), New York University, 2009.

Sommer, Monika, ed. *Mythos Alt-Wien: Spannungsfelder urbaner Identitäten*. Innsbruck; Wien; Bozen: StudienVerlag, 2009.

Stanford Friedman, Susan. "Planetarity: Musing Modernist Studies." *Modernism/ modernity* 17.3 (2010): 471–99.

Stewart, Janet. *Fashioning Vienna: Adolf Loos's Cultural Criticism*. London; New York: Routledge, 2000.

Syson, Damon. "'Make It Hard' exhibition of work by Helmut Lang." *Wallpaper** 22 July 2011. <http://www.wallpaper.com/art/make-it-hard-exhibition-of-work-by-helmut-lang/5364> accessed 1 June 2013.

Thompson, Ben. "The First Kiss Takes So Long." *Sight and Sound* 5.5 (May 1995): 20–1.

Thompson, E.P. "Commitment in Politics." *Universities & Left Review* 6 (Spring 1959): 50–55.

Thun-Hohenstein, Christoph, Hartmut Esslinger, and Thomas Geisler, eds. *Made 4 You/Design für den Wandel/Design for Change*. Nürnberg: Verlag für Moderne Kunst, 2012.

"Tiberius." *Unlike City Guides*. <http://unlike.net/vienna/shop/tiberius> accessed 1 June 2013.

Tien, Chieh-Ching. "The Formation and Impact of Museum Clusters: Two Case Studies in Taiwan." *Museum Management and Curatorship* 25.1 (2010): 69–85.

Trenkler, Thomas. "Richtungsstreit um Zukunft des Wien-Museums." *DerStandard Web* 25 May 2012. <http://derstandard.at/1336697980227/Richtungsstreit-um-Zukunft-des-Wien-Museums>.

Turner, Graeme. *Understanding Celebrity*. London: SAGE, 2004.

Urban Guide Vienna. Vienna: INOPERAbLE, 2012. <http://www.inoperable.at/> accessed 31 May 2013.

Vana, Gerhard. "'Wien…, der Ort ist hier nebensächlich.' Zur Ausstattung von *Die freudlose Gasse*." *Wien, die Inflation und das Elend: Essays und Materialien zum Stummfilm Die freudlose Gasse*. Ed. Armin Loacker. Wien: Filmarchiv Austria, 2008. 131–56.

Varnedoe, Kirk, ed. *Vienna 1900: Art, Architecture & Design*. New York: Museum of Modern Art; Boston, MA: Distributed by New York Graphic Society Books/Little, Brown, 1986.

Vienna Now or Never. Brand Manual. Vienna Tourist Board. <http://www.vienna.info/> accessed 1 June 2013.

Vocelka, Karl. "Die Stadt und die Herrscher." *Wien: Geschichte einer Stadt*. Eds Peter Csendes and Ferdinand Opll. Wien: Böhlau, 2001. 13–45.

———. *Geschichte Österreichs: Kultur – Gesellschaft – Politik*. Graz: Styria, 2000.

Waechter-Böhm, Liesbeth. "Kontinuität und Bruch." *Tradition und Experiment: Das Österreichische Museum für Angewandte Kunst, Wien*. Ed. Peter Noever. Salzburg; Wien: Residenz, 1988. 77–100.

"Was ist chic?" *Das Blatt der Hausfrau!* Okt. 1901–Sept. 1902, 870.

Webster, Patrick. *Love and Death in Kubrick: A Critical Study of the Films From Lolita Through Eyes Wide Shut*. Jefferson, NC: McFarland & Company, 2011.

Wegs, J. Robert. *Growing Up Working Class: Continuity and Change Among Viennese Youth, 1890–1938*. University Park, PA: Pennsylvania State University Press, 2008 (1989).

Weiss, Kirsten. "Recycling the Image of the Public Sphere in Art." *Thresholds* 23 (Fall 2001): 58–63. Original URL: <http://architecture.mit.edu/thresholds/issue-contents/23/weiss23/weiss23.htm>; also available at <http://www.davidtinapple.com/comaff/Recycling_the_Image.pdf> accessed 3 June 2013.

Weixlgartner, Roland and Achim Zeilmann. *Drehort Wien – Wo berühmte Filme entstanden.* Berlin-Brandenburg: be.bra Verlag, 2011.

Whitinger, Raleigh, and Susan Ingram. "Schnitzler, Kubrick, and 'Fidelio.'" *Mosaic: A Journal for the Interdisciplinary Study of Literature* 36.3 (2003): 55–72.

Wien im Film: Stadtbilder aus 100 Jahren. Eds. Christian Dewald, Michael Loebenstein and Werner Michael Schwarz. Wien: Wien Museum, Czernin Verlag, 2010.

Wilder-Okladek, Friederike. "A Note on Jewish Research in 'Tainted' Countries." *Jewish Social Studies* 30.3 (July 1968): 169–74.

Wilson, Elizabeth. "Fashion and Modernity." *Fashion and Modernity.* Eds. Caroline Evans and Christopher Breward. Oxford; New York: Berg, 2005. 9–14.

Wirth, Louis. "Urbanism as a Way of Life." *American Journal of Sociology* 44 (1938): 1–24.

Zimmermann, Michael F. *Seurat and the Art Theory of His Time.* Antwerp: Fonds Mercator, 1991.

Zoglin, Richard. "Theater: Room for Improvement." *Time* 28 December 1998, 184–87.

Zukin, Sharon. *Landscapes of Power: From Detroit to Disney World.* Berkeley, CA: University of California Press, 1991.

Zweig, Stefan. *The World of Yesterday: An Autobiography.* Introduction by Harry Zohn. Lincoln, NE; London: University of Nebraska Press, 1964.

Filmography

Amadeus. Dir. Milos Forman. The Saul Zaentz Company, 1984.

Die Ära Kreisky. Dir. Karin Moser, Peter Huemer, Erich Loibner, and Wolfgang Hackl. Film Archiv Austria, 2011.

L'Arrivée d'un train en gare de la Ciotat (Arrival of a Train at La Ciotat). Dir. Lumière Bros, Lumière, 1896.

Ausländer Raus! Schlingensiefs Container (Foreigners Out! Schlingensief's Container). Dir. Paul Poet. Bonus Film, 2002.

Bambi. Dir. David Hand. Walt Disney Productions, 1942.

Bad Timing: A Sensual Obsession. Dir. Nicholas Roeg. Recorded Picture Company (RPC), Rank Organisation, 1980.

Before Midnight. Dir. Richard Linklater. Sony Pictures Classics et al, 2013.

Before Sunrise. Dir. Richard Linklater. Detour Filmproduction, Filmhaus Wien, Universa Filmproduktions (in association with) (as F.I.L.M.H.A.U.S., Wien), Sunrise Production, Columbia Pictures Corporation, 1995.

Berlin: Die Symphonie der Großstadt. Dir. Walther Ruttmann, Deutsche Vereins-Film, Les Productions Fox Europa, 1927.

Berlin Express. Dir. Jacques Tourneur. RKO Radio Pictures, 1948.

Berliner Ballade (Berlin Ballad). Dir. Robert A. Stemmle. Comedia-Film GmbH, 1948.

Blow-Up. Dir. Michelangelo Antonioni. Bridge Films, Metro-Goldwyn-Mayer (MGM), 1966.

Blutrausch. Dir. Thomas Roth. Dor Film Produktionsgesellschaft, Österreichischer Rundfunk (ORF), 1997.

Bock for President. Dir. Houchang Allahyari. Allahyari Filmproduktion, 2009.

Bride of the Wind. Dir. Bruce Beresford. Alma UK Limited, ApolloMedia, Firelight Films, Kolar-Levy Productions, Terra Film Produktion, Total Film Group, 2001.

Burgtheater. Dir. Willi Forst. Willy Forst-Filmproduktion GmbH, 1936.

A Dangerous Method. Dir. David Cronenberg. Lago Film, Prospero Pictures, Millbrook Pictures, 2011.

Daybreak. Dir. Jacques Feyder. Metro-Goldwyn-Mayer (MGM), 1931.

Dazed and Confused. Dir. Richard Linklater. Alphaville Films, Detour Filmproduction, 1993.

De Mayerling à Sarajevo. Dir. Max Ophüls. B.U.P. Française, 1940.

The Emperor Waltz. Dir. Billy Wilder. Paramount Pictures, 1948.

Eyes Wide Shut. Dir. Stanley Kubrick. Hobby Films, Pole Star, Stanley Kubrick Productions, Warner Bros. Pictures, 1999.

Fast Food Nation. Dir. Richard Linklater. Recorded Picture Company (RPC), Participant Productions, Fuzzy Bunny Films (I), BBC Films, 2006.

A Foreign Affair. Dir. Billy Wilder. Paramount Pictures, 1948.

Die freudlose Gasse (Joyless Streets). Dir. G.W. Pabst. Sofar-Film, 1925.

Geboren in Absurdistan (Born in Absurdistan). Dir. Houchang Allayhari. Epo-Film Produktionsgesellschaft, 1999.

Germania anno zero (Germany Year Zero). Dir. Roberto Rossellini. Produzione Salvo D'Angelo, Tevere Film, 1948.

Höhenangst (Fear of Heights). Dir. Houchang Allahyari. Epo-Film Produktionsgesellschaft, 1994.

I Love Vienna. Dir. Houchang Allahyari. Epo Film, 1991.

Immortal Beloved. Dir. Bernard Rose. Icon Entertainment International, Majestic Films International, 1994.

Killer's Kiss. Dir. Stanley Kubrick. Minotaur Productions, 1955.

Kinopioniere. Filmarchiv Austria, 2009.

Klimt. Dir. Raoul Ruiz. EPO-Film Vienna, Film-Line Munich, Lunar Films London, Gemini Films, 2006.

La Ronde. Dir. Max Ophüls. Films Sacha Gordine, 1950.

La ronde. Dir. Roger Vadim. Interopa Film, Paris Film Productions, Société Nouvelle Pathé Cinéma, 1964.

Leise flehen meine Lieder (Unfinished Symphony). Dir. Willi Forst. Cine-Allianz Tonfilmproduktions GmbH, 1933–34.

Letter from an Unknown Woman. Dir. Max Ophüls. Rampart Productions, 1948.

Liebelei. Dir. Max Ophüls. Elite-Tonfilm-Produktion GmbH, 1933.

The Living Daylights. Dir. John Glen. Eon Productions, 1987.

Lola Rennt (Run Lola Run). Dir. Tom Tykwer. X-Filme Creative Pool, 1998.

Marie Antoinette. Dir. Sofia Coppola. Pricel, Tohokushinsha Film, American Zoetrope, 2006.

Maskerade. Dir. Willi Forst. Sascha-Verleih, Tobis Filmkunst, 1934.

Mayerling. Dir. Anatole Litvak. Nero Films, 1936.

Mayerling. Dir. Kirk Browning, Anatole Litvak. Showcase Productions, 4 Feb. 1957.

Mayerling. Dir. Terence Young. A Winchester-Corona Production, 1968.

Me and Orson Welles. Dir. Richard Linklater. Framestore, Hart-Lunsford Pictures, Detour Filmproduction, 2008.

Merry-Go-Round. Dir. Rupert Julian and Erich von Stroheim. Universal Pictures, 1923.

Mit Ihren Augen. Dir. Tereza Barta. ORF, 1992.

The Moderns. Dir. Alan Rudolph. Nelson Entertainment, 1988.

Die Mörder sind unter uns (The Murderers Are Among Us). Dir. Wolfgang Staudte. DEFA, 1946.

Nordrand (Northern Skirts). Dir. Barbara Albert. Fama Film AG, Lotus Film, Zero Film GmbH, 1999.

Operette. Dir. Willi Forst. Deutsche Forst-Filmproduktion GmbH, Wien-Film, 1940.

Prater. Dir. Ulrike Ottinger. Kurt Mayer Film, Ulrike Oettinger Filmproduktion, Westdeutscher Rundfunk (WDR), Österreichischer Rundfunk (ORF), 2007.

Vizi privati, pubbliche virtù (Private Vices, Public Virtues. Dir. Miklós Jancsó, Filmes Cinematografica, Jadran Film, 1975.

Pratermizzi. Dir. Gustav Ucicky. Sascha-Film, 1927.

Razzia. Dir. Werner Klingler. DEFA, 1947.

A Scanner Darkly. Dir. Richard Linklater. Warner Independent Pictures (WIP), 2006.

Le Secret de Mayerling. Dir. Jean Delannoy. Codo Cinéma, 1949.

Sissi. Dir. Ernest Marischka. Erma-Film, 1955.

Sissi – Die junge Kaiserin. Dir. Ernest Marischka. Erma-Film, 1956.

Sissi – Schicksalsjahre einer Kaiserin. Dir. Ernest Marischka. Erma-Film, 1957.

Slacker. Dir. Richard Linklater. Detour Filmproduction, 1991.

Song Without End. Dir. Charles Vidor and George Sukor. William Goetz Productions, 1960.

The Third Man. Dir. Carol Reed. London Film Productions, British Lion Film Corporation, 1949.

Tragödie im Hause Habsburg (Tragedy in the House of Habsburg). Dir. Alexander Korda. Korda Film, 1924.

Die verrückte Welt der Ute Bock (The Crazy World of Ute Bock). Dir. Houchang Allahyari. Allahyari Filmproduktion, 2010.

Waking Life. Dir. Richard Linklater. Flat Black Films, Detour Filmproduction, 2001.

The Wedding March. Dir. Erich von Stroheim. Paramount Famous Lasky Corporation, 1928.

Wien, Du Stadt meiner Träume (Vienna: You City of My Dreams). Dir. Willi Forst. Lux-Film Wien, Sascha-Verleih, 1957.

Wiener Blut (Vienna Blood). Dir. Willi Forst. Deutsche Forst-Filmproduktion GmbH, Wien-Film, 1942.

Wiener Walzer (Viennese Waltz). Dir. Emil E. Reinert. Cordial-Film, Vindobona-Filmproduktion GmbH, 1951.

Das wilde Leben (Eight Miles High). Dir. Achim Barnhak. Babelsberg Film, Neue Bioskop Film, On the Road, 2007.